THE HISTORY LESSONS

THE HISTORY LESSONS

SHALINA PATEL

Published in the UK and USA in 2024 by
Icon Books Ltd, Omnibus Business Centre,
39–41 North Road, London N7 9DP
email: info@iconbooks.com
www.iconbooks.com

ISBN: 978-183773-161-9
ebook: 978-183773-163-3

Text copyright © 2024 Shalina Patel

The author has asserted her moral rights.

No part of this book may be reproduced in any form, or by any means, without prior permission in writing from the publisher.

Typesetting by SJmagic DESIGN SERVICES, India

Printed and bound in the UK

ACKNOWLEDGEMENTS

The History Lessons was conceived after a LinkedIn message from Emma. I am so grateful for all your wise words and for so firmly believing in the importance of not only sharing these stories but also the importance of my voice within them. Everyone I've worked with at Icon has been so brilliant, from Keira, to Clare, Sophie and my final editor Connor, whose insightful guidance shaped this book into its finished product.

People often ask, 'how do you have time to do all of this and also teach?' – and the truth is it wouldn't be possible without Nicki and Alice. Thank you for always allowing me to say yes and for encouraging me from day one. My number one cheerleader at school was always Sula – I miss you every single day and I know you'd have been the most excited about all of this.

Most of all, thank you to my family; Mum, Keyur, Shaneil and Kavi. You have done nothing but support my dreams and none of this would be possible without you – special shout out to Izzie for supporting all my research! And to all my brilliant friends who have been so excited about this book even when I've doubted myself. I am so lucky to have you all in my life.

My interest in marginalised histories was sparked at LSE by the incredible Dr Joanna Lewis and I've never forgotten this. Thank you to my brilliant students whose questions in the classroom continue to inspire me.

To George, Matt, Laura, Zara and Georgia, the History department of my dreams! We have shaped this meaningful, rich and evolving curriculum together and I could not have written this book without you all. You introduced me to so many stories, including Tomoe, Rosa, Abe, Licoricia and of course, Ernst. I thank you with every fibre of my being.

Finally, thank you to Sam. You've supported and encouraged me every single day since we met and there's no one else I'd rather have by my side.

CONTENTS

Introduction   ix

1 Early History   1
2 The Tudors   25
3 Abolition and the Age of Revolution   51
4 Victorians (at Home and Abroad)   83
5 The Suffragettes   111
6 The Great War and Beyond   145
7 The Second World War   179
8 'Modern' Britain   211

Conclusion: Every Day Is a School Day   239
Bibliography   243

INTRODUCTION

Hands up – who were the historical figures you most enjoyed learning about at school? Or perhaps you didn't enjoy learning history at school, but have (hopefully) developed an interest in it later in life? Regardless of how you got here, there's a space for you in this classroom.

Think back to your school history lessons. In terms of events, people and places, it's likely that you barely even scratched the surface. Even if your entire timetable had been back-to-back history, it would have been impossible to learn *everything*.

It's a challenge faced by anyone teaching history. The Holocaust is the only compulsory historic event to be included in the Key Stage 3 curriculum (the first three years of secondary school). The rest is up to individual history departments. In the department I have the pleasure of working in, we often agonise over what we have time to include and, most tragically, what – or indeed who – we have to cut. We do not see the curriculum as a static entity, but rather as ever evolving and something we need to consistently reflect on.

Similarly, history itself operates within this state of flux, with so many aspects of the subject being uncovered that then reframe how we look at familiar contexts. One such example is Miranda Kaufmann's 2017 book *Black Tudors*, which fundamentally changed how so many of us teach that period of time.

When I started @thehistorycorridor on Instagram it soon became abundantly clear to me that there was a real appetite for adults to return to their school history classroom, and to learn the sort of lessons students like mine are having now. The idea for this book was born out of the sentiment I continue to receive from followers and people I meet at events: 'I wish you'd been my history teacher.'

Through this book, which is limited by the same challenge facing anyone teaching history – you can't even begin to hope to cover *everything* – I will take you on a chronological journey through some of the key elements of British history from the medieval period to the 1980s. You'll encounter many of the people my students meet in their history lessons from Year 7 to Year 9 along the way. And it's worth bearing in mind that this book would not be possible without the countless historians whose work uncovering hidden histories in particular has been so helpful to us on the front lines of school history education.

Give yourself 30 seconds to think about what you consider to be the key dates from your school history lessons – many of those will feature here. But what I hope to do with this book is use these familiar dates and stories as a foundation for exploring the lesser-known aspects – to use what was happening in Britain as a window of opportunity to visit another part of the world, allowing us to appreciate the bigger picture.

Have a look at the chapter titles – what do you already know about these historical periods? From the medieval to the world of the Tudors, the Suffragette movement and the World Wars, you'll meet recognisable figures here as well as some that might surprise you. Some chapters will hone in on aspects of history that are perhaps not as familiar to you from school, such as Abolition and the Age of Revolution, or the Victorians at Home and Abroad, both of which have the British Empire as their main backdrop, an area of history so many people tell me is something they know frustratingly little about. The final chapter will focus on the experience of migrant communities who moved to Britain after the Second World War, who in many ways fought their own civil rights movement, and to which many of us owe so much.

Along the way I hope you are able to make connections between the past and your own life. I hope to offer you a richer and broader version of what you previously knew. My aim with this book has always been to write an accessible history that blends the familiar and the hidden, which will inspire you to perhaps take your first steps towards embracing history in ways you may not have done so before. I hope that reading this book will act as a springboard of sorts, encouraging you to delve further into some of the people and places you meet throughout these chapters.

Let's go. You don't want to be late for your first lesson.

EARLY HISTORY 1

Roman Britain was more diverse than you might think

August 1901 was a typical British summer, a classic mix of sun, wind and rain. The country was between monarchs, with the formidable Victoria dying in January, and her son Bertie formally crowned the following year. This Edwardian era was just as noisy as its predecessors thanks to all the heavy machinery of the time.

At the turn of the century York was a bustling city full of tourists because of its rail connections. The Scarborough Rail Bridge was built in 1845, and it was just a short walk away from here, on Sycamore Terrace, that a team of builders was working on expanding the street when they hit something rather unexpected. Just a foot below ground level they had discovered a large stone sarcophagus. No doubt the team were stunned into silence when they saw what was inside it: the skeleton of a woman, which was later dated to the 4th century. The contents of the woman's grave, goods for the afterlife, included a selection of jewellery (bangles, a bracelet, silver and bronze pendants and a pair of earrings), a glass mirror and a blue glass jar. A rectangular bone mount was also found. The inscription upon it translates as, 'Hail sister, may you live in God.'

Later analysis of her teeth suggested she consumed above average amounts of fish, a reflection of her high status. She most likely enjoyed other symbols of wealth of the time, such as underfloor heating and expensive imports like wine and olive oil. Based on these items alone it's easy to imagine what kind of life this Roman woman must have led. No doubt you're picturing her now, reclining on a couch. Perhaps she's deciding what new food item to try. She may even be enjoying produce now seen as quintessentially British, such as cucumber, apples and plums.

What did she do in her spare time? While we can draw likely conclusions about her lifestyle, there's so much we'll never know. Did she enjoy a classic Roman day out at her local amphitheatre, where a thumbs up or down dramatically signalled the fate of a gladiator? Did she enjoy wearing make-up, which during this period involved grinding your own eyeliner using soot or wearing brightly coloured eyeshadow ground from saffron and precious stones like lapis lazuli? Despite her careful burial, did she have enemies?

Cursing those who had wronged you was relatively straightforward in Roman Britain. All you needed to do was address your lead tablet to Minerva, the Roman goddess of wisdom, justice and victory, and make your vengeful wish as clear as possible. Writing it backwards was thought to make the curse even stronger. Curse tablets found in Bath reveal a variety of wrongdoings, including a request for a stolen bronze vessel to be 'filled with the blood of the thief', while others simply request that 'those who are badly disposed towards me' should no longer be allowed 'to stand or sit, to drink or eat'. It was the Romans who first brought domestic kittens to our shores, which begs the question – was she an early cat lady?

The bone mount tells us her religious beliefs, while the burial tells us that she was well-respected. After all, the dead are buried by those still living.

We know for certain that she lived after the time of Boudicca, who raised her infamous army in AD 60, and after Emperor Hadrian's decision in AD 122 to build a 73-mile-long, 10-foot-high wall to keep the 'barbarians' at bay. Although we can't be certain of the timing, she may have lived during Constantine the Great's rule as Roman Emperor. There are even a few connections between them: he was the first emperor to convert to Christianity and was even proclaimed emperor in York. Constantine was, however, the only one of the two to name a new capital city (Constantinople – now Istanbul) after himself.

One of her bangles was made of ivory. The existence of ivory in Roman York reflects the migration of both objects and people from across the Roman Empire, which at its peak required 300,000 soldiers to guard its borders. It was this migration, combined with economic prosperity, that kept the empire relatively stable for over two centuries, with trade flourishing in goods from grain to the enslaved. The ivory bangle originates from North Africa and, irrespective of whether it is an heirloom, it reflects the diversity of goods this 1.7 million-squaremile empire encompassed. If it was purchased in York then it's likely to have been made into a bracelet in northern Italy before being imported to Britain, to be sold perhaps at a local market.

When the Ivory Bangle Lady was unearthed in 1901, archaeologists of the time marvelled that this was absolute proof of local acceptance of Christianity during the early Roman occupation of York. Over a hundred years later, when she was analysed by archaeologists in 2010, a far more startling discovery was made. The woman was of North African ancestry. This was surely something those in 1901 could scarcely have imagined. She was around five feet tall and twenty years old when she died, with no clear indicators of the cause of death. In the short span of her life what we do know is that she migrated to York and prospered.

In the wake of this discovery, Hella Eckardt from the Department of Archaeology at Reading University declared, 'We're looking at a population mix which is much closer to contemporary Britain than previous historians had suspected.' This is a real eye-opener – a reflection of how dynamic and evolving our history can be.

Science has played a huge role here, shown by the details we are able to glean from the Ivory Bangle Lady compared with those in the centuries before us. She was a woman of colour in 4th-century Britain, not in a position of enslavement but one of privilege, something the science critically confirms. Her buried bones showed no significant muscle markings, indicating that she did not live a particularly strenuous life. It begs the question, what other histories are yet to be known?

Perhaps this young woman was the daughter of a soldier, military-based migration being common across the Roman Empire. Or she may have been the daughter of rich African merchants who settled in Britain. Either way, her very existence and elaborate burial tells us not only that African-origin Romans lived in Britain, but that some of them did so as wealthy, high-status individuals. Her bangles alone tell the story of Roman Britain: the white ivory one made in Africa teamed with black jet bangles produced in Whitby.

By the early 5th century, Rome had withdrawn its troops from Britain in order to fight invaders elsewhere. The Huns, who originated in Central Asia, were one of the key invaders to distract the Roman Empire at this point. Their most famous leader was the formidable Attila, who was so committed to his aims of conquest that he assassinated his own brother. With the Romans gone, Britain was then inevitably invaded and settled by a variety of different groups, most famously the Angles and Saxons.

Even during this period, the movement of relatively normal people across continents was not unusual. There's another burial that spectacularly shows that the medieval world was far more connected than we may have assumed. An excavation prompted by Edith Pretty in 1939 of the mounds of land surrounding her Suffolk home provided a mirror into life here before the 'kingdom of England' was established in 927 under King Athelstan. The site at Sutton Hoo included an Anglo-Saxon ship burial, the richest ever found in northern Europe, shattering prior illusions that after the Romans left we were plunged into the Dark Ages. In fact, this was a time of immense wealth, international connections and a continued desire to show respect to those whose lives had passed. It's likely to have been the grave of Raedwald, who was king of East Anglia (present-day Norfolk and Suffolk) till his death in 624.

The 27-metre wooden ship in which he was buried understandably did not survive millennia underground, unlike the masses of jewellery and weaponry he was buried with. The objects reveal so much to us about their possessor and the time in which he lived. The wear on the sword tells us he was left-handed, and many of the objects have surprising global origins, including silverware from the Byzantine capital Constantinople and garnets from Sri Lanka. One of the most iconic finds was the Sutton Hoo helmet, decorated with animals, including a dragon. Edith donated all of the finds to the British Museum, where you can find them on display in Room 41. If you ever visit Sutton Hoo itself, be sure to look out for a pair of roller-skates. Edith's son Robert left them in one of the burial sites back in 1939.

Traditionally, secondary school history starts a few decades after this spectacular burial, with a central story we all know from the year alone: 1066. So why introduce these burials first? Firstly, to show that global connections and, indeed, non-white presence precede the start of the first notions of 'Englishness' formed by the Anglo-Saxons. While Roman Britain may not have been 'multicultural' in a modern sense, it was certainly a more diverse place than has always been pictured, both in terms of the people and the goods that passed through it. The Ivory Bangle Lady specifically provides a typical example of other stories we'll come across. Whilst her existence cannot be disputed, the details of her life are gaps we have to fill, just as we'll do with so many unexpected characters whose personal experiences we have to piece together and infer from the small traces they left behind.

The last person to successfully invade England

If you were to make a 1066-themed bingo card I can only assume that the Battle of Hastings, William the Conqueror and the Bayeux Tapestry would all feature. You may even remember supressing giggles when you saw the word 'bastard' in your school textbook, a term used disparagingly for William because his birth was the result of an affair his father Robert, Duke of Normandy had with a local woman called Herleva. In 1047 William cut off the hands and feet of several local residents who mocked his mother's peasant-class heritage. But the fact that gets the most stunned reception in the classroom is that when William of Normandy invaded these shores in 1066 and beat the English king, Harold Godwinson, he was the last person to successfully do so.

He was not warmly welcomed, however. The northern population of England considered themselves somewhat independent from the rest of the country, and they did not take kindly to a man who had killed their beloved King Harold and who didn't even speak their language. Rebellions spread across the country, led by people with fantastic names like Edric the Wild. William even faced resistance from his own earls, some of whom he promptly blinded or murdered.

By 1070, the English rebels in some parts of the country had additional support from Danish forces, so William had to take more serious action, which came to be known as the Harrying of the North. York, for instance, faced serious retribution, with essentially a 'scorched earth' policy in place, meaning livestock were killed and fields were either burned or 'salted' to prevent crops growing.

After 21 years of ruling over England, William was fatally injured at the age of 59 while attempting to seize Mantes in France. And he endured his own grisly postscript when, having had his size grossly underestimated, his corpse burst as his body was crammed into his stone sarcophagus.

It wasn't just in the north where trouble was brewing. The Normans built castles on all their borders, most notably along the Welsh Marches, in order to prevent the Welsh from attacking England, which at this point was an entirely separate country. By the 1200s much of Wales was in fact under English rule, largely thanks to invasions under the instruction of King Edward I. This was partly thanks to divisions among the Welsh, with different kingdoms within the country vying for control. The might of the sword was used to infiltrate Wales, but the English used a variety of other methods to subjugate them. A 'ring of fire' was created – a fortification of castles, with towns filled with English people to show who was now in charge (the official language of Wales was English from 1284). The Welsh leader Llywelyn ap Gruffudd had called himself the prince of Wales, something English monarchs had initially accepted as long as appropriate homage was paid. From 1301, however, Edward I decided this title would no longer belong to a Welshman. Instead, it would be exclusively bequeathed to the oldest son of the English monarch, a tradition which, of course, continues to this day.

Edward I also had his eye on Scotland, imprisoning the rebellious King Balliol and taking the Stone of Destiny, an ancient block of stone that all previous Scottish monarchs had been crowned on, to London. The Scots had the infamous victory at Stirling Bridge in 1297, led by William Wallace, but he was captured in 1305 and promptly executed. In 1314, Robert the Bruce defeated Edward II's forces in just two days, meaning this king of Scotland secured his borders from English control for three more centuries.

The Stone of Destiny was returned to Scotland in 1996, under the promise that it will be returned to England temporarily every time a new monarch is crowned. Medieval kings like Henry II, Richard II and John similarly failed to conquer Ireland thanks to strong military opposition, with the only area they controlled referred to as the Pale, hence why being 'beyond the pale' became a phrase used for those perceived to be behaving unacceptably.

While William the Conquerer's wife Matilda stood at just four feet and two inches, her small stature did not stop her from making quite a name for herself. Her family ties were impressive, with links to many royal European bloodlines, including the King of France, Charlemagne, and King Alfred the Great. At a time when the wives of kings were very much on the sidelines, Matilda wished to be recognised as a queen in her own right. Unsurprisingly, women in medieval England endured many inequalities, some of which will feel familiar to the modern woman. Take the gender wage gap, for example – a female sheep clipper earned two pence less per day than their male counterparts. Most girls were married by the age of sixteen and would have several children by their mid-twenties, although not all children would be expected to survive to adulthood. Women in towns had far more opportunities than those who lived in the countryside, thanks to the possibility of learning a trade. For example, women were known to brew ale, be shopkeepers and even blacksmiths.

Although the wage gap may not have been an issue for a queen, Matilda still faced problems of her own, chiefly that she was acutely aware of how disparagingly many across her English realm viewed her husband. Unlike William, Matilda learned the language, possibly in an attempt to enamour herself to her sceptical subjects. She was so determined for the English to see her children as rightful heirs to the throne that she insisted on giving birth in York, where rebels operated at their fiercest, although the sudden onset of labour meant she gave birth to her ninth child in Selby, fourteen miles away. Her coronation was also the first to be organised just for a queen, complete with its own soundtrack (special chants were written for the occasion). Sadly, the crown that was probably made for the occasion was lost, most likely in 1216 when King John's baggage train was swept away in the boggy marshes of Lincolnshire, never to be found again.

Nicola de la Haye, the unlikely Sheriff of Lincolnshire

Lincoln Castle was built by the Normans in 1068 for the same reason they built castles across the country – as physical symbols of their power. Nicola de la Haye inherited her father's land in Lincolnshire and his position as castellan of Lincoln Castle, a medieval term to describe a governor of sorts. Typically, Nicola's right to this land and role was expected to be fulfilled on her behalf by her husband, Gerard. However, Nicola was left in command during her husband's absences, despite the usual custom of a male deputy taking on such a role. Clearly, many people didn't know what to make of her, shown by chronicles of the time stating that she defended the castle 'manfully' in 1191. After the death of her husband, she was appointed Sheriff of Lincolnshire by King John in 1216, a reflection of her loyalty to him, something he desperately craved since he had been forced to sign the Magna Carta by his barons. In 1204 they had stood firm against John for a variety of reasons, including the scutage tax that they were being charged to fund his wars in France, which, coincidentally, he always seemed to be losing.

Later that year King John was determined to take Rochester Castle back from rebel barons. John asked for the castle to be mined so that the wooden props holding up the foundations could be exposed. Forty large pigs were slaughtered and set on fire, the walls collapsing as the wooden props burned away. The castle was stormed and the siege was over. The barons had another card up their sleeve, though; they'd promised Prince Louis of France the throne in exchange for his help in dealing with John. And it's here that we meet Nicola again. Louis' forces lay siege to Lincoln Castle for almost three months, while Nicola refused to give in. Despite the constant bombardment Nicola kept guard, commanded a garrison and oversaw the safe transfer of hostages. No wonder John had refused to accept her resignation and the return of the castle keys a few months earlier. The rebels and their French allies eventually surrendered, Magna Carta was reissued in 1216 to get consent from a new generation of barons, and John's young son Henry III was crowned.

Nicola's commitment to the crown, however, was ignored; Henry's regents seized her position as sheriff, perhaps demonstrating their unwillingness to praise a woman who many had already struggled to describe without referencing men. Nicola did not accept such treatment, and she immediately travelled to London to appeal directly to the King. This worked temporarily, but everything was eventually seized from her again only two months later. Nicola lived into her seventies, a formidable woman who continued to contribute to local life by issuing charters and providing financial support to the community. We can remember her as a woman who defiantly played an unexpected role in the defence of Magna Carta, a document whose significance – the right to trial by jury, the monarch is not above the law – continues to live on despite the centuries that have passed since its signing.

Yes, there were female versions of samurai

From the early 900s, nobles in Japan began hiring warriors to safeguard their interests, creating a class known as the samurai. They supported a military style of dictatorship called the shogunate. Different classes had distinct roles within Japanese society: the daimyo were the mirrors of European nobles or barons, controlling large pieces of land on behalf of the shogun; peasants made up the majority of the population and their main job was to grow rice, Japan's main crop. Upward movement between the different classes was very unlikely, just as in Europe. But being downgraded was, of course, possible, particularly if you had wronged those more powerful than you.

The position of knights within European feudal systems was very similar to the samurai class in Japan. Samurai devoted their lives to Bushido, the way of the warrior. The consequence of failing to uphold Bushido was seppuku, or rather, ritual suicide. However, the military role of the samurai was carefully balanced by the cultural expectations placed upon them. Most samurai committed time to cultivating a range of other skills, including flower arranging, which was regarded as a martial art of sorts, allowing one to achieve a sense of focus before going into battle. Poetry was something else samurai were encouraged to get involved in. The samurai poet Minamoto no Yorimasa wrote a heartbreaking death poem about his regrets at not having any children, before he was forced to commit seppuku. The samurai label was specific to men, but this isn't to say that female warriors did not exist. Onna-bugeisha was the name given to women who were trained in martial arts.

One famous warrior was Tomoe Gozen. Much of her life is shrouded in mystery and legend, her story told within an epic called *The Tale of the Heike*, compiled not by a singular person but based on ballads. She is described as a skilled archer who fought with a katana, a weapon usually only used by male samurai, rather than a ningata – a pole with a curved blade at the tip – the weapon usually reserved for female warriors. Tomoe is described as being worth a thousand warriors, 'ready to confront a demon or god, mounted or on foot'. She single-handedly fended off attackers during the Gempei War, and she decapitated the enemy leader while he attempted to drag her from her horse. At the Battle of Awazu in 1184 she was one of the last warriors standing and was ordered to leave, as her commander stated that he would be ashamed if he died fighting with a woman.

Tomoe's life after this is a mystery, but some believe that she may have committed seppuku. Either way, her story is understandably hugely popular in Japan, where she has been immortalised in films, comics and even video games. The story, along with that of Nicola de la Haye, shows that some medieval women were able to fulfil roles in society traditionally occupied by men and did so unapologetically and with absolute gusto. If the two women ever crossed paths they'd have had plenty to talk about, both having wielded weapons among medieval men at a time when attitudes and even language weren't quite ready for them. While Nicola's history is closely tied to the Magna Carta of 1215, around the same time a similar set of principles was being drawn up in a completely different continent.

Meanwhile, in Timbuktu

Timbuktu – the name conjures images of a faraway place. The idea permeates our consciousness, yet our factual understanding of the city often leaves a lot to be desired. Timbuktu was, in fact, a key hub in the 13th century and a centre for trade and cultural exchange within the Mali Empire. It was also a centre for education, with the University of Sankore housing the largest collection of written text since the Great Library of Alexandria. Many intellectual pursuits flourished within the city, including the study of astronomy, poetry and law.

The commitment to enshrining human rights formally during this period often centres around Magna Carta in England, but there was also the Manden Charter, its contemporary, likely adopted in the 1230s in medieval Mali. Articles within the charter are both familiar (Article 5 – Everyone has the right to life) and perhaps unusual for the time (Article 14 – Never offend women, our mothers). Some of the articles give a fascinating insight into the way Malian society operated, such as Article 7, which essentially gives permission to 'jokingly' mock the king, officially enshrining banter into the law. Clearly this was a society with core values, one which wished to protect its citizens but also valued community spirit and didn't take itself too seriously.

Here it must be noted that one of the difficulties historians face when studying a context like precolonial Africa is the nature of the source material. While much of Western history is written based on extensive archives, the history of West Africa was largely passed down via oral tradition. Some written archives do exist from those who visited at the time, however, such as those from Ibn Battuta, a Moroccan explorer whose original plan to visit Mecca (assumed to take just over a year) became a 29-year journey spanning parts of Africa, Europe, the Middle East and Asia. He travelled further than anyone else before him, four times further than Marco Polo, a Venetian merchant famous for his extensive writing about Asia. Exploration is often framed as a Western pursuit, but for every Columbus and Drake there was a Battuta and Zheng He (a Chinese mariner). Despite what we may have been led to believe when we were at school, the desire to explore beyond one's borders was not limited to Europeans.

When Battuta returned home he dictated an account of his travels, although many believe his recollections of visiting China might have been plagiarised. Even so, he provides us with a valuable insight into the wider world of the 14th century.

One stopover on his accidentally epic tour landed him in medieval Mali, in the presence of Mansa Musa, the tenth Mansa of Mali – the richest man who ever lived. It's estimated that he would have been worth approximately $400 billion today. He became ruler in 1312 when Abu Bakr II embarked on a voyage of discovery of his own to the New World and never returned.

The Mali Empire was founded a century before Mansa Musa came to power, and by the time of his rule it was the most powerful empire in West Africa, largely due to its trade in two incredibly precious commodities, salt and gold, which had allowed Mali to grow both geographically and financially.

Ibn Battuta wished to see both the city of Timbuktu and the ruler behind it. But his assessment of meeting Mansa Musa seems to be one of slight disappointment. Despite being wowed by the ceremony and entourage that surrounded Musa, Battuta appears to have had certain expectations that were not met. He was personally offended at not being bestowed with any gifts, stating, 'He is a miserly king, not a man from whom one might hope for a rich present.'

However, Musa's generosity was demonstrated in 1324, when his dedication to his religious beliefs meant an inevitable and infamous decision was made to travel on a pilgrimage to Mecca. The details of this Hajj were well-documented due to the sheer size of the operation. Musa spared no expense and left with his entire royal court, resulting in a caravan of over 60,000 people dressed in finery. Dozens of camels formed part of the procession, all carrying gold dust, while 500 enslaved people marched ahead of him, each carrying a staff made of pure gold. Musa spent so much gold in Cairo that it caused its value to depreciate. It's no wonder that Musa is depicted in the 1375 Catalan Atlas holding a gold sceptre in one hand and a gold nugget in the other, which shows us that his European peers were very aware of his achievements at the time. The gold that originated from the Mali Empire found its way to Europe, to be immortalised in crowns that adorned the heads of royalty or gilded on paintings that hung in palaces, courts and churches.

West Africa during this period is clearly a context rich in fascinating individuals, art, traditions and advancements of all kinds – in clear contrast to Victorian notions of Africa being a 'dark continent' with little history, something which later underpinned their desire to embark on 'civilising' missions there. By studying it again now, we can begin to piece together connections between those individuals and England, and widen our understanding of the medieval world, to see a less-familiar place within this well-trodden period. It's also imperative that we remember the thriving civilisations that existed in West Africa prior to the inception of the transatlantic slave trade. Too often this part of the world is first encountered in the classroom through the prism of slavery.

Medieval Baghdad was a perfect circle

If you could build a city from scratch, what shape would you build it in and why? What would your shape of choice say about you as a leader, as well as the hopes and dreams you have for your city? In July

762, the Abbasid caliph Al-Mansur laid the first brick of the Realm of Peace, having had royal astrologers confirm that this was the most auspicious time for the work to start. He had carefully planned the city, supervising workers as they laid out his design in lines of ash. Here was Baghdad, and it was going to be a perfect circle.

Built in the fertile land between the Tigris and Euphrates rivers, it took 100,000 workers to turn his vision into a reality and was the most ambitious of all construction projects in the Islamic world. At the centre of the Round City lay a magnificent mosque and the Golden Gate Palace, whose roof had domes that were over a hundred feet high. Four straight roads ran towards the centre, with squares and bazaars selling goods that reflected the international links the city enjoyed, including glass from Lebanon, dyes from India and enslaved people from African and Central Asia. If you travelled across the Silk Roads it was likely you would have passed through Baghdad. At this point the Muslim empire stretched from Spain to India, hence Baghdad was a centre of trade but also a centre of learning, where goods and ideas were exchanged within and beyond its borders.

Being a librarian in medieval Baghdad was a position of great honour. And there was no greater honour than working in the House of Wisdom. This was both a library and astronomical observatory, which catered to the interest in a variety of scholarly work, including maths, philosophy and science. It was an important place in the medieval world, not least because without these Muslim scholars meticulously translating the great works of the Greeks and Romans into Arabic, it's likely this knowledge would have been lost for ever. Familiar names to us such as Galen and Hippocrates, Plato and Aristotle were translated here first before being filtered to the West.

The dedication to translating such work had unexpected consequences, with the Abbasids specifically capturing Chinese paper makers as prisoners of war after the Battle of Talas in 781 so they could share their secrets. By 796 a paper-making factory was established in Baghdad. History has always been written by the victors, but knowledge relating to that history has been translated by those who value learning. This was a clear priority for this city where free paper, pens and lamps were provided for those wishing to write notes in their libraries. By casting our eyes beyond the cities of Europe, our understanding of life in this 'medieval' period starts to include grand libraries and mosques in addition to church towers and castles.

Despite building the city gates precisely high enough to let a lancer pass through without lowering his lance and having gates of iron so secure that a company of doormen were required to open and close them, Baghdad fell to the Mongols and their impressive siege weapons in 1258. Some 700,000 people were killed and all the notable buildings, including the libraries, were set on fire. Any books that did not burn were thrown in the Tigris River.

The destruction of medieval Baghdad by the Mongols is exactly why it is such a crucial stopover on our tour. While little physical evidence of the city remains, the learning they nurtured lives on. There's also another important lesson to be learned from this city – that of mutual understanding and respect. Despite the divisive Crusading rhetoric of the time, scholars of all faiths were invited to the city's libraries and universities to share their knowledge.

The Black Death was the most devastating pandemic in human history

The most sinister thing to travel across the medieval world was the plague of the 1340s, resulting in the death of millions. Where exactly it originated from is unclear, but the fleas who carried the deadly disease had no boundaries, killing a third of the European population in five years. Three quarters of the population of Venice perished, while in Egypt the number of taxpayers fell by 98 per cent – from 6,000 to 116.

Our understanding of what it's like to live within the context of a deadly pandemic changed dramatically from 2019, with many of us never expecting words like 'bubble' to take on such new meaning. Just as we have witnessed in the 21st century, this deadly disease and its variants that swept across the world in the 14th century did so with total disregard for religion, class or nationality. Its impact on the population alone highlights why this plague is a classic feature of school history.

The Black Death was in fact a combination of two types of plague – bubonic and pneumonic. The first had symptoms such as fever and the development of 'buboes', large boils filled with pus and blood, usually in your armpit. You'd also get a rash in the form of black and red spots. Pneumonic plague, however, was the deadlier of the two. This was caught through breathing in infected air, leading to symptoms like coughing up blood. Theories behind the cause of this widespread plague varied. Some were closer to the truth, with the air or 'miasma' being blamed. Other ideas reflected the beliefs in society at the time, such as the misalignment of the planets.

European understanding of medical science left a lot to be desired, so visiting a medical professional wouldn't have helped much. After all, this was the era when even hobbies could be hazardous. Take the medieval pastime of mob football, for example. It had no limit on player numbers, a football made of a pig's bladder stuffed with peas, and absolutely no rules. It's therefore hardly surprising that one in twenty people at the time had a broken or fractured limb. It was also the time when barber-surgeon was a genuine option as a portfolio career. And how would you know your barber of choice offers surgery too? Just look out for the fresh bowl of blood in the window. Disclosing even the simplest of ailments in medieval England could have dire consequences, a 'cure' for headaches including trepanning, which involved a hole being drilled into your skull to release the evil spirits who were causing your pain.

Knowledge at this point in England was largely based on fundamental misconceptions about how the body worked. The belief in the body being made up of four humours shows this perfectly, the idea that the body was a careful balance of blood, yellow bile, black bile and phlegm. It was therefore the job of a doctor to figure out how to restore this balance. An unlucky patient thought to have an excessive amount of blood might be advised to follow a course of bloodletting, possibly involving leeches. If they were lucky they might simply be advised to drink more red wine. A person's internal humoral balance explained their temperament. For instance, melancholic people were said to have an excess of black bile, while too much yellow bile could make a person prone to anger.

Another form of medical diagnosis was through inspecting a patient's blood, urine or faeces. It was entirely possible that you could present the exact same symptoms as another patient but leave with an entirely different course of action because your urine or even blood tasted different. Much like the medical posters adorning the walls of hospital rooms today, medieval physicians had urine charts to analyse your sample.

Faced with medical options like this, many inevitably turned to a variety of preventative measures to avoid catching the plague. One such measure was from flagellants who felt that publicly punishing themselves was the only way to avoid the plague. They would beat themselves with leather straps studded with metal shards in the hope that God would appreciate their commitment and spare them, showing just how much religion lay at the centre of medieval belief systems. Some measures were even more dangerous, like drinking a combination of mercury and vinegar. Those who developed buboes were understandably willing to try anything at that point; many tried strapping chickens and even dried out frogs to themselves in the hope that would help them survive.

The language we associate with contagious diseases like the plague originates from this period, with the word 'quarantine' coming from the 40-day isolation imposed on sailors arriving in the ports of Venice. Words like 'social distancing' and 'furlough' are surely the 21st-century versions of this, with 'lockdown' at the top of that list. While Covid-19 travelled across borders, international efforts to combat its impact are a testament to the importance of understanding and exchanging ideas in the context of global health.

There's no doubt that the Black Death, which wiped out 40 per cent of England's population, was insurmountably devastating for those who survived it, having witnessed their loved ones and other members of the community hastily buried in shallow pits, which only exacerbated the spread of the disease. Plague pits were dug due to the sheer number of bodies. A stark reminder of this came in 2013 when forensic testing confirmed that 25 skeletons unearthed during the building of the London Crossrail network were interred in one of the two emergency burial grounds dug outside the city walls for victims of the plague.

Jewish people were expelled from England in 1290

As a result of the Black Death, anti-Semitism grew in prominence in medieval Europe, but not in England, due to the expulsion of Jewish people in 1290. To try to understand this decision we must retrace our steps back to William the Conqueror, who invited Jewish people to England in 1070 to help fund various projects like castle-building, as Jewish people, unlike Christians at the time, were allowed to lend money with interest.

One such moneylender was a woman known as Licoricia of Winchester, and we can learn a lot about the experiences of Anglo-Jewish people through her story. This is not to say all Jews in England were moneylenders, of course; while there were restrictions on the type of work they could pursue, they did a huge variety of jobs, from doctors and teachers to fishmongers.

The religious zeal of the Crusades legitimised religious violence, erupting in places like York, where Jewish people were massacred in 1190. Daffodils have since been planted at the base of Clifford's Tower in York to commemorate the estimated 150 Jews who were killed, the yellow flower chosen for its six-pointed shape which echoes the Star of David. 'Blood libels' – false claims that Jews were abducting and murdering Christian children – fuelled anti-Semitism across Europe from the 12th century, with some even believing they were using the children's blood to make matzos with. This started in Norwich in 1144, when Jewish people were falsely accused of killing a young boy, something Licoricia's first husband (Abraham of Kent) was also accused of in 1225. There are many other examples of anti-Jewish violence during this period, such as in 1255, when eighteen Jewish people were executed at the Tower of London for killing an eight-year-old boy whose body was found in a cesspool attached to the house of a member of the Jewish community.

Licoricia herself was imprisoned in the Tower of London a decade before this, but for a different reason. Her second husband, David of Oxford, was a well-connected moneylender who went to great lengths to marry her. Licoricia was clearly quite the catch: she travelled with armed guards, wore fur-lined silk gowns and was highly educated, shown by her grasp of both numbers and languages. David had to divorce his first wife, Muriel, in order to marry Licoricia, which proved tricky when Muriel refused to give her consent. The marriage was eventually nullified, although only after the intervention of the King.

Licoricia and David soon had a son, and after David's death, Licoricia intended to continue leading his business. She was imprisoned while the debts owed to him were assessed, the authorities fearing she would somehow interfere with the process. It's likely she was fairly comfortable, though, and given allowances such as kosher meals. Eventually she was released and was informed that she could purchase the rights to the debts owed for a fee, much of which was then used to fund renovations at Westminster Abbey.

Her relationship with the royal family did little to protect her from prejudice, however. She was sent to the Tower again in 1258, falsely accused of stealing a gold ring meant for King Henry III. Her neighbour Ivetta, who led the accusations, was subsequently charged. Similarly, Abraham of Berkhamsted, also known as 'the king's Jew' due to his financial connections to the monarch, was falsely imprisoned in the Tower, accused of doing the most 'filthy and unmentionable' things to a statue of the Virgin Mary, which he allegedly kept in his bathroom.

Despite this clearly being a dangerous time for Jewish people, Licoricia's tenacity meant she was able to simultaneously raise her family and run a successful business as a single mother of five, although after 1279 she was a mother of four. Her son Benedict was found guilty of 'coin clipping', which involved illegally cutting the edges of coins and melting them down to make new ones. Stories of coin clipping exacerbated existing prejudices, and Christian–Jewish relations in England soon reached boiling point. Hundreds of Jewish people were imprisoned in the Tower, with approximately 300 executed, including Benedict.

From 1275, Jewish men and women, and children over the age of seven, were required to wear badges on their chests to differentiate them from the rest of the population. There were also limits placed on where Jews could live, meaning whole communities were forced to move. Just two years later, Licoricia and her maid were found murdered in her home, possibly during a robbery, though it's not beyond the realm of possibility that she was deliberately murdered by one of the many powerful people still indebted to her. No one was charged and two of her sons tried to get justice, but to no avail.

In 1290, Edward I, under increasing burden of debt, promised parliament that he would expel the Jewish community from England in exchange for £116,000, the largest single tax of the Middle Ages. This marked the first permanent and forcible expulsion of Jewish people in Europe. The Jewish community, numbering around 3,000, were given three months to leave, and not all were able to do so safely, with one group told to disembark onto a sandbank where they were then abandoned and left to drown. Those expelled included all of Licoricia's remaining children. The Edict of Expulsion meant that Jewish people would not return to England for 365 years, when Oliver Cromwell extended an invitation to them in 1655. When you think of governments forcing Jewish people to identify themselves with a badge or patch, remember that while this was mostly famously adopted in 1930s Germany, it also happened in 13th-century England, in the shape of stone tablets rather than yellow stars.

A statue of Licoricia now stands in Winchester, opposite her home in 13th-century England. She's mid-stride, clearly a defiant woman on a mission, while also holding the hand of her youngest son, who is playing with a dreidel: a woman from a religious minority who juggled family life and a career before her tragic murder. Her statue grasps a demand for tallage (taxation) in her other hand, a reminder of how the Jewish community were increasingly taxed prior to their expulsion.

Had she lived till 1290, despite all her resilience, she too would have found herself being forced from the island she'd called home her entire life.

The peasants found their voice in 1381

A 1348 chronicle of the Black Death describes the inevitable shortage of workers that followed: 'Alas, the mortality devoured such a multitude of both sexes that no one could be found to carry the bodies of the dead to burial.' Some English peasants who had miraculously survived felt empowered to demand higher wages, sparked further by food shortages and price increases. Those in power were keen to remind the peasants of their place, and in 1351 the Statute of Labourers was introduced. This law limited the freedom of peasants to travel in pursuit of new employment and it froze their pay at pre-plague levels. By 1380, King Richard II had inherited the crown, who, much like Richard I, was not necessarily expecting to be king so soon. Unusually, Richard II inherited the throne from his grandfather, Edward III, in 1377 (at the age of ten), as Richard's father had died rather unglamorously of dysentery in 1376. Richard II found himself knee-deep in the Hundred Years' War against France and had to raise taxes regularly to support the campaign, which would rage on for another 73 years. The latest tax was a blanket poll tax that quadrupled the previous payment and was imposed on everyone over fifteen. In 1381 the Peasants' Revolt started, targeting those who they saw as responsible for their hardship.

This is widely known as the first example of ordinary people starting a revolt, with previous uprisings commonly led by nobles and barons. As Richard was only fourteen at the time, anger was mostly directed elsewhere. The first target was John Bampton, a tax collector whose clerks were beheaded by peasants angered by his attempts to clamp down on supposed tax evaders. This violence of the peasants lies in stark contrast to scenes in Coventry circa 1050, when Lady Godiva nakedly rode a horse after her husband, Leofric, Earl of Mercia, told her he would only yield to her demands for lower taxes in the city if she did so.

Religious leaders were attacked too, partly due to growing resentment towards the church, with preachers like John Ball encouraging peasants to question social inequalities. The Archbishop of Canterbury was dragged from the Tower of London onto Tower Hill, where he was brutally executed, his head, which had received eight blows from an axe, placed triumphantly on a spike. Buildings representing royal authority and government were also attacked. Savoy Palace, the home of the King's economic advisor John of Gaunt, was infiltrated by rebels who proceeded to consume all of his wine. Not all the barrels in the house contained wine, though; the entire building was destroyed when two barrels of gunpowder exploded.

The elite and the church were not the only groups the peasants aimed their anger at. Say these three words aloud: 'Bread and cheese'. In 1381, if you were asked to say this and your reply revealed an accent, you may well have lost your life. Flemings were migrants who primarily arrived from modern-day Belgium, the Netherlands and Luxembourg. They migrated here as labourers and did a huge range of jobs, from brewing to brick making. Flemish weavers in particular were a key component of the expanding English cloth trade, who were given permission to set up their own guilds. This was because it became clear that higher profits could be made if wool were weaved into cloth before being sold, and the Flemish were the most skilled weavers in Europe. They had a lasting impact: weavers who moved to Manchester in 1363 laid the foundation for the thriving textile business that industrial Britain would be built on 500 years later.

It should come as no surprise to learn that some peasants in London specifically targeted these early migrants. It's estimated that 150 migrants were killed, most likely beheaded. Was 'bread and cheese' the brutal medieval version of the seemingly innocent question 'Where are you *really* from?' This means of identifying native speakers was not new, of course; in 1302 the phrase 'shield and friend' was used to identify French speakers, resulting in the death of approximately 2,000 people.

The Peasants' Revolt was over by the middle of June. Their main leader, Wat Tyler, was decapitated after their demands were rejected by the King, his head displayed on London Bridge. A further 1,500 rebels were executed as a warning to anyone considering restarting the revolt. The poll tax was never repeated in the medieval period, though it was infamously reprised in 1989. Over the next century peasants would be able to gradually loosen themselves from the land they'd been traditionally tied to, becoming 'freemen' at last.

THE TUDORS 2

In 2010 the Redland Hotel in Chester was undergoing redevelopment. The bed from the honeymoon suite had seen better days, so was dismantled and placed in the car park to be auctioned. Advertised as a 'Victorian four poster bed', it was purchased for £2,000 by someone who suspected the provenance of the bed might be earlier. Dendrochronology, the scientific method of dating tree rings, confirmed that not only was this bed made in the 1480s, but it was made for the marriage of Henry VII, the first Tudor king, and Elizabeth of York, who tied the knot at Westminster Abbey in 1486. This 'state bed' is one of the few early Tudor furnishings we have, as so much of it was destroyed by anti-royalists during the English Civil War of the 1640s. It is ironic that this bed was intended to celebrate a royal couple, while its alleged disappearance was fuelled by negativity against royals so sharp that Charles I lost his head. Paint analysis reminds us of the wealth of this period and how connected the world continued to be, with the blue identified as lapis lazuli, originating from Afghanistan and worth more than gold at the time.

The wedding feast likely had a menu that left little to the imagination, with more subtle servings of chestnuts, pistachios and pine nuts thought to stimulate one's libido, in addition to the inclusion of phallic-shaped food like asparagus. The final event of the night was the infamous bedding ceremony, where blessings would be given, followed by both parties consuming a drink of wine and spices thought to provide the 'necessary' strength. The onlookers, including musicians, attendants and priests, might not have left until they saw the couple's naked legs touching, a reflection of how their privacy was secondary to the realm's investment in the heirs it was hoped the couple would have. It's likely that Henry VIII was conceived on this bed, meaning it's now valued at around £20 million. It may also have been where their daughter Margaret was conceived, the Tudor that Queen Elizabeth II's lineage can be traced through.

Why start with the state bed? Marriages are almost synonymous with the word Tudor. The first six decades of the Tudor reign saw an abundance of royal weddings, mostly thanks to one man, while the last four significantly saw none, despite the number of proposals that came Elizabeth I's way. This chapter will touch on, but won't centre around, such marital dramas. Instead, we'll reach beyond the palaces and tournaments to show how surprisingly vast the world of the Tudors really was.

Henry VIII was the spare

Henry VII ruled for 24 years as the first monarch of the House of Tudor, until his death in 1509. His marriage with Elizabeth of York was seen as successful, and the couple had their first child, Arthur, in 1486. When Henry VII died, however, it was not Arthur who inherited the crown. Why? Arthur had been struck down with an unknown illness in 1502 at the age of fifteen. Therefore, the 'spare' was now next in line to the throne, in the form of second son Henry. A prince not destined to be king was now firmly placed on that path. Arthur had been married for less than six months when he died. His wife was Catherine, daughter of Isabella I of Castile and Ferdinand II of Aragon. Their marriage was a strategic one, with this Anglo–Spanish union seen as a helpful bulwark against the French by both sides.

Seventeen-year-old King Henry VIII inherited a wealthy and relatively stable kingdom from his father. At this point in his life he was the epitome of health, towering at 6 feet and 2 inches, with a 42-inch chest and 31-inch waist. Within eight weeks of his father's death he married his ex-sister-in-law, Catherine. Their marriage was given the green light after a papal dispensation confirmed that her first marriage had not been consummated. Henry VIII claimed he was simply fulfilling his dying father's final wish. We all know what happens next. In the classroom the wives of Henry VIII are usually reduced to one word: 'Divorced, beheaded, died; divorced, beheaded, survived'.

In 1511, Catherine of Aragon gave birth to a baby boy named Henry. To honour this occasion, Henry VIII held two days of celebrations and commissioned a parchment to record the event.

The Black Tudor trumpeter who knew his worth

The parchment, known as the Westminster Roll, shows six trumpeters, one of whom we now know to be John Blanke. He is Black and wearing a brown and gold turban. The turban itself suggests he may have been Muslim, with the flat shape similar to North African styles of the time. African presence was far more limited in England than it was in the rest of Europe at this time, particularly Spain, or even Scotland, where Peter the Moor, for example, was paid a pension by King James IV between 1501 and 1504, enjoying perks of the job like travelling to France.

Blanke likely came to England as one of the African attendants of Catherine of Aragon, when she first came to the country in 1501. The Spanish court she was brought up in would have been fairly multicultural, due to its proximity to Moorish North Africa. Blanke was present at many significant events of the early Tudor period. For example, he was given a new black outfit for the funeral of Henry VII in 1509. A few weeks later, Blanke played at the joint coronation of Henry VIII and Queen Catherine and was given four and a half yards of cloth, which he used to make a gown and hood. The colour he was given was scarlet, to symbolise that he was a high-ranking servant.

Blanke was one of fifteen trumpeters who would have been working solidly for the two days of the tournament celebrating the birth of Henry, an event that would have cost two hundred times the amount of Blanke's wages. One of the final tasks for the trumpeters was to welcome the King and Queen to the post-tournament banquet.

Sadly, the first-born child of Henry VIII and Catherine died only 53 days after his birth, less than a fortnight after the extravagant tournament that had been organised in his honour. Catherine was pregnant six times during her marriage to Henry, with only one, Mary, surviving.

Written records show wages being given to 'John Blanke, the Black trumpeter'. He was paid 8d a day, the wages parallel to those earned by skilled craftsmen. Blanke petitioned Henry VIII for a pay rise, arguing that he was being paid less than the previous trumpeter. During this time wages were based loosely on experience, which by this point Blanke had in spades. Henry VIII clearly thought so and his wages were swiftly doubled. In 1512, Blanke got married and Henry VIII gave him a wedding present of a gown of violet cloth as well as a bonnet and a hat. We know that it was customary to do this, with Henry VIII issuing various gifts to servants depending on the sort of job they had. After the document noting the wedding present, Blanke disappears from the records.

Irrespective of the mystery surrounding the later part of his life, what we do know is that he lived in Britain in the 1500s, was a Black Tudor, had a job in the service of Henry VIII and decided to marry here. He was treated just as other servants were, shown by the wedding gift he received. The pay rise petition provides us with an intriguing insight into his character: he knew his worth. His ethnic origin does not appear to have impacted his ability to be in such close proximity to royalty; he played a part in events of real significance, from funerals to coronations. He clearly disrupts our traditional understanding of Tudor England. We will be meeting more Black Tudors throughout this chapter, although Blanke remains the only one for which we have a definitive image. Out of the hundreds of people of African origin we know lived in England and Scotland during this period, his is the only face we can be absolutely sure of.

Christopher Columbus did not 'discover' America

Finish the sentence that starts with 'Christopher Columbus ...' Most people will go with '... discovered America'. This, of course, negates the reality that approximately a hundred million people already lived in the Americas, roughly the same population as Europe at the time. The more accurate term would be that Columbus landed on the Americas. He wasn't the first European to do so, however; Viking Leif Erikson's voyage to Newfoundland likely takes that award.

Columbus, an Italian merchant with dreams of maximising riches from abroad, shopped around the royal courts of Europe, determined to find someone to sponsor his endeavour to sail westwards and reach Asia. As we already know, the Silk Roads had long connected Europe with Asia. Columbus was hoping he could find a route to Asia across the seas that essentially cut out the middlemen along the way. Of course, what Columbus didn't know was that there was a rather large land mass that lay west, and maps like the one from 1489 by German cartographer Henricus Martellus would radically shift as a result of Columbus' voyage.

Queen Isabella and King Ferdinand of Castile, Catherine of Aragon's parents, gave Columbus the green light, and in 1492 he sailed west, bound for the Indies, assuming he would reach China. He set sail with three ships and around a hundred men. After six weeks or so, land was spotted, much to the joy of those aboard, as supplies were running low. The island they landed on was promptly 'claimed' as Spanish territory and was named San Salvador (translated as 'Holy Saviour'). It was assumed this was an island in Asia, hence they referred to the indigenous people they encountered there as 'Indians'.

We now know this was in fact the Bahamas. Columbus continued to explore the islands, taking much interest in what he named Hispaniola, now modern-day Dominican Republic and Haiti. Columbus wrote to his benefactors, describing the riches he had encountered, such as gold, silver and pearls. Word of Columbus' letters spread like wildfire across Europe, supported by what he brought back with him:

chillies, pineapples, tobacco and captured members of the Taino, the indigenous people of the region.

Columbus made three successive voyages back to the 'West Indies'. One of the motivating factors was the possibility of enslaving indigenous people, and on his second voyage Columbus sent 500 Taino to be sold in Spain, with many dying en route. His other focus was on procuring as much gold as possible. Any Taino above the age of fourteen would have their hands chopped off if they failed to fulfil their quota. Columbus imposed 'iron discipline' across Hispaniola, with brutal punishments like mutilations commonplace and dismembered body parts paraded in public. It was this that led to Ferdinand and Isabella removing his role as governor of Hispaniola in 1499. He died in 1506, though his family were embroiled in legal battles with the Spanish monarchy till 1790, arguing that they were owed money.

The significance of Columbus' voyage in 1492 was far-reaching, sparking others to set sail in the same direction, egged on by technological advances that allowed more accurate navigation. And the Spanish continued to build on their hold over the Americas, as did Portugal.

The Aztec Empire was based in Central Mexico and is usually a feature of primary school history, starring flat-topped pyramids upon which priests made human sacrifices. This was based on the belief that the sun god Huitzilopochtli needed human hearts and blood to keep the sky moving. The Aztecs used cocoa beans as currency and had derived a multitude of ways to use cacti, from fuel to paper and wine. Understanding the destruction of the Aztec Empire is essential in order to comprehend the strength of Spain, one of the key rivals of Tudor England.

The heart of the Aztec Empire was Tenochtitlan, and it was this city that became the target of Spanish conquistador Hernán Cortés in 1519. Central America was relatively unexplored by Europeans at this stage; by 1521 it would become known as New Spain. The Aztecs ruled by fear, intimidating neighbouring cities, which meant Cortés was able to lure some of these indigenous groups, such as the Tlaxcalans, to ally with them. The Spanish had already inadvertently given themselves an advantage in the form of smallpox, which was sweeping through the indigenous population, resulting in the death of the city's ruler Cuitláhuac after a mere 80-day reign following the death of Montezuma II.

In advance of the Spanish assault on Tenochtitlan, food supplies were cut, canals were filled and buildings destroyed. Cortés also had a secret weapon – an indigenous woman called La Malinche or Malintzin. She was sold into slavery by her mother, who then faked a funeral for her rather than tell anyone the truth. She was eventually sold to Cortés, who soon realised her grasp of languages was an invaluable asset. She quickly rose to prominence as a translator as well as strategic liaison; she would frequently gain intel from locals and pass it on to the Spanish. She also had a child with Cortés, a son named Martin. She was, ironically, an interpreter who has since been interpreted in such different ways. For some, she likely had no choice in her actions, an enslaved woman who was simply trying to survive. For others, she was and always will be a traitor, with her name still used as an insult in Mexico today.

The Spanish military tactics were a surprise to the Aztecs, who mistook Spanish horses for gods. The Aztecs were also used to a different type of warfare, the aim of which was to keep the enemy alive for sacrificial purposes. After an 85-day siege, the new ruler, Cuauhtémoc, was captured while attempting to flee by canoe. He was tortured in an attempt to reveal the location of additional Aztec treasure and was later executed by the Spanish.

Overall, it's estimated that 240,000 Aztecs died, through a combination of combat, starvation and disease, in contrast to the Spanish, who lost fewer than 1,000. Mexico City was built on the rubble that was Tenochtitlan, the capital city of New Spain. Christianity spread across Central America along with the increasing wealth and power of the Spanish.

In 1525 another Spanish conquistador, Francisco Pizarro, followed Cortés' example when he successfully subjugated the Incas in Peru. This European conquest of Central and South America, which began in the 1490s and was very much led by the Portuguese and Spanish, had far-reaching consequences. Their actions led to countries like Britain beginning to formally colonise other Caribbean islands in the 1620s.

Henry VIII loses his favourite ship

While previous monarchs largely relied on the ships of their subjects, Henry VIII was keen on funding a navy and had his own ships commissioned. It's reputed that his favourite warship was the *Mary Rose*, which saw fighting against both the French and Scots. It was constructed from 1510 and refitted in the 1530s, but the *Mary Rose* sank in July 1545 during a battle with the French.

Henry VIII was staying at Southsea Castle and actually watched the *Mary Rose* sink, with the situation made even more tragic by the fact that its commander, Sir George Carew, was a close friend of his. The actual cause of the ship's demise is still debated, with some arguing it was burdened with too many weapons and men, while others suggest it was the work of a French cannonball. It was hoped that the entire ship could be recovered, given the waters were shallow enough for the masts to still be visible above sea level. The Venetian salvage operators tasked with the recovery made little progress, snapping the masts and failing to move the wreckage as planned. Coincidentally, their team had consumed almost 36,000 pints of beer that month, which they billed to the King. When the recovery of the whole ship became unlikely, focus shifted to the recovery of guns onboard, which were worth the equivalent of nearly £2 million today.

Italian salvage diver Piero Paola Corsi was tasked with this operation. His team was led by a Guinean diver called Jacques Francis, who may well have been joined by two other Black Tudors, John Iko and George Blacke. Jacques Francis was born in the 1520s and it is likely he learned to free dive in Africa, where he was possibly employed as a pearl diver. In contrast, most Europeans at this time did not know how to swim. The team assembled managed to recover some, but not all of the guns. It would be 1836 before anyone would lay eyes on the wreck again, and in 1982, some 437 years after it sank, the remains of the *Mary Rose* were finally recovered.

It was through Francis' subsequent employment under the same boss that he came to be the first known African to give evidence in an English court of law. Piero Paola Corsi was accused of stealing tin from a wreckage the team were salvaging in Southampton. Francis was asked to testify, in which he defended Corsi. Attempts were made by the other side to discredit Francis on the basis that he was enslaved, but this was, in fact, not the case, as several witnesses confirmed he received wages for his work. It is unclear what happened to Francis after this, but what we can be certain of is that the skills of this Black salvage diver were sought after and rewarded in Tudor England. Interestingly, thanks to recent multi-isotope analysis of the teeth of the crew members, it's come to light that the crew aboard the *Mary Rose* when it sank in the Solent may have been more diverse than previously assumed. Although we can't be certain, it seems that when Jacques was attempting to recover goods from the ship, he may well have passed the sunken remains of other Black Tudors, who had originally hailed from Morocco.

Henry died two years after the sinking of his beloved *Mary Rose*, on 28 January 1547. The funeral was as lavish as the man himself, complete with a wax effigy of Henry covered in velvet and precious stones. He was buried, at his request, next to Jane Seymour. What followed was the short reign of Edward, and then the years of 'Bloody Mary'. It's estimated that 280 people were burnt at the stake during her reign, as the heresy laws made it punishable by death to deny papal supremacy. However, this number pales in comparison next to the tens of thousands estimated to have been executed overall during Henry VIII's reign – even if only 81 people were executed for heresy under him.

Why, then, is Mary so closely associated with executions? Again, we come to the issue of who writes history. Writers like John Foxe were incredibly influential during the Elizabethan age of emphasising the torture and treatment of Protestants under Mary I's reign. His book contained 60 woodcuts, many of which depicted horrific scenes of people being executed, which certainly contributed to how Mary has been remembered.

The end of Mary's life was plagued with personal tragedy: she suffered from a phantom pregnancy, which may well have been an ovarian tumour that eventually killed her. Eleven days before her death, Mary named Elizabeth as her heir. Elizabeth became queen in 1558, at the age of 25. Elizabeth had been educated under the assumption that she would be married off to a foreign prince, hence her fluency in English, French, Italian, Greek and Latin. But while Henry VIII's legacy has been so closely tied to his six marriages, the reign of his third child, Elizabeth I, was carefully constructed around her single status.

Elizabeth I gets the ick

Think back over your life and consider: what's the most romantic gesture someone has done for you? Because whatever it is likely pales into comparison with how Robert Dudley, the Earl of Leicester, made one final attempt to woo Elizabeth in 1575. He put on quite the public display when he housed her for a staycation at Kenilworth Castle, from designing a symmetrical Italian-style garden complete with bejewelled aviary and 18-foot-high fountain to actually stopping all the clocks once she arrived, presumably to signal that he felt time literally stopped in her presence. Dudley hired the playwright George Gascoigne to write plays especially for her visit, which included not too subtle hints that she should get married. He built apartments especially for her, with spectacular views overlooking the lake and which featured rich tapestries, ornate fireplaces and the tallest sequence of windows anywhere in England at the time. He also had direct access to her private chamber discreetly built into one of the walls. He wanted to show her that he knew her well, by including a private dancing chamber and a basement to house her huge travelling wardrobe.

This three-week proposal stay is regarded as the most expensive party of Elizabeth's 45-year reign. When she arrived at 8pm she got quite the welcome, including cannon fire and actors reciting speeches. Dudley had organised a programme of spectacular entertainment, including bear baiting, dancing and a fireworks display. The latter was particularly risky, given that on her last visit Dudley had put on a battle re-enactment for her, complete with pyrotechnic dragons, during which a cannonball had accidentally set fire to a neighbouring town, whom Elizabeth understandably then compensated.

Despite clearly partying like it was 1575, Elizabeth left Kenilworth earlier than planned, with Dudley hoping it was the poor weather rather than overkill on his part. He even had matching portraits of them made and hidden behind curtains, to be revealed when she agreed to marry him. She therefore never set eyes on either of them.

Yasuke, the first Black samurai

Portraits we have of Elizabeth consistently depict her as young and ... pale. Many women followed her example and started to wear a form of Tudor make-up called ceruse, a dangerous combination of lead and vinegar, the highest quality of which came from Venice and was mixed with water or egg white to form a paste. This would not receive positive reviews from the beauty influencers of today; the paste would have looked grey after a few hours of wear, and it would have a long-term impact on one's skin, with some resorting to using artificial eyebrows made from mouse hair, as the lead could stunt hair growth.

The fascination with pale skin during this time was in direct contrast to the experience of a man who found himself in Japan in the 1570s. In fact, so many people in Kyoto were desperate to see this particular man that it's reported some were crushed to death when they attempted to get a glimpse of him. Luckily, he managed to hide out in a church to avoid such dangerously enthusiastic crowds. But why were they so intrigued by him? Well, he was at least a foot taller than the average Japanese citizen, and he was Black. The powerful warlord Oda Nobunaga was so fascinated by his skin colour on meeting him that he asked for his body to be scrubbed.

Yasuke's origin story is highly disputed, but it's possible he hailed from Mozambique and arrived in Japan under the service of an Italian Jesuit priest called Alessandro Valignano. It is unclear whether he was enslaved or not, although the ranks he so quickly rose to indicate he had some kind of warrior background.

Within a year he achieved something extraordinary: he was the first foreign-born man to become a samurai warrior, illustrated by his possession of the katana sword. He learned to speak Japanese and was allowed to dine with Oda Nobunaga, which would have been a great honour. He also joined him in battle, and was present when Nobunaga performed seppuku. The warlord requested that Yasuke take his head rather than allow it to fall into enemy hands, a sign of clear trust between these two men. What happened to Yasuke in later life is unclear, but his legacy is incredibly powerful. He was a man who was able to overcome barriers of language and customs, able to thrive in a society that was becoming increasingly closed off.

His unexpected presence as an African-born samurai in 16th-century Japan is, once again, an example of how history can continue to surprise.

Elizabeth I laid the foundations of the British Empire

Elizabeth I used portraiture as propaganda, with symbolism used to signal various messages to her subjects, from nods to her Tudor lineage and therefore her legitimacy as queen, to references to her support for the navy, which also served as a reminder of her father. The first thing most people probably notice, however, are her spectacular dresses.

If you're not a morning person then you certainly would not have enjoyed getting dressed as Elizabeth. It took an entire team of people, including a 'pinner', as up to a thousand pins could be used with one outfit alone. She frequently had to be sewn into her dresses, meaning each stitch would have to be carefully unpicked before she could retire to bed that night. This was particularly important, because in stark contrast to her father, Elizabeth was known to frequently repair and re-wear her dresses, several centuries before tabloid commentary on the recycled outfits of royal women today. The colours she wore were chosen carefully, with white used often due to its links with virginity.

The embellishments added to her dresses were often symbolic, representing messages she wished to convey publicly. My favourite of these is seen in the *Rainbow Portrait*. When you first look at the dress, it appears to be an orange dress with a seemingly innocent pattern across it. But when you look closer you realise the patterns are in fact tiny eyes and ears, a symbol that shows nothing got past Elizabeth.

The famous *Armada Portrait* contains a wealth of symbolism, including an ermine (member of the weasel family), which had a double meaning. Firstly, ermine fur was only worn by royalty, so its presence in the painting served as a reminder of her status. Secondly, legend has it that ermines would rather die than soil their white fur, so they were also a symbol of purity.

On the *Armada Portrait* Elizabeth is resting her hand on a globe, and her fingers are closing in on the Americas, a sign of what England desired most: an empire. Building an empire relied on what were euphemistically referred to as 'explorers'. A key player for Elizabeth was Sir John Hawkins, who became the first Englishman to enslave West Africans in this period, formally creating the foundation for what would become the English triangle of trade. In 1564 he captured 300 African people from Sierra Leone. He transported them via ship and they were sold to the Spanish in Hispaniola in exchange for pearls, hides and sugar.

Elizabeth sponsored his subsequent voyages, even providing him with a large ship called the *Jesus of Lübeck*. During his four voyages to Sierra Leone between 1564 and 1569, he sold approximately 1,200 Africans into slavery. At this point the Portuguese were enslaving up to 12,000 Africans annually. Hawkins was simply the first Englishman to do so, adding a bound and enslaved man to his coat of arms.

Interest in this particular trade had formed under the previous queen, when, in 1555, five West Africans, from Shama in modern-day Ghana, were brought to England for a very specific purpose. Merchant Jon Locke had thought of a way to muscle in on Portugal, who were dominating this trade. He thought that if he could teach these men English, they could then act as interpreters for English enslavers in the future. On the same journey, proof of what else could be traded for profit was displayed at the home of another merchant, Sir Andrew Judd, including 36 casks of pepper and 44 pounds of 22-carat gold. It was probably the elephant's head that caused the biggest stir, though, which was accompanied by 250 tusks.

Over the course of the next century the English would come to dominate the transatlantic slave trade, until the early 1800s, creating many more wealthy merchants. Lots of these newly wealthy families were able to commission family portraits of their own, just as Elizabeth had done throughout her reign.

Meanwhile, elsewhere: the Mughals ruled over India

Elizabeth faced many threats throughout her reign, including those from Catholics who believed her to be illegitimate and wished her cousin Mary would rule instead. Elizabeth was not alone in having to carefully manoeuvre religious policy as a ruler in the 16th century, however. To the east, in India, the Mughal emperor Akbar was trying his utmost to keep religious divisions as stable as possible. The history of the Mughals is inextricably linked to British history, as it was during this time that the foundations were being laid for the British takeover of India.

Akbar the Great shared many similarities with Elizabeth I. They had both inherited their kingdoms at a young age and at a similar time (Akbar was crowned in 1556, aged thirteen, while Elizabeth was crowned at 25 in 1559), and they died two years apart. Their grandfathers were of vital importance to the stories of their respective families, with Henry Tudor's victory at the Battle of Bosworth securing the Tudor dynasty, while Babur the Conqueror beat the Delhi sultan Ibrahim Lodi in 1526, making him the first emperor of the Mughal dynasty. Babur had actually been invited to invade North India by Lodi's rivals. The Lodi sultans were, like the Mughals, a Muslim dynasty whose power was wavering thanks to internal rivalry. In contrast, Babur had been going from strength to strength, conquering

Kabul in 1503, a city of trade that joined India with Central Asia. The odds were in his favour, as despite being outnumbered by five to one, Babur's investment in Ottoman weaponry like cannons and muskets paid off. After the Battle of Panipat, treasures were seized from Agra, including a very special diamond that we'll meet again.

Henry Tudor had come from royal stock, the Lancaster line of the House of Plantagenet running through his veins; meanwhile, Babur's family descended from the Mongol warlord Timur. Babur doubled the size of the empire across his four-year reign, something his grandson Akbar extended further west to include Afghanistan, Bengal to the east and Gujarat to the south. Had Elizabeth and Akbar met, they may well have bonded over their mutual love of hunting, although perhaps Elizabeth would be taken aback by Akbar's interest in taming wild elephants. Tales of family drama could also have been a point of discussion, with the execution of Elizabeth's mother something not too far removed from the Mughals' experience. Although Akbar's father Humayun had not been willing to execute his own rival brother, he had not been beyond blinding him.

There were, however, many differences between the two. The 'marriage question' that plagued Elizabeth throughout her reign was not something Akbar experienced. Akbar had multiple wives, with his successor Salim, later known as Jahangir, born in 1569 to his Rajput wife, a matrimonial alliance which gave him control over Rajasthan, echoing the role Catherine of Aragon played in England. In 1600 Akbar's empire included around a hundred million people, while Elizabeth ruled over fewer than five million.

Akbar's chronic dyslexia meant he never learned to read and write, but this did not limit his intellectual curiosity. He ensured his court reflected his interests, hiring scholars and scribes to support the expansion of the imperial library to over 24,000 books. He would often disguise himself and slip away from his royal apartments to mingle with ordinary people, who were unaware that they were in the presence of their emperor. Much like Elizabeth's attempt at the 'middle way' early on in her reign, which included policies like allowing Catholics to worship in private, Akbar was conscious of repairing religious divisions, repealing policies like jizya tax, which was a poll tax imposed by the Delhi sultanate on all non-Muslims. Akbar took this further, celebrating Hindu festivals like Diwali. To that end he was mindful that power should be distributed among different groups, ensuring the mansabdars (nobles) were Afghans and Persians as well as Hindu and Muslim Indians.

Akbar's religious tolerance is reflected through the Fatehpur Sikri in Agra, a palace complex he had built in 1571, which translates as City of Victory. Every aspect of the design had a purpose, from the entrance gate where Akbar would greet the public every morning to the 'peerless pool' where he would sit most evenings surrounded by musicians and dancers, breathing in the perfumed water. It was Persian in style but with clear influences from Hindu and Jain temples. To that end, Akbar encouraged leaders of all faiths to join him in debates every Thursday in his new palace. He would host Catholic missionaries from Portuguese Goa as well as Hindus, Jains, Muslims, Jews and Zoroastrians. This is not to say everyone agreed with Akbar's policies, however; he experienced rebellions during his reign led by men like Pratap Singh, who were resistant to his territorial expansion.

It was at the Fatehpur Sikri that Akbar met Ralph Fitch, the first recorded Englishman to visit India. Fitch was sent to India by Elizabeth, complete with a letter of introduction for the emperor that made clear the reason for Fitch's mission: trade. It was the Portuguese who had sparked English interests in India following Vasco da Gama's expedition in 1498, which made him the first European to successfully sail to India. The Portuguese were also interested in establishing an empire, annexing Goa in 1510, which allowed them to enjoy a huge amount of revenue due to their monopoly of the spice trade. Other European nations, such as the Spanish and Dutch, sought a slice of this trade too.

Setting sail in 1583 and hoping the letter from Elizabeth would protect him, Fitch was accompanied by John Eldred (a jeweller) and William Leedes. They were soon arrested as spies by the Portuguese, but they were released and made their way to meet Akbar. It turned out that the letter from Elizabeth wasn't particularly useful, but all wasn't lost, as Eldred found himself a new job as Akbar's jeweller – presumably not what Elizabeth had in mind when she sent him to India. Fitch's travels took him around Asia for eight years, arriving back in 1591, much to the surprise of his family, who'd presumed he was dead. He shared all he had learned and wrote an account of what he'd seen, such as the Indian markets filled with gems, spices, dyes and cloth.

In the same year that Fitch returned, a merchant called Sir James Lancaster embarked on a trading voyage to India. He was not successful, with one of his ships sinking. He did, however, learn a lot about how the Portuguese operated. In 1601, Lancaster was chosen to command the East India Company's first expedition on a ship called the *Red Dragon*, formerly a pirate ship called the *Scourge of Malice*. They had been spurred on by the Dutch, and this group of unassuming merchants decided that they too wanted to trade directly. They met at Founders' Hall in London and formed a company, the Honourable Company of Merchants of London Trading with the East Indies. In December 1600, after being lobbied by said merchants, Elizabeth granted them a royal charter. Lancaster was part of that initial drive to set up trading stations in the East, which would flourish beyond imagination over the next two centuries. The East India Company (EIC) would eventually control much of the Indian subcontinent, with this then leading to almost a century of direct British rule over India.

By the time the EIC visited the court of the Mughals in 1615, it was Akbar's son Jahangir who was emperor. In 1615, Thomas Roe was sent to Agra to secure trading rights. An image of this scene can be found in the Houses of Parliament, in a gallery of canvases united under the theme of the 'Building of Britain', a clear reflection of how significant this meeting at Agra was, marking as it did the beginnings of Britain's commercial relationship with India.

Jahangir succumbed in 1618, allowing an English trading post to be secured at Surat. By the end of the century they'd set up a huge number of these all across the country. One of the most intriguing images of Jahangir depicts a weighing ceremony, a tradition which started under his father Akbar. This image gives us an extraordinary insight into life inside Mughal India under Jahangir's reign. The ceremony itself reflects the wealth of the Mughals; the prince (the future emperor Shah Jahan) is being weighed against different precious goods, including gold, silver and grain. Beyond the ceremony itself there are other indicators of wealth, such as the Persian rugs and Chinese porcelain, signs of the international connections the empire had fostered. The gold, silver and grain, or the equivalent value in coins, were then distributed to those in need. The continuation of religious tolerance is also clear, as this ceremony was derived from an ancient Hindu ritual called Tulabhara. Shah Jahan's mother was Jahangir's first wife, Jagat Gosaini, a Rajput princess. Had this ritual taken place after 1611, the coins may well have borne the name of Jahangir's 20th and final wife, Mehr-un-Nissa, later known as Nur Jahan – Light of the World.

Nur Jahan held an unusual level of responsibility within Mughal politics, essentially ruling as co-sovereign. She is the only empress to have coins engraved with her name, a physical symbol of her influence over the administration of the court and the Mughal Empire as a whole. She also became a co-signatory of the emperor, which meant she signed documents and laws on his behalf and did so with her own name. She even led an army in 1626 to save Jahangir when he was taken captive by Mahabat Khan as part of a coup to overthrow him. Nur Jahan on a war elephant demanding the release of her husband must have been quite the sight.

Discussions about the Mughals often centre around the emperors, but here was an empress who ruled among those men, just as Elizabeth had ruled into the beginning of the 17th century. In Mughal India, however, the tradition that noble women were largely secluded from public view under the purdah system makes Nur Jahan's role as such a powerful and influential figure incredibly unusual for this time and context. Nur Jahan had a huge breadth of interests, from being a patron of poetry to using her status to support the rights of women and girls.

The two women had other connections, too. They both experienced imprisonment by family members, and they had a penchant for hunting, though Nur Jahan slayed tigers rather than deer, with some sources claiming that during one particular hunt she slayed six tigers with just four bullets. Portraits portrayed Elizabeth as chaste, wealthy and wise, while Mughal paintings show Nur playing polo with her ladies and even holding a gun. No doubt Elizabeth would have had a lot to share with Nur Jahan had they crossed paths, even if Elizabeth's power formally lay on the throne, rather than behind it.

After Jahangir died in 1627, his son Shah Jahan's first act as emperor was to execute his chief rivals and imprison Nur Jahan, his stepmother. He also ordered several executions, including those of his own brother Shahryar, as well as his nephews and cousins. Shah Jahan's reign is seen as the golden age of Mughal architecture, featuring complexes like the Red Fort in Delhi as well the Pearl Mosque in Lahore and the Shah Jahan Mosque in Sindh, the interior of which contains dazzling multicoloured geometric tile work.

But the building synonymous with this period is the one he famously had built for Mumtaz Mahal, Shah Jahan's second wife and mother of fourteen of his sixteen children, who died in 1631 while giving birth to their last child. Shah Jahan ordered the construction of the Taj Mahal, a magnificent mausoleum, to commemorate his favourite queen. Some say the building was inspired by Nur Jahan's architectural interests. The tall doorways are inscribed with texts from the Quran. Precious stones such as onyx, malachite and lapis lazuli stud the mosaics, the latter of which you'll recall was one of the pigments found in Henry Tudor's marriage bed and in the goods found at Sutton Hoo.

We still don't know what happened to the residents of Roanoke

In 1584, the year after Ralph Fitch set off for India, Elizabeth granted Walter Raleigh a royal charter to explore North America and colonise any land not ruled by Christians. Raleigh sent two vessels that got to Roanoke Island, which today is part of North Carolina. They were met positively by the Algonquian-speaking indigenous people, and two of them, Wanchese and Manteo, were brought back to England to teach the scientist Thomas Harriot their native language. They were returned to Roanoke in 1585. In 1586 there was an initial attempt to settle there, which failed miserably because of disease, a lack of food supplies and increasingly strained relations with a Native American chief called Wingina, whom the English settlers beheaded. Francis Drake rescued the attempted colonists, who brought tobacco and potatoes to England for the first time.

One of the key reasons we can picture what was seen is thanks to the artist John White. His are the first English images of North American Native Americans and were used extensively as a form of propaganda, paving the way for the 'successful' American colonies of the 17th century. In 1587, men, women and children travelled from England to Roanoke in another attempt to permanently settle there. John White left Roanoke to bring back more supplies from home, leaving behind his daughter and granddaughter, Virginia Dare, who was the first English child to be born in North America. However, White was delayed for three years, partly due to the Armada. When he eventually returned to Roanoke, the 116 people he had left behind were gone. The only clues were a 'Cro' carved into a tree and 'Croatoan' carved into a post (which we later learned was referring to a nearby island). The glass half-full version of the 'lost colony' story assumes that the English, including White's family, assimilated into Native American communities in the three years he was gone. You can imagine how the glass half-empty version ends. The reality remains a mystery.

Light the beacons, the Spanish are coming

While Elizabethan colonists faced hostility abroad, Elizabeth herself faced problems of her own, in the form of her cousin. Mary, Queen of Scots arrived in England in 1568 not expecting to be placed under house arrest for the next two decades. She came with a lot of baggage, in the form of three marriages and indirect involvement in at least two murders. She'd been forced to flee Scotland without her only child, James, who was now the thirteen-month-old king of Scotland.

Elizabeth made her feelings about Mary's arrival quite clear; when Mary sent a request for clothes, Elizabeth sent some of her most dishevelled dresses.

Mary's arrival gave hope to those in England and abroad who wished to restore a Catholic monarch to the throne. In August 1586, Mary was involved in a plot to assassinate Elizabeth I. Mary had been involved in previous plots to take the throne, but none of those had provided enough clear evidence. Coded letters hidden in beer barrels had been intercepted this time, by Elizabeth's spymaster Sir Francis Walsingham, which confirmed Mary's involvement. The stage was set to put Mary on trial, and she was pronounced guilty in October. Mary opted to wear crimson for her execution, the colour of Catholic martyrdom. It took three blows of the axe to behead her. The executioner held her severed head and declared, 'God save the Queen,' not realising that she was wearing a wig; her head tumbled to the ground. Witnesses also claim that Mary's dog was present at the execution and hid under her dress during the whole ordeal.

In May 1588, King Philip II of Spain dispatched his 'invincible Armada', a 130-ship fleet with 2,431 guns and 30,000 men, to England with the intention of overthrowing Elizabeth I and restoring the Roman Catholic faith in England. Philip II was the most powerful man in Europe and saw himself as the champion of Catholicism, hence the 180 priests and monks also aboard.

Philip II's plan to overthrow Elizabeth I had been in the making for several years, with the execution of Mary, Queen of Scots offering the final excuse needed. Licences had been granted to English privateers to raid and disrupt Spain's trade routes, making England a fortune. The most notable privateer was Sir Francis Drake, who was deemed an enemy in Spain and earned himself the nickname the Dragon. He had already weakened the fleet when he attacked and destroyed a dozen Spanish ships in Cádiz in 1587, known as 'singeing the King of Spain's beard'. This state-sanctioned piracy understandably enraged Philip.

Drake had his first taste of the profit that could be obtained on voyages when he accompanied his cousin Sir John Hawkins to West Africa to capture people with the intention of enslaving them and selling them in the Spanish Caribbean. By 1619, some 370,000 people had been transported from Africa to the Spanish Americas. A community called Cimarrons quickly formed, made up of those who had escaped their enslavement. It's estimated that there were 3,000 Cimarrons in Panama by 1573. The Spanish resented Drake's encroachment, so in September 1558 they attacked the English at San Juan de Ulúa and destroyed five of their seven ships. Drake swore to get revenge, and it was during his attempts to steal Spanish treasure from Nombre de Dios that he met an enslaved man called Diego.

Diego told Drake not to attack the town, warning him that there were many Spanish reinforcements in the area. Diego introduced Drake to local Cimarron leaders, eventually resulting in the capture of 150,000 pesos of gold and silver, and before the English set sail for home, they did two things. Firstly, they provided the Cimarrons with iron to make arrowheads. Secondly, they agreed to let Diego sail with them.

Diego arrived at Plymouth in August 1573, perhaps the same port where John Blanke disembarked. Diego likely worked in Drake's household before they set out on the most famous of Drake's voyages, the circumnavigation of the globe. Not that Drake told anyone that was the plan – he told the crew they were heading for Egypt, assuming that few would accompany him if they knew the truth. Diego's skills as an interpreter were incredibly helpful on the journey, which had a secondary motive of avenging the Spanish. By November 1578, Drake became the first Englishman to sail through the Straits of Magellan. Drake and his crew landed near Chile, where they were met positively by the indigenous people there, known as the Mapuche. Relations turned sour, however, and Diego was wounded in the ambush that followed, dying within the year. Diego's story is an important one that shows the role of a free and Black Tudor within the familiar context of Elizabethan exploration and the Age of Discovery. It is, however, imperative to link the positive treatment he received from Drake with the invaluable assistance he could offer.

In June 1579, Drake landed on the coast of California and called it New Albion. Although there was no attempt to colonise the land at this point, these claims of sovereignty would have far-reaching consequences, showing English ambition went beyond simply undermining the Spanish. When Drake returned in April 1581, he arrived with a ship full of treasure worth more than the Queen's entire royal income from the previous year. He was knighted by Elizabeth onboard his ship the *Golden Hinde*, much to the anger of the Spanish, who considered him to be nothing more than a pirate.

When the Armada stopped at Calais in France in 1588, Drake attacked by filling ships with oil and tar and setting them on fire, known as the 'fireship' tactic. In the panic, the defensive Spanish crescent formation broke, giving the English the advantage. Battle commenced near Gravelines: the English culverin cannons allowed them to fire at the Spanish from a distance, while the Spanish had unfortunately brought a large number of the wrong cannonballs with them.

On 9 August, Elizabeth went to speak to her troops at Tilbury. She wore a military-inspired outfit, including a plumed helmet and a steel breastplate over a white velvet gown. She was on a white horse and holding a gold baton when she said the famous line, 'I have but the body of a weak and feeble woman, but I have the heart and stomach of a king, and a king of England too.' No doubt this gave the English the boost they needed.

By mid-August, 'God's Protestant wind' blew the Armada into the North Sea, where they were chased by the English fleet. The Spanish had to return home by sailing round the north of Scotland and the west coast of Ireland, where many ships were destroyed by storms. The defeat of the Spanish Armada secured Elizabeth I's international position as a female ruler of a Protestant country, adding to the idea that her reign was a 'golden age'. She had seen off the most serious foreign threat since the Norman invasion in 1066.

The unexpected connection between Tudor England and Morocco

Upon hearing about the defeat of the Armada there were celebrations in the streets, complete with fireworks, banquets and dancing. Effigies of Philip were set on fire in triumph. It might surprise you to learn that these scenes were not in fact in England, but in Marrakesh. The Armada changed how Ahmad al-Mansur, Sultan of the Saadi dynasty in Morocco, viewed England and Elizabeth. His court historian described her as 'Sultana Isabel' and echoed how the English felt about the Armada, that God was on their side and had demonstrated that support through the 'reehan sarsaran', or divine wind.

Morocco's first ever ambassador to England was Abd el-Ouahed ben Messaoud, and he was under orders to negotiate an Anglo–Moroccan alliance to take on the Spanish once and for all. The portrait of him during this visit in 1600 is the first English painting of a Muslim sitter. This visit had other artistic consequences, possibly influencing Shakespeare's depiction of Othello three years later. The trading relationship between Morocco and England was already well established, with England importing 250 tons of Moroccan sugar a year by the 1560s. Elizabeth famously had blackened teeth from the sugary desserts she had so enjoyed in life. Much like the symbols in her many allegorical paintings, her teeth were a sign of the international connections of the age.

Ahmad al-Mansur's reign marked a high point in Moroccan power, not only uniting the country after years of civil war, but also conquering the Songhai Empire in 1591, now modern-day Mali, that had once been ruled by Mansa Musa. Since his infamous reign the empire had continued to flourish in many ways, with the city of Gao as its capital, acting as a central city for trade. Timbuktu also continued to thrive, becoming a centre for Islamic jurisprudence and scholarship. Al-Mansur had English muskets, which the weaponry available in Mali was no match for. Anglo–Moroccan trade allowed English cloth and weapons to be exchanged for gold, sugar and saltpetre, a key component of gunpowder. By 1567, England's trade with Morocco was double that of their trade with Portugal and estimated at £3.3 million in today's money.

There were many other ways the influence of the Islamic world was evident during the Tudor period, from the Ottoman-style clothing we associate with Henry VIII and the materials like silk and velvet and accessories such as the turban, to the currants and rhubarb that was consumed and the words that entered the English vernacular like 'tulip' and 'crimson'. Turkish carpets were so sought after that they were displayed on tables rather than placed on the floor. Efforts had been made before to build on these economic and linguistic exchanges. In 1579, for example, Ottoman sultan Murad pulled out all the stops, commissioning an introductory letter meant to impress. It was dusted with gold, sealed with a beautiful calligraphic monogram and delivered in a bag of satin tied with a silver capsule.

These connections with the Islamic world not only meant that visits such as the Moroccan ambassador's occurred, but that some people moved permanently. Mary Fillis was born in Morocco in 1577 and likely moved to London when she was around six years old. She started off as a servant to the Barker family, headed by the MP and merchant John Barker. At the age of twenty, Fillis started working for Millicent Porter, who was a seamstress in West Smithfield. Although not as wealthy as the Barkers had been, the Porters offered Fillis an opportunity to learn valuable skills like sewing, which were a possible gateway to more independence in the future.

It seems that sewing was not the only new knowledge Fillis picked up while working for Porter. Fillis would have been born into a Muslim family in Morocco, but her decision to be baptised in Aldgate in 1597 shows that she lived out her life as a Christian, complete with three godparents (including Millicent Porter), a reflection of her acceptance into their community. Fillis, like so many other ordinary Tudors, vanishes from the records after this. We can hope that she was able to use her skills to become a seamstress of her own accord, or to have gone to work elsewhere, possibly even as a married Christian, Black Tudor woman. Fillis is just one of the few hundred Africans we know lived freely in Britain during this period.

Elizabeth I reigned for a total of 44 years and 4 months. She had successfully defeated the Spanish Armada, overseen a Golden Age of art, theatre and technology, and laid the foundations of empire, granting a charter to the East India Company. She also commissioned John Hawkins to be a privateer, allowing him to become the first

Englishman to profit from the triangle of trade which enslaved West African people. The Tudor period had overseen a religious rollercoaster as well as a time of growing international connections, from Morocco to Mughal India and the New World, reflected in so many ways, from the food people consumed to the Black Tudors who lived and thrived in England.

ABOLITION AND THE AGE OF REVOLUTION 3

If you were to be invited to dinner at the start of the 17th century, there are a few things you'd need to remember. Firstly, when it comes to cutlery, forks are not a thing until the end of the century, when we are eventually influenced by the Italians to utilise this utensil. Completely necessary, given that it's during this time that English dinner tables start to serve pasta. Knives are used, but not provided by your host. You'll need to bring your own, alongside a napkin to wrap it up in for your journey home. Secondly, much of the meat and fish you encounter will be pickled or potted in order to preserve it for several months. The average person will cook meals in a large cauldron, and many cottages were rebuilt to include an absolute necessity: a bread oven. Carbs really do reign supreme at this point, with potatoes a staple crop.

But it wasn't just in the kitchen where revolutionary change was in the air. Hangovers were aplenty, thanks to the abundance of alcohol now available. Wine was something of a status symbol, with port and sherry rising in popularity alongside spirits like brandy, whisky and rum. However, war with France meant heavy duty imports were imposed; a domestic option was needed and gin stepped in. The taste for gin distilled from the juice of juniper berries led to other, less successful attempts to distil anything and everything, including snails. By 1751 the government had to intervene, heralding the passing of the Gin Act, which sought to reduce the consumption of spirits, as this was seen as synonymous with rising crime. The notorious case of Judith Dufour heavily influenced this. She had allegedly strangled her two-year-old son and sold his clothes to pay for her gin habit. No wonder the spirit was often referred to as 'mother's ruin'.

There are, of course, many non-alcoholic tipples on offer. Coffee houses begin popping up all over the country, after the first one in 1650, although only men are permitted in such establishments, as subjects like politics are, of course, not the concern of 'ladies'. Perhaps this is why serving tea becomes so closely associated with women, with wealthy households investing in porcelain tea sets to keep up with this new trend. They took theirs slightly differently, though; rather than the usual, 'Do you take milk and sugar?' they'd ask if you'd like an egg yolk or two in your tea. After the British capture the island of Jamaica, the cacao trees there mean hot chocolate becomes a popular breakfast drink in the late 1600s, partly based on the belief that it settles the stomach.

Other parts of the world influence and change British habits during this time. British diplomats to the Middle East bring back a new-found appreciation for regular bathing, having noted that Muslims in Turkey, for example, bathe for the sake of cleanliness and not just on the advice of a doctor. And when it comes to diseases that even a good bath can't cure, there are plenty of options. There are outbreaks of plague across the 17th century, although less so after the 1670s, though this is not related to the Great Fire of 1666, despite what you may have been told at school. Tuberculosis, scarlet fever and typhoid are common diseases, and by the end of this chapter, in the 1830s, cholera has almost certainly caught up with some of your nearest and dearest.

The workshop of the world

In 1771 former wig-maker Richard Arkwright opened the first factory in Britain to house a machine he had invented called the 'spinning frame'. The machine was powered by a waterwheel, meaning it could be operated 24 hours a day, producing far more cloth than could be done by hand and eventually making Arkwright a tidy fortune of approximately £200 million in today's money.

The Industrial Revolution meant that Britain became the world's first industrial nation, and the landscape of the country changed dramatically to meet the needs of these new industries. In parts of Wales and Scotland, mines opened to produce the coal that was now essential for powering steam engines across the country. Roads and canals meant that travel from one end of the country to the other now took a matter of hours, rather than a fortnight. The explosion of factories, from textile mills to metal foundries, led to the creation of towns as people were pulled into this work. By 1850 there were more people living in British towns and cities than in the countryside.

The story of the Industrial Revolution is often associated with children working in dire conditions. The average age children started to work was around ten years old, though some worked as young as four, working as 'trappers' in coal mines and 'scavengers' in factories – both of which could result in broken limbs and crushed fingers. But for some people, industrialisation provided unprecedented opportunity. Samuel Catton now earned significantly higher wages in a chemical works compared with his previous employment as an agricultural servant. Some, like Adam Rushton, even earned enough to emigrate to America. Joseph Livesey gave up manual labour to make a living selling cheese to those earning factory wages. Eliza Mitchell is a rare example of a woman who learned shoe-making, a skill which offered her a route out of domestic service.

Unsurprisingly, Britain was known as the 'workshop of the world', producing two thirds of the world's coal and steel and half of the world's cotton cloth. This is where the Empire came in, as cotton would be imported (from American plantations and India, for example) in to Britain, manufactured into cloth in factories and then sold back to those colonies for huge profit. The British Empire grew exponentially, from having a few colonies in 1750 to controlling a fifth of the world's land mass by 1900. Industrialisation aided this expansion, from the railways and steamships that sent goods within and across the Empire, to the manufacture of guns, an important and necessary tool of empire.

Neither witches nor Wahunsenacawh's daughter fared well under James I

Did you know that the average execution rate for those accused of witchcraft was five times higher in Scotland compared to anywhere else in post-Reformation Europe? One of the key reasons for this was the Scottish ruler King James VI (who was James I of England from 1603). He even published a treatise in 1597 called *Daemonologie*, in which he outlined his beliefs about witches and explaining that their executions were justified, as they had made a pact with the devil. The attributes we so closely link with witchcraft were also outlined, including the ability to fly and to conjure storms, and the 'familiars' – the animals witches could turn into, hence their association with cats and toads. James, like many European rulers of the time, wished to prove his godliness in a time of tumultuous religious reform. Between 1590 and 1662 there were five large-scale witch-hunts in Scotland.

Elderly women were mostly associated with witchcraft at this time, and approximately 84 per cent of all convicted witches were women. Quarrels between neighbours often resulted in accusations of witchcraft. Witch hunters created evidence through torture as well as by finding the 'Devil's mark', which involved physical searches for visible blemishes, or a professional witch-pricker might be employed to, you guessed it, prick you with pins till the mark unsurprisingly then became visible. Ducking stools were also used sometimes, with the accused floating if guilty due to the belief that water was pure and they were therefore being rejected by it.

In most European countries, convicted witches were burned. In Scotland it was custom to strangle suspected witches at the stake first before burning them. The only known grave of an accused witch in Scotland belonged to Lilias Adie. She was accused of sleeping with the devil and actually died by suicide while in prison in 1704. She was buried in a wooden box by the beach at Torryburn Bay, with a huge sandstone slab placed on top to ensure she stayed there. In 2017 images of her skull were used to create a digital reconstruction of her face, bringing life to a woman who represents so many whose lives were ended in such unnecessary tragedy. The last woman to be tried and executed for witchcraft was Janet Horne in 1727. She was accused of turning her daughter into a horse.

It was not only women at home who suffered under the auspices of King James. In 1607 the Jamestown colony in Virginia was established, a mere four years after the death of Elizabeth I. James had chartered the Virginia Company for the colony, with Christopher Newport captaining one of three ships carrying 104 colonists. Newport always brought gifts back from his voyages and had previously given King James two baby crocodiles from the Caribbean. In 1608 he brought James a large deer-hide hanging decorated with shell beadwork. It had been gifted from Wahunsenacawh, the leader of the Powhatan, the Algonquian-speaking people living in Virginia when Newport arrived.

At first the English maintained relatively peaceful relations with the Powhatan, but in 1613 they resorted to kidnapping one of Wahunsenacawh's daughters, Mataoka. You may know her as Pocahontas. She was lured onto an English ship under the pretence that she was going to be given a tour. Pocahontas is thought to have been sixteen at this point. She was held as a hostage and taught English, and was baptised and renamed Rebecca. She was then married to widower John Rolfe, who is thought to have first brought tobacco to Jamestown in 1610. Tobacco planting was one of the key reasons why Jamestown succeeded where previous colonies had failed. There were high profits to be made from growing crops like tobacco, cotton and corn, which could be sold in Britain. Within three years, tobacco exports from Virginia skyrocketed from 500,000 pounds to 1.5 million. This encouraged migration to the New World, eventually meaning Britain had developed the 'thirteen colonies' along the east coast. The most famous of these groups were the Pilgrim Fathers, who arrived on the *Mayflower* in 1620.

Pocahontas was brought to England in 1616, along with Rolfe and their son, in the same ship used for her kidnapping. She attended events at court, including the elaborate annual Twelfth Night Masque, an immersive experience copied from the Italians in which guests could participate in the dances alongside professional actors and entertainers – the Secret Cinema of its day. During her short time in England she became a source of intrigue, a walking advert for the 'opportunities' of the New World. The Virginia Company aimed to emphasise how 'civil' she had become thanks to their influence. They hoped people would invest as a result, and they provided her with 4 pounds a week (the equivalent of £500 today) to ensure she dressed in the latest fashions. This clearly worked, with many Londoners writing about her in their letters and diaries. A portrait of her by Simon van de Passe was even replicated as souvenirs to mark her visit, like modern-day celebrity merchandise.

Pocahontas fell ill in March 1617 on her return to Virginia. The ship stopped at Gravesend so she could receive medical help, but unfortunately she died shortly after. She is buried in Gravesend, but the exact location is unknown due to a fire there in 1727. Her story has been romanticised to most of us thanks to the 1995 Disney animation, which centres around her relationship with Captain John Smith. While Smith was a colonist in Jamestown, historians remain sceptical of the story that he himself wrote: that she saved him from being clubbed to death by placing her head upon his. We'll likely never know the true story, but what we can be certain of is that the Disney version certainly leaves out several key points, most notably her kidnapping, conversion to Christianity and forced marriage. The facts remain that she was buried as Lady Rebecca Rolfe, a 21-year-old Christian wife and mother, in a land far away from her home and family.

Artichoke juice couldn't save Charles I from losing his head

The Civil War was something you almost certainly would have learned about at school. You may remember some of the causes, such as the fact that Charles I staunchly believed in the 'divine right of kings' and therefore introduced a range of unpopular measures, from raising taxes to religious changes spearheaded by the Archbishop of Canterbury, William Laud. Outspoken Puritans were warned that punishments would follow for anyone who refused to comply with these changes, and indeed John Bastwick, Henry Burton and William Prynne had their ears cut off in 1637. We know that witnesses clambered to dip their handkerchiefs in the blood that fell from them as a sign of support.

When Laud's reforms were extended to Scotland that same year, rioting was sparked during the first reading from the new prayer book, when market-trader Jenny Geddes threw a stool at the minister's head in disgust at what she was hearing. By 1642 the relationship between Charles and Parliament had deteriorated to breaking point, after Charles raised an army and attempted to arrest the Five Members of Parliament who were leading the cause against him. The civil war was fought between those who supported Charles, known as the Cavaliers, against the Parliamentarians, who were known as the Roundheads. The leader of the Roundheads, Oliver Cromwell (MP for Cambridge), trained the New Model Army, who would prove to be integral in defeating the Royalists once and for all. They were recruited based on their ability rather than rank, and the temperate rules they had to follow, such as not swearing and drinking, were a sign of what was to come.

There were technically two civil wars, one between 1642 and 1646, and the second from 1648 to 1649. These wars involved the Welsh, Scots and the Irish, as well as foreign mercenaries like the Croatian captain Carlo Fantom, who when asked why he came to fight responded with, 'I care not for your cause, I come to fight for your half-crowns and your handsome women.'

John Lilburne was a particularly influential figure, a very public-facing critic of Parliament. His wife, Elizabeth, organised for the first all-women petition, which amassed an impressive 10,000 signatures. MPs were unimpressed, however, with one retorting, 'It was not for women to petition; they might stay home and wash their dishes.' The term 'fishwife' was often used to describe women who involved themselves in politics, a derogatory term referring to how loud the women were.

Women like Jane Whorwood certainly did not spend her time during the Civil War quietly washing dishes. She was a key player within the Royalist network, and between 1642 and 1644 she successfully smuggled over £83,000 of gold in several soap barrels for the war effort. By 1647 she was so determined to reach Charles directly that she consulted the astrologer William Lilly for guidance.

Whorwood was crucial in more than one attempt to free Charles from his imprisonment at Carisbrooke Castle. The first attempt failed on account of Charles getting stuck when attempting to climb out of a window. By the second attempt, Whorwood was feeling confident. She had chartered a ship to take Charles to Holland and had ensured nitric acid had been smuggled into the castle to loosen the window bars. It was her choice of confidante that scuppered her success, however; Lilly had likely tipped off Parliament and the plan was abandoned. Female spies at the time used everything they could to pass on their intel, from Lady d'Aubigny concealing documents in her wig, to Susan Hyde's role in the secret Sealed Knot organisation, which included sending letters in 'invisible' ink made from raw artichoke juice that only became visible when exposed to an open flame.

A courtroom was prepared in Westminster Hall (there is a plate on the floor to mark where Charles sat during his trial). Only 67 of the 135 judges appointed to oversee the trial actually turned up, presumably through fear of retribution. The main judge, John Bradshaw, wore a special metal-lined hat, as he was so concerned he might be assassinated by Royalist supporters. Charles refused to plead either way, on the basis that the trial had no legal basis. Fifty-nine judges disagreed with him, charging him with treason.

King Charles I was publicly executed by beheading on 1 January 1649, in one clean blow of the axe. He wore a thick shirt so that he didn't shiver from cold; he was keen to ensure that no one would mistake this for him shaking with fear. The executioner and his assistants wished to hide their identities altogether, so each insisted on wearing a wig and false beard. Charles I is the only English monarch to have been tried and executed for treason. After the restoration of the monarchy in 1661, his son Charles II did eventually get his revenge, rounding up many of the men who had signed his father's death warrant and executing those who didn't manage to escape.

Oliver Cromwell, king in all but name

The time between the reigns of Charles I and Charles II is known as the Interregnum, meaning 'between kings'. Our short spell as a republic is associated with Cromwell, whose statue resides outside the Houses of Parliament to this day, a reflection of the Victorians who revered him; he even has over 250 roads named after him across Britain.

Cromwell famously closed Parliament in 1653 after a brief spell of Parliament ruling the country. He became Lord Protector and was as powerful as a king but refused to take a royal title and crown. Attempts made by Charles I's son (another Charles) to revive the civil wars in Scotland were swiftly dealt with, meaning Cromwell controlled all of the British Isles by 1651. Life under the Protectorate meant strict Puritan laws were passed, meaning no more trips to the theatre, Sunday football or ... swearing, which was now punishable by fine, although if you kept swearing you'd end up in prison. The fact you probably remember the most from school is that Christmas was banned, with soldiers patrolling the streets and seizing food they assumed had been prepared for festive celebrations. From 1656, shops and markets were told to stay open on 25 December to reflect its relegation to being just another day. An attempt to ban make-up in 1650 was not passed, but there was a Puritan crackdown on 'night walking', with some brothel owners having a 'B' branded on their foreheads. Legislation became more extreme, shown by the deportation of 400 sex workers from London to Barbados in 1656.

In 1654 Cromwell backed calls for Jewish readmission, following their expulsion in 1290. This meant Jews from outside the country were able to move to Britain and practise their faith freely. The

Bevis Marks Synagogue in Aldgate, which opened in 1701, represents the impact of this change in policy. Commissioned by Spanish and Portuguese Jews who had now made London their home, it is the oldest synagogue in the country as well as the only one to have been continuously open for 300 years, thus also making it the oldest working synagogue in the world.

It was under Cromwell that Ireland was formally conquered, through sheer brute force. The most heavily cited incidents are the 1649 massacres at Drogheda and Wexford, with the number of civilian deaths as a result of these atrocities disputed but estimated to be in the thousands. These massacres were partly seen as revenge for the 1641 Irish Rebellion, which had resulted in thousands of Protestant settlers being killed, which in turn was motivated by attempts to show opposition to the Irish plantation system, which had been displacing Irish owners from their land in favour of English colonists. This was having a visible impact on the demographic of Ireland, with the balance of the ruling communities now tipped in favour of those who identified as British and Protestant rather than Irish and Catholic.

One of the consequences of these 1649 massacres was that thousands of Irish men, women and children experienced a similar fate to the previously mentioned sex workers: they were shipped off to the West Indies. Once again, the figures and nature of this transportation are heavily disputed, but what is clear is that thousands of Irish Catholics were placed (either willingly or forcibly) into indentured service, which is when people are required to undertake unpaid labour for a fixed period. English ships took them to colonies like Barbados where they worked unpaid for approximately seven years. It was under Charles I that tobacco plantations were established in Barbados, and the treatment of indentured servants working on plantations harvesting sugar and tobacco was appalling. Until the late 1650s these white indentured servants made up the majority of the unpaid workforce across the British Caribbean colonies. Additionally, military prisoners or those deemed as vagrants were transported. Eventually, Australia would replace the West Indies as Britain's preferred penal destination. By 1680 the last of the Irish servants were freed, many either returning home or settling in British North America. There was increasingly less need for an indentured workforce when the enslaved were so readily available.

Cromwell was actually struck down by malaria in 1658 and, just like William the Conqueror, his body was embalmed in drama after his death. In 1661 his body (alongside John Bradshaw's and Henry Ireton's) was hauled out of Westminster Abbey and stored overnight at the Old Red Lion pub in Holborn. The next day they were posthumously 'beheaded' for regicide. Their bodies were hung in chains and their heads were placed on spikes above Westminster Hall, where the trial of Charles I had taken place. In 1685 Cromwell's head fell from its spike and was allegedly scooped up by a guard. The head changed hands and was sporadically on display before being buried at Sidney Sussex College at Cambridge University, where Cromwell had once been a student.

What we don't like talking about: Britain and the transatlantic slave trade

Throughout this chapter, I will use the term enslaved people instead of slave, as the latter dehumanises those forced into this process. I will also use the term enslavers as opposed to master/owners, as the latter options empower those who orchestrated such practices.

Britain's role in the slave trade is not one that many of us will have been taught at school. If we were taught about slavery, it was usually focused on American plantations, with Britain's role firmly fixed in the abolition story. The information in this chapter is therefore disturbing and can feel very confronting. This is an incredibly complex history to teach and has been incredibly challenging to write.

As exemplified by the teeth of Elizabeth I, sugar was considered a luxury and a symbol of wealth. To that end, the rich would typically adorn their banquet tables with a selection of sugar sculptures fashioned into anything from ships to mythical creatures. This was something Europeans likely adopted from the Islamic world, with the specialist sculptors known as sukker nakkasarli. For example, in 1562, Queen Elizabeth was given a marzipan model of St Paul's Cathedral; thankfully, it was not life size. Inevitably, sugar became less of a status symbol once it was accessible to more than just the highest in society. Middle-class Brits soon found sugar to be a staple ingredient within cookbooks, a reflection of the booming sugar trade that Britain was deeply involved in.

Portugal was the first European nation to enslave Africans for labour in sugar plantations, on São Tomé. It was the Spanish and Portuguese who first took sugar cane across the Atlantic, and by 1600 more than 200,000 enslaved Africans had been shipped to the Caribbean and Brazil. We know from Chapter 2 that it was from the 1560s when Britain began to take part in the transatlantic slave trade. But it was from the 1650s that British merchants became entrenched in the transatlantic slave trade, and it was after 1698 that this 'triangular trade' expanded once ports outside of London were allowed to participate. This was embraced in Liverpool and Bristol in particular, and the legacy of this is still visible today, such as in the frieze featuring African faces that adorns Liverpool's town hall. All of the city's mayors were involved in the slave trade in some way between 1787 and 1807.

Between 1690 and 1787, 11,000 British ships transported enslaved Africans to the Americas. The sailing route taken by British enslavers was carried out in three stages. Ships carrying manufactured goods would set sail from Britain, bound for West Africa. One of the most lucrative exports was guns; in 1765, 150,000 guns were exported to Africa from Birmingham alone. The cost of an enslaved person varied from one to five guns.

The circumstances under which West Africans were captured varied hugely. In some areas, local chieftains were complicit, exchanging prisoners of war for the goods they had begun to rely on from Europe, like cloth and gunpowder. The West African people also played their part, acting as messengers as well as utilising their expert knowledge of the coastline to evade capture themselves. Tomba, chief of the Baga, who were based in Sierra Leone, attempted to organise a rebellion, but unfortunately he was captured and promptly enslaved.

Nearby, the British had set up a trading station at Bunce Island in 1670, and until 1808 thousands of Africans passed through Bunce Island on their way to being transported west to the Americas. One of the main British organisations that operated out of the island was the Royal African Company, who were responsible for transporting tens of thousands of African people into slavery, more than any other British company. The company was issued a charter by King Charles II in 1663. Enslaved people had their skin branded with the company's initials (RAC), or (DY) to reflect the initials of the company's governor, the Duke of York.

Edward Colston became deputy governor of the Royal African Company in 1689 and made huge profits, much of which was spent on schools and other public enterprises in Bristol and London. During the period he was involved with the company, 84,000 people were transported, with approximately 19,000 dying before reaching the Americas. His name has loomed large over Bristol ever since, and his statue was infamously pulled down in the summer of 2020, with schools, pubs and venues across the city replacing his name accordingly.

Bunce Island offers a unique insight, as it is one of the few sites not to have been inhabited after the abolition of the slave trade. Reminders of those connected to its past are still littered across the island. Cannons marked with the crest of King George III confirm the relationship between this place and royals of the 18th century. Rusted nails remind us of the presence of blacksmiths on the island and the fact that captives were shackled before being loaded onto ships for their final journey. It's worth noting that this did not deter attempts at rebellion, which, although proved unsuccessful, serves as another important reminder that even in an almost inescapable reality, people tried to fight their way out anyway. Remains of wine bottles are another inconspicuous debris that reveals a sinister aspect of this island, that for some this was a chance to unwind and revel in luxury. For the traders there were fine dinners of antelope and wild boar. Unusually, the island even had its own ice store and golf course, with caddies clad in tartan loincloths. It is estimated that 50,000 African people were transported from Bunce Island alone.

This next part of the route was known as the middle passage and could last between one and five months, depending on the weather. One of the most reproduced images used by abolitionists was a 1787 image of the *Brookes* slave ship, which showed 454 people crammed into the hold. This image is one of the first examples of print propaganda, with the image going what we would now describe as viral, being seen everywhere from newspapers to tavern walls. While the provenance of the image is useful in showing us how abolitionists appealed to the public to support their cause, the image is limited in depicting how truly horrific the conditions aboard would have been. The accompanying text provides us with some details pertaining to the experience of the enslaved, such as the fact that men were chained together while women and children were not. We also learn that occasionally they were taken to the main deck to exercise, which primarily involved being forced to 'dance' to a drumbeat or flute.

The image shows the enslaved neatly packed into the ship's hold in a uniform manner, but the reality was far worse. Women endured brutal treatment onboard. Below deck the enslaved were unable to move, diseases such as dysentery and smallpox spread rapidly, and often those who perished were left among the living for long periods. The heat alone was unbearable, as campaigner Olaudah Equiano, who had experienced the conditions first-hand, wrote: 'The closeness of the place and the heat of the climate, added to the number in the ship which was so crowded that each scarcely had room to turn himself, it almost suffocated us.'

His account also describes the suicide attempts he witnessed while onboard, an observation supported by examples such as in 1796, when approximately a hundred people jumped overboard on the Bristol-owned *Prince of Orange* slave ship, which was heading for St Kitts. There were also 485 attempts at rebellion onboard officially recorded. Statistics like this highlight the need for us to approach the *Brookes* image with caution, as such propaganda does not allow us to appreciate that enslaved people not only overcame the horrific conditions they were trapped in, which took approximately three in ten lives, but also barriers like language, in order to orchestrate acts of rebellion, be it suicide or attempted uprisings.

An incident in 1781 highlights another horrific facet of the middle passage, when approximately 133 enslaved Africans were thrown overboard the British slave ship *Zong*. A navigational error extended the crossing to Jamaica by several weeks, and with limited water supplies a decision was made by the crew to drown a proportion of the enslaved people aboard. The crew assumed they would be able to claim insurance upon their return home, based on the fact that the enslaved were categorised as 'cargo'. The crew were tried in 1783, under the guise of an insurance dispute, not a murder trial. The campaigner Granville Sharp got involved at the behest of campaigner Olaudah Equiano, although this did not result in any of the crew being successfully prosecuted, despite the judge ruling that the *Zong*'s bosses were unjustified in their insurance claim. The immediate public reaction to the case was lukewarm, although this subsequently shifted when abolitionists including Sharp and Equiano used it to illustrate the horror of the middle passage.

For those who survived the middle passage, they then had the humiliation of being sold to contend with. Experiences varied depending on the time of year, as well as the location, but what was consistent was the dehumanisation that took place. When enslaved people were auctioned they may well have been physically 'prepared' beforehand, which involved covering any marks or bruises with gunpowder and slathering them in oil to accentuate their muscle definition. The enslaved may have been scrutinised inhumanely closely during an auction itself, such as inside their mouths to inspect their teeth.

Pricing may have varied, but huge profits could be made every time. The captain's landing bill from the Liverpool-based ship *Thomas* provides a window into the profits. A total of 630 enslaved people were taken on the middle passage, with 530 sold upon arrival at Jamaica and 100 dying on the journey. Each was sold for an average of £60. Once all the bills were paid this resulted in a profit of £24,000, something like at least £1 million today. Those who were not successfully sold at auction may have been subjected to a 'scramble' auction, which involved exactly what you are already likely to be imagining. The enslaved would be held in a pen, much like cattle. At the sound of a drumbeat or gunshot, buyers would grab whichever individuals they wanted, sometimes paying a set price.

The mental toll this process would have exacted on the enslaved was something that those who profited from the trade were well aware of and took advantage of. The process of 'seasoning' was potentially lengthy, but traders could enjoy higher profits at the end of it. Seasoning involved acclimatising enslaved people to their new surroundings; essentially conditioning them for a life of enslavement. This process involved a whole host of things, from getting used to the climate and limited diet of life on a plantation as well as possibly acquiring skills, from language to the processing of different crops. Brutal violence was used alongside this, to inflict physical pain as well as breaking the enslaved psychologically and allowing enslavers to more easily 'control' them. This is why a 'seasoned' enslaved person often fetched a higher price compared to those who were sold immediately.

From 1698, the Royal African Company lost its monopoly, opening the floodgates for independent traders, as long as they paid a 10 per cent tax to the RAC. These '10-percenters' transported approximately 75,000 enslaved people between 1698 and 1707, compared with the 18,000 carried by the RAC in the same period. Those who made the most out of the slave trade were the enslavers: the owners of the plantations in North America and the Caribbean. Wealthy British landowners would often buy vast tracts of land in the New World to run for profit. Most would rarely visit the plantations, preferring instead to remain in Britain while managers and overseers organised their business in the colonies.

By 1800, as trade increased in products produced by enslaved labour (such as cotton, sugar, tobacco and coffee), small towns became important cities and individuals made small fortunes. New docks were built in ports such as London, Liverpool, Cardiff, Bristol and Hull. Thomas Leyland was one such person, his associated ships carrying over 22,365 African people to the Americas in the late 18th century. Leyland actually won £20,000 in a lottery and used some of his winnings to invest in the trade. The profits he made primarily from slave ships departing from Liverpool allowed him to seek a banking partnership that eventually became a popular high street bank. Similar stories can be found across the country. In Birmingham, over 4,000 people were employed in the factories to make guns that were sold to slave traders. Penrhyn Castle in Wales, originally built as a medieval manor house, was rebuilt in the 1820s from profits made by the Pennant family's Jamaican sugar plantations and the subsequent compensation they received. The slave trade contributed to the development of the financial, commercial and insurance institutions, all of which endorsed and profited greatly from the trade.

One of the key reasons we know about the vast range of enslavers in Britain is because of the records from the Slave Compensation Commission. Four years after the 1833 Slavery Abolition Act came the Slave Compensation Act. When students are presented with the name of the Act, they often assume that this was compensation granted to those who had been enslaved. In fact, this money was given to approximately 46,000 British enslavers as compensation for their 'loss of human property'. They argued that the 1833 Act had granted unfair powers to the government to 'confiscate their property' – their enslaved workers. This led to the 1837 Act – a £20 million payout to be set aside specifically as compensation – which taxpayers were paying off until 2015. The value of that payout in today's money equates to approximately £17 billion. Meanwhile, formerly enslaved workers were forced into tied apprenticeships and extreme poverty. To finance the slave compensation package, the British government took out one of the largest loans in history. The total sum was equivalent to 40 per cent of the government's annual income at the time, and it was the largest state-sponsored payout in British history before the banking crisis in 2008.

The Slave Compensation Commission, a team of ten men working in Whitehall, processed the claims. Each of the 46,000 claimants had to complete a form, providing details to prove their claim was valid. One of the largest sums was given to John Gladstone, the father of

Prime Minister William Gladstone. He received £106,769 (approx. £83 million today) for the nine claims he made, including the Vreed en Hope (Peace and Hope) plantation in the Demerara region of Guyana (formerly British Guiana), which in 1832 had 243 enslaved women and 229 enslaved men working primarily on sugar processing. However, the records illustrate that enslavers were not necessarily confined to a particular class or even gender. A quarter of the claimants were women, including Agnes and Martha Montgomerie from Perthshire, who received compensation of £63 for a single enslaved person in Trinidad. These records show the deep connection between Britain and its enslaving past, also highlighting just how widespread those connections were across the country, all the way from those in the highest echelons of politics to physicians, bakers and shopkeepers. Other countries involved in slave-owning, including France, Denmark, the Netherlands and Brazil, followed the British example of compensating enslavers.

The Barbados Slave Codes of 1661 formally legalised that enslaved people were essentially chattels. The preamble to the Act describes enslaved Africans as 'heathenish, brutish and an uncertain dangerous pride of people'. Enslavers were given the legal right to use punishments including severe whipping and face branding. Until the 18th century, if an enslaved person was killed on a plantation, legally no crime had been committed. These codes were eventually adopted by many other colonies, including in Jamaica. The use of terror and violence as a means of controlling the enslaved is depicted in illustrations from the time, as well as via first-hand accounts of the perpetrators of this violence.

One such example can bed found in Thomas Thistlewood's diaries, written between 1748 and 1786, amounting to a 37-volume and 2-million-word insight into the life of an English-born, Jamaican-based enslaver. His diaries reveal particularly brutal realities of plantation life, such as the systematic rape of enslaved girls and women. When we consider the sorts of punishments enslaved people could endure for the slightest mistake, such as allowing a pot to overboil, flogging most certainly comes to mind. However, the freedom wielded by enslavers meant that men like Thistlewood could invent their own uniquely cruel methods of torture. Not seeing flogging as enough of a punishment, he would have chilli, salt or lime juice rubbed into the wounds they'd just acquired. The 'Derby's dose' – a method I would not mention in the classroom – involved an enslaved person being forced to defecate into the mouth of another, who would then be gagged for several hours. It's important to note that Thistlewood was well regarded by other planters in Jamaica, and he was well known for his interest in reading and gardening.

This did not, however, prevent enslaved people from engaging in acts of resistance, be it covert or overt. Covert resistance can be characterised as daily acts of defiance, from feigning ignorance of runaways to deliberately breaking tools or working slowly. The maintenance of cultural traditions and the retention of language was another form of resistance, particularly given that in some plantations it was deemed a punishable offence to speak in African languages. Women could defy these limitations in very particular ways, maintaining childcare practices from home as well as passing on wisdom, from the medicinal properties of plants to storytelling, knowledge of food preparation and dancing.

In 1668 a law was passed in Barbados which prohibited 'masters' from permitting enslaved people to 'beat drums, blow horns or use any loud instruments'. Although this law had a limited impact, its very existence reflects fears present at the time: that enslaved people would utilise West African practices like drum signalling to organise revolts. Drums played a key role in Akan culture, and were used to send messages across vast areas, be it for celebrations or declarations of war. Cultural resistance was evidently something the British feared.

Such fears were not unfounded, as shown in 1675 when a rebel leader called Caffee set up a court modelled on those from Akan traditions at which he intended to be crowned in a ceremony introduced by traditional horn music. And while his planned revolt was discovered by the British and he never got to have the coronation ceremony he'd dreamed of, this nonetheless highlights the prevailing nature of West African customs within enslaved communities, and their intention to maintain and celebrate these in the event of their freedom. The British Museum's original collection included an Akan drum obtained by the collector Hans Sloane in Virginia circa 1730. It was not until 1906 that the origins of the drum were no longer assumed to be Native American.

The Newton Slave Burial Ground in Barbados is the earliest and largest undisturbed plantation cemetery for enslaved people in the New World. Some of the graves have been excavated, with two in particular of relevance here. Once again, we find ourselves confronted with the grave of a young woman of African birth, known as Burial 9. This was a prone burial, meaning she was buried face down. Unlike others around her, she was also buried alone. All of this implies that she may have been associated with negative traits, possibly as someone who practiced witchcraft.

In contrast, Burial 72 included grave goods such as an iron knife and bracelets. Most of these items have been determined as being of African origin and he was likely a healer or medicine man. Grave goods were gifted based on a variety of ideas, such as the belief that the ancestors of the deceased would expect gifts, or that such goods would help maintain the status the dead had enjoyed while alive in the afterlife. The most intriguing item is an elaborate necklace made up of different components. While the origin of the fish vertebrae and canine teeth cannot be confirmed, the cowry shells originally came from the Indian Ocean and were used as currency in West Africa; they were believed by some to have spiritual powers.

Almost 900 beads were found among twelve of the burials at Newton. Beads were a key element of West African material culture, used as accessories as well as for religious ceremonies and as markers of political power. Beads from Africa were often made out of materials like bone and ivory. A carnelian bead from the necklace originated in southern India, a reminder of the geographical connections of the time.

The contrasting ways in which Burial 9 and Burial 72 were organised provides a fascinating insight into the enduring influence of West African traditions and beliefs; their status within the enslaved community was then reflected in their final resting place. Such cultural influences were particularly clear in Jamaica, where a preference was shown for 'Koromantis', the term used by enslavers to describe those from the Akan region of the Gold Coast (modern-day Ghana), prized for their military prowess. The influence of Akan culture is clear with the language of maroon communities today, from not only the words themselves but also the way in which these words are pronounced. The endurance of Akan culture in the Caribbean is a testament to the resilience of those who, despite the gruelling process of seasoning and consistent attempts to repress such beliefs, masterfully maintained some form of agency.

It wasn't just MPs who campaigned to end the slave trade

Abolitionists used many methods to publicise their cause. They would use physical objects such as manacles, whips and thumbscrews, or imagery such as that of the *Brookes*, but Thomas Clarkson took this one step further. He produced two models of the slave ship, one of which he took on his national speaking tours, while he gave the other to William Wilberforce, who showed it to his fellow MPs in the Commons. It is these two men who are synonymous with the abolitionist movement.

Religion was integral too, with Quakers at the heart of the formation of the Society for Effecting the Abolition of the Slave Trade in 1787. Former slave ship captain John Newton jumped ship and famously joined the abolitionist cause, having converted to Christianity after surviving several weeks at sea following a severe storm. Undoubtedly you know some of the lyrics from the hymn that he debuted in 1773, 'Amazing Grace'.

William Wilberforce first introduced a bill to abolish the slave trade in 1791 and introduced new bills every year between 1794 and 1799. The bills often included lengthy speeches by Wilberforce pertaining to evidence collected by Clarkson, which included first-hand testimonies, data and images.

Other than the *Brookes*, the other image most associated with the abolitionist campaigns was one created by potter Josiah Wedgwood. His image of an enslaved African kneeling, manacled hands outstretched, with the title *Am I Not a Man and a Brother?*, is viewed as the symbol of the struggle for abolition. It was placed on ceramics as well as being reproduced on medallions, hairpins and necklaces. There were many other accessories too, like sugar bowls emblazoned with 'West India Sugar – not made by Slaves', specially made to hold sugar from South-East Asia – Indonesia or the Philippines, for example – which was also meant to provide a springboard for conversations about abolition. Sugar boycotts were often orchestrated by women and were successful in encouraging approximately 350,000 people to join in. Women like Hannah More encouraged others to join the abolition movement, and her penning of 'Slavery, a Poem' was regarded as incredibly influential at the time. She was not the only author involved in abolition, however; those who had endured enslavement first hand wrote about their experiences and no doubt changed hearts and minds as a result, though their legacy has not been as prominently recognised.

Mary Prince was born into an enslaved family in Bermuda in October 1788 and was first sold from her family at the age of ten. For years she was forced to work up to her waist all day in the salt ponds of Turks and Caicos, which would often result in severe boils and sores. Interestingly, when writing about this she states, 'Oh that Turk's Island was a horrible place. The people in England, I am sure, have never found out which is carried on there.' She describes the cruel treatment she and others, including children and pregnant women, received not only from men in positions of power on the plantations, but women too. Mary herself was left with a lifelong back injury after one particularly brutal beating at the hands of her enslaver in Bermuda. She ended up in Antigua, having been sold to the Woods family. She travelled to England with them in 1828 and managed to run away.

During her time in England, Prince worked alongside the Anti-Slavery Society. She became the first woman to present an anti-slavery petition to Parliament – she petitioned for her freedom so she could return to Antigua without being enslaved again. She became the first Black woman to write and publish an autobiography, in 1831. It was so popular that three editions were published that year. The book particularly highlighted the effect of slavery upon domestic life: the break-up of families, the absence of 'normal' married life, the sexual abuse and the humiliation endured by enslaved women. She also touched on issues we would now describe as misogynoir, delving into her treatment by others in regards to her race and gender.

Two lawsuits for libel were filed against the book's publisher in 1833, and Prince testified at both, effectively rebuking any claims that her story was exaggerated. Unfortunately, the remainder of Mary Prince's life is a mystery. It is unknown whether she died in Britain or was able to return, free, to Antigua. She wanted to ensure that 'good people in England might hear from a slave what a slave had felt and suffered', which she most certainly achieved. As Mary's story shows, when enslaved people were brought to Britain, their legal status was unclear. While the Barbados slave codes clearly outlined that enslaved people were essentially property, no such laws existed in Britain.

The enslaved people brought to Britain largely worked as servants in the households of wealthy enslavers. Visitors from abroad came to London and sometimes wrote letters home, describing the numbers of enslaved people they saw working for the rich. When the Russian Tsarina (Queen) decided she wanted enslaved people to work as servants in her court, she sent her agents to London. Many paintings from this period reflect the attitude that having Black or Asian servants was fashionable and a way to show off wealth, paralleling the sugar sculptures mentioned earlier. These wealthy Georgian Britons would be dressed in all their finery, as would their servants, who were used as a vehicle to demonstrate the wealth and status of the family they served. A 1682 portrait of Louise de Kéroualle, Duchess of Portsmouth and mistress of Charles II, with her 'unknown female attendant' is a clear example of this. This image takes things one step further, with the young servant gazing up at the Duchess while holding a shell full of pearls, placed symbolically in the centre of the painting as an indicator of her mistress's beauty.

There are hundreds of newspaper adverts from this period that offer rewards in exchange for finding runaways, which, as the paintings already suggest, indicates that having enslaved people working in a household was a publicly acceptable practice at the time. For example, one advert from the *London Gazette* in 1700 offers a 'guinea' in reward for the return of Quoshey, a boy of sixteen. While Quoshey may have been wearing very different clothes to his counterparts on Caribbean plantations, such as a 'plush cap with black fur' and a waistcoat, the fact that he was 'branded on his left breast with E.A' after his enslaver, Captain Edward Archer, is a stark reminder of the reality of his situation. Adverts were made for runaway 'Indian' servants too. A 1707 advert from the *Daily Courant* is for an 'East-Indian boy named Caesar', who 'has a handsome face and is tall for his age'. His name reminds us that no matter how flattering the description of him was, attitudes towards those bound into this type of servitude meant their identity was secondary.

In 1772 the 'Somerset case' dealt with a prevalent issue for many runaways: the fear of being caught and then taken to the Caribbean. Somerset had been brought over to London three years earlier by Charles Stewart, who had enslaved him for twenty years. Somerset escaped, but Stewart hired someone to kidnap him. He was then placed on a ship set for one of Jamaica's sugar plantations. Somerset escaped again and convinced Granville Sharp to take his case (Somerset vs Stewart). Stewart's lawyers argued that slavery was legal in Britain and therefore Somerset should be returned to him. The judge, Lord Mansfield, ruled that Stewart did not have the right under English law to deport Somerset, as he was a free man and should be 'discharged'. Celebrations erupted for many, as it was more broadly interpreted as meaning slavery was illegal in Britain, while for others the ruling was narrower, focused on it now being illegal to remove an enslaved person and deport them. Either way, the threat of being deported was theoretically lessened. The fact that adverts offering rewards for 'runaways' still existed after this illustrates that however it was interpreted, bound servitude to enslavers in Britain remained, leading some to take matters into their own hands. George Germain Foney, for example, ran away from his enslaver, Captain Thomas Ralph, in Liverpool on 18 April 1780. Interestingly, George is described as 'not only the slave, but the apprentice of Captain Ralph'.

Not all of Britain's Black population were in the same position as those named in these newspaper adverts. Dido Elizabeth Belle (1761–1804) was a member of an aristocratic family in Georgian Britain. Born in the Caribbean, she was the daughter of a Royal Navy officer, Sir John Lindsay, and a former enslaved African woman, Maria Belle. By 1765, Dido had been brought to England. She was entrusted to the care of her father's uncle, William Murray, Lord Chief Justice and 1st Earl of Mansfield, owner of Kenwood House in north London and, of course, the judge who presided over the Somerset case. She was brought up alongside her cousin Lady Elizabeth Murray, whose mother had died. Dido was taught to read, write and play music, while also receiving an annual allowance. She served as Lord Mansfield's legal secretary, and had other domestic responsibilities within the estate, such as looking after the dairy, which were all typical tasks taken on by gentlewomen of the time.

A 1779 painting of Dido and her cousin Elizabeth, which now hangs in Scotland's Scone Palace, is largely responsible for generating interest in Dido. In the painting, both Dido and her cousin are dressed in finery, and unlike the portrait of the Duchess of Portsmouth, both women are standing beside each other on what appears to be equal terms.

In his will, Mansfield made sure to protect his niece's rights, clearly stating that Dido was a free woman. Perhaps this was also because he knew that his 1772 ruling was open to interpretation and therefore Dido's status required such specificity. She received a substantially smaller sum than her cousin; whether this was due to her race or the fact that she was viewed as illegitimate is unclear. In comparison to her earlier years, Dido's later life was relatively humble. She went on to marry John Davinier, a French steward with whom she had three sons. The family lived in London until her death in 1804, aged 43. She is regarded as Britain's first Black aristocrat, her image exquisitely immortalised on canvas.

Another Black Briton with impressive penmanship was Olaudah Equiano, who was encouraged to write his life story. It was a first-hand account about the terrible reality that was enslavement, called *The Interesting Narrative of the Life of Olaudah Equiano, or Gustavus Vassa, the African*. Equiano was born in the Kingdom of Benin and was kidnapped as a child with his sister and sold to enslavers, eventually being trafficked to Virginia. He was sold on twice more, but in 1766 Equiano was able to buy his freedom at the age of 21 before travelling to Britain in 1777.

The rest of his life would be dedicated to ending slavery. It was he who told Granville Sharp of the *Zong* massacre, which gained a great deal of attention and revealed the horrors of slavery and the middle passage to the British public. And he shared other experiences, such as his time spent working in the Royal Navy and his travels to the Arctic. It was a bestseller by 1792 and was read across the continent. His public readings were vital in securing support for the abolitionist cause, and Equiano embarked on the first British author tour of its kind between 1789 and 1794. During his tours he would sign copies of his book and engage with people by going door to door, as well as encouraging audiences to boycott sugar. He also actively engaged with working-class communities, such as miners, across Manchester and Newcastle, which he mentions in the sixth edition of his book. Inevitably, he received what we would now deem to be trolling across various newspapers, and he even expressed concerns for his own safety when he went to visit Bristol in 1793.

Equiano also co-founded an abolitionist group called the Sons of Africa, possibly Britain's first Black political organisation. These Black Britons were united in their experience of and desire to abolish slavery. They wrote letters, made speeches and worked alongside the heavyweights of the movement like Granville Sharp. We know Equiano did not live to see the abolition of slavery, as he died in 1797, but his impact on those who continued the fight cannot be understated. He also was a charitable man, raising money for poor members of the Black community and campaigning for the working class to be given the vote. Today, there are plaques dedicated to Equiano, but sadly his burial plot is lost. A statue stands in his memory in Telegraph Hill Lower Park, in south London.

Revolution helped end the slave trade

Outside of the British Empire, the Haitian Revolution was the largest revolt led by enslaved people in modern history and lasted for over twelve years, from 1791. It started in the French colony of Saint-Domingue and ended with Haiti as its own independent state, led by the formidable Toussaint L'Ouverture. The revolution's success inevitably led to paranoia in Britain's colonies, understandably, given that Jamaica at that time had already been the site of numerous attempted enslaved uprisings (and indeed would continue to be). Rebellions led by enslaved people certainly influenced the decision by the British government to abolish the slave trade in 1807. Queen Nanny of the Maroons, featured on Jamaica's $500 note, is an iconic symbol of resistance. So much of what we know about her is wrapped in legend due to her links to Obeah, a system of Jamaican spiritual folk practice. Some assert that she was even able to catch bullets.

Maroon communities were formed by runaway enslaved people, and their presence alone undermined as well as threatened the colonial hierarchies of power. They came into direct conflict with the British, raiding and freeing enslaved people on plantations. We know the Maroons were feared by the British, shown by the fact that they were tortured and burnt to death if captured alive.

Nanny was a key strategist in the First Maroon War, which started in 1728. The Maroons used guerrilla tactics expertly – which L'Ouverture would later utilise – and were able to use camouflage and breathing techniques to avoid being seen or heard. By 1739 a peace treaty was achieved, which gave the Maroons their own lands. There were many years of peace between the Maroons and the British in Jamaica, though this did not last.

The British found themselves in almost constant battle with enslaved people on the island. Tacky's Revolt in 1760 was eventually supressed after eighteen months, but intense British military tactics were needed to do so, including transporting 500 enslaved people to Nova Scotia to try to minimise reprisals. This did not stop the rebellions, in places like Demerara, Antigua, Barbados and the Bahamas.

The Baptist War of 1831–2 in Jamaica was led by Samuel Sharpe, and is seen as the greatest rebellion in its history. He was inspired by Christian teachings and preachers who taught the enslaved about equality, leading him to demand greater freedoms and payment for the labour of the enslaved. When the enslaved refused to work unless their demands were met, things escalated into a violent uprising involving 60,000 enslaved people on the island. There was over a million pounds' worth of damage done to property.

When Sharpe was captured he did not deny the role he had played. He was executed in Montego Bay on 23 May 1832. His last words were 'I would rather die upon yonder gallows than live in slavery.' When Sharpe was executed, his enslaver was paid £16 compensation. Sharpe is remembered as a Jamaican national hero and has been immortalised on their $50 note. It is no coincidence that a year after the Baptist War, slavery was abolished in most of the British Empire.

As demonstrated by these stories of bravery and defiance, the design of the kneeling enslaved African by Josiah Wedgwood clearly requires interrogation, as it shows the enslaved as passive and pleading for freedom. It is an image that does not depict the resistance and revolutions carried out by enslaved people, as well as the campaigning of figures like Equiano and Prince. It also doesn't reflect the physical brutality and mental anguish that enslavement created, nor the way that cultural traditions, values and beliefs endured against the odds through the generations to the present day. The image presents one particular view of the enslaved, given its intended audience; the design was aimed at the British public and Parliament, who saw themselves as being solely responsible for freeing the enslaved. Examples of resistance both within and beyond the British Empire contributed far more to abolition than they have been given credit for. This paternalistic view of the reasons behind abolition has endured for centuries. Those most associated with the abolition of slavery are the men with the influence, platform and connections to write themselves as the central figures of this narrative.

Despite opposition from the 60 MPs of the West India Lobby (possibly the first organised parliamentary lobby in history), who had consistently defended slavery for decades, the bill of 1807 gained a majority in Parliament, overseen by Prime Minister Lord Grenville, who supported it. The British slave trade was abolished in 1807, or rather the buying and selling of newly enslaved people was; the already enslaved people were not freed until 1833, when Parliament abolished slavery in the British Caribbean, Mauritius and the Cape.

The West African squadron was established by the Royal Navy in 1808 to clamp down on the trade. With its base in Portsmouth, it patrolled the West African coastline from Sierra Leone to Angola, supported by African sailors from the Kru coast (now Liberia) intercepting slave ships. This was dangerous work, dubbed 'the white man's grave', as crews fought diseases as well as those attempting to maintain the trade. Approximately 1,600 ships had been seized by 1860, and 150,000 Africans aboard these vessels were freed.

On 1 August 1838, some 800,000 enslaved people living in British colonies throughout the Caribbean were set free, following the passage of the 1833 Slavery Abolition Act. This was passed by Parliament two years after the publication of Mary Prince's book. The economic reality was that the slave trade was less profitable than ever before, which was compounded by the work of the abolitionists alongside the fear stoked by uprisings and rebellions. It's also worth noting that Britain was several decades behind the Dutch, who had abolished the trading of enslaved Africans in their colonies in 1792.

Meanwhile, the British Empire rules the waves, mostly

The Enlightenment was a time of new ideas and inventions that evidently fuelled discoveries, wars and revolutions. This was the time of individuals and moments deeply entrenched within our consciousness and in the lyrics of some of Queen's greatest hits. In 1610, Galileo was the first person to see the four moons of Jupiter. Sir Isaac Newton sat under an apple tree in 1686 and identified the force of gravity. Writers like John Locke advocated that revolutions may be necessary under some circumstances.

By 1775 there were 2.5 million people living across the thirteen colonies on the eastern seaboard of America. Many of those colonists now considered themselves to be American and wished to rule themselves, rather than be ruled by the British government. Tax legislation like the Stamp Act of 1765 meant that all printed materials like pamphlets, newspapers and even playing cards had to be made from taxed paper, uniting many colonists under the slogan of 'No taxation without representation'. The words of Thomas Paine in his 1776 pamphlet 'Common Sense: addressed to the inhabitants of America' fuelled the colonists further, with his arguments encouraging American independence and arguing against the divine right of kings.

In the same year, on 4 July, the thirteen colonies published the Declaration of Independence. That summer many began to celebrate independence prematurely, arranging mock funerals for King George III. What ensued was five years of war, with the balance tipping in favour of the colonist army with support from the French, who supplied them with troops and weapons. In 1781 the British surrendered at Yorktown, and then marched out to the band playing 'The World Turned Upside Down'. The song title undoubtedly reflected how this made Britain feel. This was, after all, the first time any colony had fought against their 'mother country' to become independent.

Australia was chosen as the destination for Britain's new penal colony now that America was no longer a viable option, though Australia was, in fact, Plan B. Plan A had been to imprison people on 'hulks', essentially old warships turned into floating prisons along the English Channel. Overcrowding and the spread of diseases meant an alternative solution was needed. Those awaiting transportation were held on these hulks until their ships were ready.

The 1787 decision to turn the area around Botany Bay (named because of the number of plants 'discovered' there) into a prison would not have been possible without James Cook, a British naval officer who left Plymouth in August 1768 and had sailed to Australia's east coast by April 1770, the first European to do so. Two Gweagal Aboriginal men tried to stop them, believing it was their spiritual duty to protect their homeland. Cook's interpretation of events, made clear in his journal, was that he believed he was under attack, hence shots were fired, wounding one of the Aboriginal men. Cook and his crew on the *Endeavour* sailed north and landed on an island that Cook named Possession Island. He also claimed the eastern coast as British territory, naming it New South Wales, despite indigenous populations having lived there for thousands of years. By the time the British returned to Australia, however, Cook was already dead. He was fatally stabbed on Valentine's Day in 1779 in Hawaii during his third trip to the Pacific.

The First Fleet of eleven ships left Britain in May 1787 and arrived in Australia eight months later, with approximately 750 convicts between them. Australia Day is celebrated on 26 January to mark the day the fleet arrived in Sydney. Australia was considered to be an 'infant settlement', reflected in the name given to medallions made by Wedgwood to commemorate the landing of the First Fleet.

By far the most common reason for transportation to Australia was theft, for both men and women. For example, Elizabeth Anderson was sentenced to transportation for seven years for stealing three linen tablecloths and two aprons. Other crimes included murder, perjury and setting fire to a haystack. After the French Revolution, political prisoners were increasingly transported in order to limit their influence. For example, John Hughes was sentenced to twenty years in Van Diemen's Land (Tasmania) for his role in the 1839–43 protests led by farmers in Wales against the taxes they were now being charged to use certain roads. These riots became known as the Rebecca Riots, as men would disguise themselves as women and attack the tollgates. There is a passage in the Bible where Rebecca talks of the need to possess the gates of those who hate them.

A lot of the political prisoners were from Ireland, particularly in the wake of the Irish Rebellion of 1798. Being transported did little to stop some political prisoners, like Phillip Cunningham, who arrived in New South Wales in 1801. He was a key leader in the 1804 Castle Hill revolt, which was an attempt to establish Irish rule. Cunningham was executed as a result.

Many convicts faced a sentence of hard labour, which would include work such as building roads or breaking rocks. Convicts working in chain gangs would be shackled together by the ankle, the weight of these chains serving as an additional punishment to the intensive work they were already doing. Despite some convicts receiving a 'ticket of leave' once their time was up, many opted to stay, particularly as infrastructure had been firmly established. They set up their own farms and were involved in work such as sheep farming and whaling, and from 1851 the focus for many was finding gold. The devastating impact the influx of European migrants had on the Aboriginal people of Australia cannot be overstated, with population numbers falling by 90 per cent in the century following Cook's arrival for a number of reasons, including diseases that Europeans brought over. Drawing parallels with the American experience, by the 1880s many settlers now saw themselves as distinctly Australian.

VICTORIANS (AT HOME AND ABROAD) 4

Some of the things we still consume today were first popularised during the Victorian era. Mr Alfred Bird's wife had an egg allergy, which led him to develop his famous custard powder in 1837, something you can still buy in your local supermarket for around £2. An 1889 experiment in London Zoo led to cod liver oil being distributed to schools and workhouses in the hope it would strengthen children as much as it had positively impacted lion cubs. This is a period of many firsts, from the first postboxes, the invention of the telephone and the first FA Cup final. In case you were wondering, toothbrushes looked similar to the ones we have today, except they would have been made from bone and pony-hair. Toothpaste, on the other hand, was not, with the two most common ingredients being powdered chalk and cuttlefish.

Despite the availability of powdered custard, the average Victorian was likely to be much hungrier than their medieval counterparts, supported by the fact that, on average, they were two inches shorter. Relying on a genuinely nutritious diet of potatoes and buttermilk, the Irish were the tallest people in Europe before 1845. Spreading from the USA across Europe, the potato famine or the Great Hunger started in 1845 and hit Ireland the worst. A combination of an unrelenting potato blight, a reliance on the potato crop and insufficient relief efforts led to the deaths of approximately a million people from hunger and disease, with two million opting to emigrate to England as well as America. The efforts to support the Irish reached the Native American Choctaw tribe, who raised $170, equating to approximately £500 today for the plight of a people far away. This friendship continues to this day in many forms, including a scholarship programme for Choctaw students to study in Ireland.

For the Victorians, school was a very serious matter, becoming mandatory in 1880, and the notion of 'exams' entered public consciousness during this time. Corporal punishment in schools was normalised on the basis that children should receive consequences for not trying their best. Physical penalties like canings with wooden rulers or leather straps were commonplace, as were methods of humiliation such as forcing a child to stand up in front of the class wearing a dunce cap.

The River Thames had been used as a dumping ground of the worst kind for centuries. The heat in the summer of 1858 meant that if you were in London, you were unfortunately in the epicentre of the Great Stink. It was so bad that when dousing the curtains in Parliament with chloride and lime wasn't enough, MPs finally decided to do something about it. The sewage system we rely on today was created as a result, the brainchild of civil engineer Sir Joseph Bazalgette. Diseases most commonly associated with this period include cholera and typhoid, the latter of which led to Prince Albert's death at the age of 42.

Learning about the Victorians is an area of history often covered mainly at primary school, where images are conjured up of children in workhouses under smog-filled skies. This chapter will, however, focus on those who lived under Victorian rule a little further afield.

Queen Victoria was also Empress of India

The Victorian era started in 1837 and lasted until 1901. Queen Victoria was born in 1819 and became queen at the age of eighteen. She would reign for 63 years, becoming the first monarch in British history to celebrate a diamond jubilee. Many of us will remember that she wore black for four decades after the death of her beloved husband, Albert.

He has been immortalised in buildings across the nation, including the Royal Albert Hall, and across the world, like Lake Albert in Uganda, a reminder that the Victorians lived at the very height of the British Empire.

The Great Exhibition of 1851 was the brainchild of Albert, who wished to showcase British and global advances in manufacturing, as well as a huge array of intriguing items, something like 100,000 exhibits, including a cannister of boiled mutton from an 1824 Arctic expedition. After the exhibition, the profits were used at the behest of Albert to found three museums in Kensington: the V&A, the Natural History Museum, and the Science Museum. The exhibition was held in a specially built 'crystal palace', consisting of over 300,000 panels of glass. Built in Hyde Park, the centre of the building held a 27-foot-high and four-ton fountain made of pink glass. Admission prices varied according to the date. The cheapest tickets could be bought for a shilling, meaning that working-class people could afford to visit, facilitated by the travel agent Thomas Cook, who arranged special low-cost excursion trains to bring people in from across the country. Most people's first look at a public toilet would have been at the exhibition – which was lucky, as more than a million bottles of Schweppes lemonade and ginger beer were sold during the six months it was open. The Schweppes logo today still features the fountain at the centre of the exhibition.

Countries from across the globe shipped over goods, and six million people visited the exhibition in the summer of 1851. The *Morning Chronicle* described one displayed item as 'having attracted more curiosity and inflicted more disappointment than anything of its size ever did since the world was created'. This was, of course, the Koh-i-Noor diamond, considered to be the largest and most valuable in the world at the time. It's now part of the British Crown Jewels and is on display in the Tower of London, as part of the crown last worn by the Queen Mother.

The Koh-i-Noor is documented in the 17th-century Mughal records of Shah Jahan's court, where it was placed atop the Peacock Throne. The history of the diamond after the invasion of Delhi by Nader Shah in 1739 is complex, and the key for us is that by 1813 it was in the possession of Ranjit Singh, also known as the Lion of Punjab, a relative of a few important figures we're yet to meet. After his death in 1839, his ten-year-old son Duleep Singh eventually had the crown. And after the British imprisoned his mother, Rani Jindan, Duleep Singh was forced to sign the Treaty of Lahore, which included the condition that the diamond should be 'surrendered' to Queen Victoria. It was presented to her in the summer of 1850 to mark the 250-year anniversary of the East India Company and was then displayed in 1851.

The diamond was, in fact, re-cut after the exhibition under Albert's instruction, as it had failed to 'wow' the crowds, despite six extra lamps and twelve mirrors being brought in to up its sparkle. A letter from Duleep Singh to the Queen in 1889 reveals that he asked for it back, stating that he was a 'mere infant' when the British 'confiscated both my diamond and my dominions'. He signed off his letter: 'To her most gracious majesty, the Queen of England and Empress of India.' To understand why she now had this additional title, we need to go further back in time.

The entrance to the medieval Powis Castle in Wales is flanked by a cannon on either side. As you get closer, it's clear they are no ordinary cannons. The muzzles are beautifully carved in the shape of an animal. Any guesses? Due to the location of the castle, you might think that the animal could be a dragon. It is, in fact, a tiger. Even more curiously, the inscription reads 'La illah ul Allah', meaning 'there is no god but Allah'. Step inside Powis Castle and you will find the largest private collection of Mughal artefacts in the world. There are, in fact, more Mughal artefacts here (over a thousand) than in the National Museum in Delhi. How did this happen?

Following the loss of America in 1775, the British focused on India as well as Australia. The East India Company (EIC) was by this point an incredibly lucrative venture, having been licensed by the Crown under Elizabeth I to import Indian goods to Britain. In 1620 the EIC bought 250,000 pounds of pepper for £26,041, which was then sold in London for £208,041. The influence of the East India Company changed dramatically over this period, as it evolved from being a trading company to effectively ruling over huge swathes of India by the mid-18th century, successfully ousting most other European influence in the region in the process. One of the key reasons for this is that the EIC developed its own army, which greatly facilitated this shift from commercial interest into political power. One man in particular played a significant role in this shift, and his statue stands today outside the Foreign and Commonwealth Office in Whitehall.

Robert Clive was sent to India in 1744 by his father at the age of seventeen, having shown himself to be somewhat of a tearaway; one of his notorious schoolboy exploits had involved extorting money from local shopkeepers. Starting out as a clerk for the EIC, by 1746 he had joined their army, despite having no formal military training. In 1757 Clive led the EIC in its most infamous victory, at the Battle of Plassey, effectively formalising their role in India as one of political rule in addition to their economic influence.

The Nawab (ruler) of Bengal, Siraj ud-Daulah, was a target for the EIC, as Bengal was an incredibly wealthy province. Mir Jafar, a key commander in Siraj ud-Daulah's siege of Fort William, was offered the role of Nawab of Bengal if he cooperated with the EIC. The bribe worked out, meaning that, despite Clive being hugely outnumbered (he had command of approximately 3,000 against 50,000) and Siraj ud-Daulah having assistance from the French, the 1757 Battle of Plassey was decisively won by the EIC. Despite his attempt to flee, Siraj ud-Daulah was found and promptly murdered, his body paraded through the streets.

This victory meant Britain now effectively controlled Bengal and could expand further into India, increasing its military and trade power. Within 50 years, the EIC controlled the Mughal capital Delhi to the north and had extended all along the eastern coastline to the southernmost part of India, hence why Clive's name is synonymous with the very foundation of the British Empire in the Indian subcontinent. Clive profited greatly from the Battle of Plassey – in today's currency, around £22 million for himself and £232 million for the company. No wonder one of the very first Indian words to enter the English language was the Hindi slang for plunder: 'loot'. Clive continued to bring back chests full of jewels, including diamonds gifted to Queen Charlotte, as well as furniture and 'curiosities'. One of the centrepieces of the Clive collection at Powis is the beautiful wooden gilded palanquin – or travelling coach – of Siraj ud-Daulah, said to have been abandoned on the battlefield in 1757.

This political and economic expansion was sealed in 1765 when the Mughal emperor Shah Alam, having been exiled from Delhi and defeated by EIC troops, was forced to sign the Diwani, which meant all taxes across Bengal, Bihar and Orissa were now to be collected by the EIC. Once again, they were proving to have powers far beyond those of a conventional company; this was corporate-driven colonialism. In order to collect these taxes efficiently, the EIC spearheaded the creation of a huge administrative structure which could be replicated across the whole subcontinent.

In 1772, two extraordinary things happened. Firstly, the EIC asked the Bank of England for a loan, the money needed a result of many factors, including rising military expenses as well as a more sinister reason: the Bengal famine of 1770, which had devastated the province, resulting in the death of approximately one million Bengalis. The death toll was almost certainly exacerbated by the EIC, who instead of following the precedent set by other provinces and introducing famine-relief measures, opted to continue tax collection and even increased it in some instances. Some EIC traders were even known to have been hoarding grain to sell for profit.

Secondly, following this bailout and the increasingly negative media coverage of the EIC, a parliamentary investigation was announced, aiming to dig into the corruption within. Clive was called and defended the fortune he had amassed from India, as well as taking no responsibility for the famine. It was also found that MPs had been bribed to pass legislation to benefit the Company. However, little changed as a result of these two events. It's surely no coincidence that, with 40 per cent of MPs at the time owning stock in the EIC, there was a personal vested interest in agreeing to their request. Parliament therefore provided the first bailout of this kind, worth £1.4 million then, and £147 million today.

While Powis Castle's 'Clive collection' might represent the pinnacle of what could be made through the EIC, there were numerous avenues through which fortunes could be made in India. George Graham, for example, having failed to prosper as a planter in Jamaica, travelled to India in 1770 hoping for better luck. Seven years later he was able to purchase the spectacular Kinross House Estate in Scotland thanks to the wealth he had quickly amassed from his involvement in supplying East India Company army uniforms in Bengal, as well as private trade. If you're looking for a venue that sleeps 48 guests, has a spa, helipads and private pier, then Kinross House is the one. Just like the immense collection at Powis Castle, these physical traces of empire are scattered all over the nation.

The East India Company was involved in a battle in 1799 so significant that the Soho mint in Birmingham was ordered to make a special medal. Each soldier was either given a tin, bronze, silver or gold version, depending on their rank, some of which were also made in Calcutta. Over 50,000 medals were made. One side of each medal shows a lion representing Britain successfully attacking a tiger representing one man: Tipu Sultan of Mysore. He defeated the EIC twice, including the 1780 Battle of Pollilur, the first time rockets were successfully used on the battlefield. He pioneered many other things, introducing a new calendar, developing roads and the navy. He saw the EIC as his true enemy and had hundreds of captives after the battle forcibly converted and circumcised, hence he was referred to as 'Tipu the tyrant'.

His disdain for the Company's encroachment on his land is reflected in a true 'curiosity' from his palace, which is now held at the Victoria and Albert Museum. Tippoo's Tiger really is the most intriguing of objects. It features a tiger mauling a Company soldier, complete in their signature red uniform. Tipu used tiger motifs on everything, from cannons to the diamond and ruby tiger heads that adorned his throne. The bronze mortars made for his army were even in the shape of crouching tigers. He's known to have said, 'Better to live one day as a tiger than a thousand years as a sheep.' This tiger's body holds quite the surprise, an organ that, when played, not only causes the arms of the soldier to flail but also emits a sound to simulate his screams. This was clearly not intended to be played as an instrument, but was used as a symbol of disgust at the Company that Tipu was constantly defending himself against.

The final incitement the EIC needed to have one last go at Tipu came when the British intercepted correspondence between him and Napoleon. Fearing relations between Mysore and France could possibly lead to a full-blown military alliance, Company troops were organised. Tipu already had French officers training his troops.

In 1799 the EIC attacked the fort at Seringapatam, Tipu's capital. As we know from the medals, the Company was successful. Tipu's body was found among a heap of corpses, recognised by the jewellery he was wearing. What ensued was the looting of the entire city, with the most precious items from the palace treasury distributed among those of the highest rank. Among those present was Edward Clive, son of Robert and now the Governor of Madras.

These items are still being auctioned today. A small jade pendant set with rubies and emeralds, thought to have been found on Tipu's body, was recently sold for £46,250 at Christie's. And there are many items from Mysore that are now part of the Clive Museum at Powis. Arthur Wellesley, the future Duke of Wellington and one of the key orchestrators of this Company victory, gave Edward's wife Lady Henrietta Clive one of the bejewelled tiger heads from Tipu's throne, which was dismantled and different parts gifted as spoils of war. The amount accumulated from Tipu's palace is estimated to have been worth £200 million in today's money. A scabbard and sword belonging to Tipu, incised with tiger stripes, are also part of the collection. Tipu's beautifully painted chintz tent, which he would have used when travelling, is now part of the Clive Museum, but was used as a garden party marquee at Powis prior to this.

Unusually, Lady Henrietta Clive was in India at the time of the battle. She actually hosted a banquet to celebrate the defeat of Tipu in Madras on 4 June 1799. Lady Clive was a keen collector and embarked on a seven-month tour of South India in 1780 with an entourage of 750 people. On this tour she largely focused on animals and plants, apparently toying with the idea of bringing an elephant back to Britain. It was during this tour that Lady Clive possibly acquired what the Guinness World Records decided in 2004 was the 'largest suit of animal armour'. Weighing in at 118 kilograms, this spectacular 5,480-plate elephant armour is now at the Royal Armouries in Leeds, but was at Powis Castle in 1809, displayed with two Indian figures riding it. The provenance, however, is not certain, with some asserting that the armour was brought back from the Battle of Plassey by Robert Clive. Either way, if you're a fan of the armoured elephant, you can buy a stuffed toy version for £19.99 from the gift shop.

After the defeat of Tipu, the EIC continued with their expansion, taking the Mughal capital of Delhi in 1803. That's not to say there was not fierce opposition along the way, of course. For example, in 1806 the Indian soldiers of the Madras Native Infantry mutinied, raising the flag of the Mysore Kingdom, showing that the legacy of arguably the Company's fiercest opponent still lived on. But by the 1850s most of India was ruled by the British due to annexations made by the EIC, facilitated by their army, which by this time contained a minority of British soldiers, while the bulk of it was made up of local Indians, known as 'sepoys'.

There was growing frustration among these Indian sepoys, particularly regarding their limited access to promotion within the army. On 10 May 1857, Indian sepoys in Meerut (northern India) mutinied against their British officers. The spark behind the mutiny came in January 1857, when each Indian soldier was given a new rifle, which used gunpowder kept in cartridge cases. These cases were covered in grease to make it easier to slide the bullets down the barrel. To load the gun the soldiers had to bite the top of the casing off. Rumours circulated that the grease was made from a mix of pork and beef fat – making it forbidden for both Hindus and Muslims. Despite the cartridges being withdrawn, the damage was done and paranoia set in. The sepoys had already been feeling some pressure to convert to Christianity, which was compounded by this cartridge scandal. It led to other items being questioned; the British interfering in cooking oil and flour no longer seemed beyond the realm of possibility.

One of the first casualties was a sepoy called Mangal Pandey, who was court-martialled and hanged for encouraging his fellow soldiers to mutiny. Sepoys rioted in support, although this was not universal by any means, partly because different groups were motivated by different reasons and desired different outcomes. For example, some wanted to restore Mughal rule under Bahadur Shah, while others wanted local leaders back. Others refused to participate at all, while some units, like the army in Bombay, continued supporting the British. The violence was therefore largely confined to the north of India.

Many others joined the fray too, including local Indian leaders who were unhappy with extensive British interference in India. Most of these local leaders were men, with one notable exception. Lakshmibai was born into a well-established noble family in 19th-century western India. The woman who was to become the Rani (Queen) of Jhansi happened to be skilled in the warrior arts at an early age. A typical day for Lakshmibai involved weightlifting, wrestling and steeplechasing – all before breakfast.

After her marriage to the Raja of Jhansi, their son, who was born in 1851, soon died, quickly followed by her husband. Then, in 1853, citing a 'lack of heirs', the EIC annexed the territory as its own, using their 'doctrine of lapse' as the justification. This meant that any area not deemed to have a 'legitimate' heir would have to forfeit their province to the Company. Many other territories had been taken this way, including Avadh, undoubtedly motivated by the Company's desire to construct railway links in the area. The letters Lakshmibai sent to the EIC were all ignored.

Four years later, Jhansi joined the rebellion against Company rule. The British attacked Jhansi in March 1858, partly in revenge for the massacre of 56 English citizens. Lakshmibai was blamed by the EIC, despite her vehement protestations that she'd done all she could to protect them. By the time British troops arrived, she'd recruited 14,000 volunteers, including women, to defend the Jhansi fort. Legend goes that when the fort was under siege, she mounted her horse, her young adopted son holding on tight behind her, and leapt to freedom from the ramparts.

The most iconic image of the Rani of Jhansi is of her last stand in battle, again on horseback, with her sword held high and the reins of her horse between her teeth. After Jhansi had been ransacked, its palace and library were burnt and around 5,000 of its citizens killed. Lakshmibai perished while fighting the British on horseback on 18 June 1858, although the exact details are unclear. British records noted that 'the rebels lost their bravest and best military leader'. Irrespective of whether this was meant sarcastically, it's understandable why she has iconic status across India. She is the main character in a stream of TV shows, films and video games: a warrior queen who is now remembered as a feminist freedom fighter.

There were brutal battles between British troops and sepoys in Delhi, Cawnpore and Lucknow. The Cawnpore massacre was seared into Victorian imperial memory, as over a hundred British women and children were killed despite their safe passage being assured beforehand. Newspapers at the time emphasised stories of women caught in the crosshairs of the rebellion, such as 'English homes in India', a cartoon from the *Illustrated Times* in October 1857 showing two Indian men who have broken into the home of a British mother of two, who is breastfeeding one child and looking suitably frightened.

Overall, the Great Rebellion lasted eighteen months and ended in British victory. The British issued extremely harsh punishments, such as massacring villages who had supported the sepoys or forcing them to eat beef or pork before publicly hanging them. Many were tied to cannons, which were then fired, killing them instantly. One such unfortunate man was Alum Bheg from the Bengal Regiment, whose skull was found at the back of a pub in Kent in 1963.

After the uprising, control of India was transferred from Company to Crown. The 'jewel in the crown' was now firmly in the hands of the government, including the army that had quelled this rebellion. Bahadur Shah was duly exiled to Myanmar, marking the official end of the Mughal dynasty. The India Office was set up in 1858 and a viceroy was put in charge of India on behalf of Queen Victoria, marking the start of the British Raj. She was given the title of Empress of India in 1877, formally cementing her association with a nation she ruled over but never visited. Her son Edward VII would be the first monarch to do so.

The uprising was very deliberately referred to as the Indian Mutiny or Sepoy Mutiny across Victorian Britain, mostly through a desire to minimise the scope of the event and confine it to being something only the military were involved in. Since India's independence, other terms to describe it have come to be more accepted, particularly in recognition of the involvement of civilians. While there is no accepted universal term, the Indian Uprising, First War of Independence and the Great Rebellion are a few examples of how this event has been revised to reflect its true scope.

Granting India independence at this point was unfathomable. This was a time of imperial expansion, and India was an integral part of the growing empire. India was also incredibly useful economically, due to her high export values and the production of goods such as indigo. There were 700 factories for indigo production in Bengal and Bihar by 1830, and it was one of the most valuable items the EIC had traded. Moreover, the Indian Army could easily be stationed to other parts of the empire, like they were in China in 1839. And Indians provided cheap and mobile labour, as shown by the fact that in the 1830s thousands of Indians had been shipped to work overseas.

Indian indentured labourers replaced enslaved workers after abolition

When slavery was abolished within the British Empire, arguments were made that indentured workers should replace the labour needed on plantations, spearheaded by John Gladstone, who approached a company that had previously sent Indian labourers to Mauritius and confirmed that expanding indentureship to Caribbean sugar plantations would work, as Indians were 'more akin to the monkey than the man'. Known as the 'Gladstone experiment', the venture was eventually abandoned after being exposed in the British press for treating the workforce 'no better than ex-slaves'.

Unsurprisingly, the system flourished anyway after a brief ban. It's estimated that approximately 1.3 million Indians moved from India to work as indentured labourers between 1834 and 1914, mostly hailing originally from southern and eastern Indian villages. They would travel by boat, with limited understanding that the journey to the Caribbean would average around three months. Some would travel alone, while others would travel with family members. Cholera outbreaks onboard were common and exacerbated by overcrowding, meaning not everyone would survive the journey. For example, in 1870 the *Shand* arrived in British Guiana having lost 98 passengers, including children. Some of the early ships used were simply refitted vessels that had taken enslaved Africans to the same destination.

This workforce was spread across the empire, including in Jamaica, British Guiana, Fiji and St Lucia. The largest number, of approximately 453,000, were sent to Mauritius. Workers were tied to an employer and were provided with a wage and accommodation in exchange for labour over a fixed period of time, often five years. In theory, the system of indentureship also included the return journey. The wages were pitiful, as little as one shilling a day. The treatment of this workforce was harsh, with beatings and assaults (particularly on women) fairly commonplace, alongside the often unsanitary living conditions. Workers had to obtain a pass to be able to leave their plantation. The barrister John Edward Jenkins confirmed this when he participated in an inquiry into the conditions facing labourers in British Guiana, which was published in 1871 under the title 'The Coolie, His Rights and Wrongs'. 'Coolie' was a derogatory term for migrant workers primarily from southern India, Indonesia and China in the Caribbean, likely derived from the Tamil word 'kuli', which translates to 'wages'. 'The Coolie, His Rights and Wrongs' reiterated that there was often corruption from the very start of the process, highlighted in the example of the *Shand*, where the doctor onboard said he would have excluded at least fifty of the passengers aboard due to their poor health. All passengers were meant to have been medically approved at the depot before departure, as shown by their immigration passes.

These passes provide an interesting insight into individual labourers, such as a 20-year-old man called Goordin, who left Calcutta for Fiji in 1882. Travelling on the *Poonah* ship, we also know he was unmarried, was five feet and three inches tall and had a scar on his right shin. What we cannot tell from these passes, however, are the reasons behind Goordin's decision, or whether he knowingly embarked on indentureship. It may have been the opportunity to escape poverty and unemployment, but, despite the passes stating that 'all matters concerning his duties as an emigrant' had been explained and signed off on, the extent to which they were aware of where they were going, how long for and the nature of the work is debatable. Various reports from the time confirm that the information they were given was often inaccurate, with some agreeing to travel on the basis that they would only be gone for a few months. There is also evidence that some were coerced and in some cases kidnapped, with women, for example, being preyed upon at pilgrimage sites and lured to depots under the false pretense of being taken to a shrine.

Jenkins' findings included the facts that workers had unfair wages, poor accommodation and were often punished and even imprisoned for arbitrary reasons. It's worth noting, however, that Jenkins reflected many attitudes at the time: that despite the conditions faced by the labourers, this was a system that benefitted Britain, was more 'morally acceptable' than enslavement and therefore should continue. Working on a sugar plantation was particularly gruelling due to the plummeting profits and a lack of investment in new machinery. Wages were therefore cut and workers had to work harder than those on tea or rubber plantations. Because some workers arrived in debt, only a third of them made it back to India. Some opted to stay where they were, and many of those who worked on the Kenya–Uganda railway between 1895 and 1902 did so.

Incidents of resistance add another angle to the lives of indentured workers, particularly given how high the stakes were; contracts could be extended, fines could be levied and incarceration was a very real possibility. In 1869 a group of workers in Demerara protested against their wages being withheld for 'unfinished work', despite this being caused by waterlogged fields. Violent protests took place consistently across Guyana, for example, resulting in injuries and even the deaths of some indentured workers.

The system of indentured labour was abolished in 1917. This system resulted in the existence of Indian diaspora communities in places like Guyana and Trinidad and Tobago, where they are the largest minority groups in those countries today. The use of indentured labourers after the abolition of slavery is not something that is particularly well known, and it is an important reminder of how much of the inner workings of the British Empire is absent from popular understanding. There are reminders of these indentured labourers in the most unexpected of places, with a town named Calcutta in Belize, a reflection of the thousand Indians sent there by the British government after the events of 1857.

The nannies hidden in plain sight

At first glance, the 1893 painting *Going North, King's Cross Station* just looks like a typical chaotic station scene. There is, however, a hidden story amongst the hustle and bustle. The station itself in many ways represents this Victorian age, with the railway system flourishing during her reign. In the centre of the image are two figures clad in red. One of them is a young girl who is being aided by another: her ayah. Ayahs were nannies and nursemaids employed to care for the young children of British families who settled across Asian colonies in places like India, Myanmar and Malaysia. An 1893 publication called *The English Baby in India and How to Raise It* reminds us that, even though these women were being entrusted with children and babies, comments about their appearance, cleanliness and penchant for trying to 'cheat' their employers reflect the unequivocal power dynamics at play. The ayahs would often travel with these families when they came back to Britain, and while some would be given a return ticket, others were unfortunately abandoned, which we know because of adverts placed in newspapers by ayahs seeking employment and help in returning home.

The Ayahs' Home in Hackney, thought to be the only one of its kind in Britain, was formed by a Christian group called London City Mission to provide shelter for approximately a hundred women a year. There is now a blue plaque on the building used as the Ayahs' Home between 1900 and 1921, thanks to the campaigning of Farhanah Mamoojee. This is an important step in remembering a group of people who were too often discarded, despite the key role they played in supporting the families of those who upheld the mantle of empire.

This celebration is even more poignant given that there are references to ayahs you may never have noticed in classics like *David Copperfield* and *The Secret Garden*. Ayahs are also featured in countless paintings scattered all over the world, often on the sidelines of family portraits in much the same way young African servants and pageboys were depicted in Georgian paintings. One of my favourites is in Berlin and features the Hancock family and their 'Indian maid', who is, rather unusually, at the centre of the painting. These images show us how they were viewed through the eyes of others, but little evidence from ayahs themselves exists. They do appear in various records, though, such as Beebee Jauneeh, who filed a petition against her employers for mistreatment in 1831, showing us that some were willing to go to great lengths to receive the appropriate pay and treatment they deserved. Whether it's stories of the ayahs who nursed young children, the violence of the Great Rebellion or the loot that made its way into private and public collections, one thing is clear. All of the connections from this period with the Indian subcontinent are part of British history and reflect a clear shared history, even if these are stories which you were not familiar with until now.

Queen Victoria's collection of imperial children

Objects relating to the British Empire continued to fascinate the public into the late 19th century, epitomised by the Colonial and Indian Exhibition in 1886. The catalogue cum travel brochure asks readers to consider trying Jamaica 'as a winter health resort', using the weather, tropical flowers and birds and the apparently soothing 'hum of the sugar mill' to entice people to take the eighteen-day journey. The catalogue introduced the reader to each place, with the entry for Fiji providing a stark reminder of who this exhibition was for: 'There are about 115,000 natives who are physically and mentally superior to most coloured races. They are a reddish-brown in complexion.'

A special building was constructed in Indian-style architecture specially for the exhibition. During the opening ceremony, Queen Victoria sat on a golden Indian throne which had been seized from Maharaja Ranjit Singh. During the national anthem, two verses were sung by the Royal Choir, in Sanskrit. 'India' took up roughly a third of the exhibition space in 1886, five times the space the country had been given at the Great Exhibition in 1851, a reflection of how important this part of the empire was to the Victorians. The gateways in particular attracted much attention. (The Jaipur Gate, paid for by the Maharaja of Jaipur, has now been in the Hove Museum and Art Gallery since 1926.)

The exhibition included a 'display' of 'native artisans'. There were 34 Indian men 'on display', including weavers, coppersmiths and stone-carvers. The eldest was a 102-year-old potter called Bakshiram. Queen Victoria had his portrait commissioned by Rudolf Swoboda, alongside seven others from the group. (This portrait is on display at Osborne House on the Isle of Wight today.) The youngest were carpet weavers, Ramphal and Ramlall, both aged nine. Two of the men had to drive a carriage around the site outside the venue. Seven others worked in an outdoor café serving Indian tea to visitors. Most of these men were, in fact, inmates from Agra Jail, and Dr J.W. Tyler, superintendent of the jail, was in charge of them. They were all invited to a reception at Windsor Castle to meet Queen Victoria in July 1886, along with other 'natives' from the exhibition, which included people from Ceylon (Sri Lanka), Hong Kong, Cyprus, Australia and the Cape of Good Hope.

Among this contingent was a servant called Abdul Karim, whom the Queen was so impressed by that she bestowed the title 'Munshi' upon him, meaning he was now her teacher and Indian Secretary. He not only wowed her with his cooking of classic dishes like biryani, but he also taught her how to read and write Hindustani, the evidence of which lies in her diaries. They had a close friendship, much to the dismay of many at the time who were particularly concerned with the kind of information he may have had access to. The Queen, however, was not to be influenced and instead provided a residence for him and his wife. The story of Karim and Victoria was depicted in the 2017 film *Victoria & Abdul*, which also highlighted the attempts of her son Edward to remove Karim from Victoria's story after her death, ordering letters and photos pertaining to their friendship to be burnt. Karim was certainly not the only person with imperial connections to grace her court, however.

In November 1850, a seven-year-old girl of Yoruba descent (modern-day Nigeria) was 'presented' to Queen Victoria at Windsor Castle. The Queen, who mentioned this initial meeting in her diary, decided she would take responsibility for her welfare and education. Born in 1843, Omoba Aina had been captured when her village was attacked by the forces of King Ghezo of Dahomey (modern-day Benin). In July 1850, King Ghezo met with Frederick Forbes, a British naval officer who, during the customary exchanging of 'gifts', brought silks as well as a letter from Queen Victoria which aimed to discourage the King from continuing to trade in enslaved people. In the gifts exchanged in return, a young orphaned girl was included, alongside less controversial ones like a keg of rum. She was described in Forbes' list as 'a captive girl'. She was baptised onboard the HMS *Bonetta* and given the name Sarah Forbes Bonetta, after the stranger she had been entrusted to and the ship she had no choice but to board.

Queen Victoria arranged for Sarah to be educated in a missionary school in Freetown in Sierra Leone, possibly based on beliefs at the time that English weather was detrimental to the health of people of African descent. This, however, does not seem to have prevented Sarah from returning to England, confirmed by her presence at the wedding of the Princess Royal, Victoria and Albert's eldest daughter, in 1858. Just like the ayahs, we largely only know about Sarah through the lens of others. The way Sarah was described often centred around intrigue about her intellect, with Victoria, for example, describing her as 'an intelligent little thing'.

In August 1862, Sarah essentially found herself in an arranged marriage to James Davies, a merchant born in Sierra Leone. Sarah clearly had her reservations about this, as shown in a letter she sent to the Schoen family, with whom she lived when she returned from Freetown. In the letter she states that despite being told she will 'soon learn to love him – that, I believe I never could do'.

It begs the question, to what extent did Sarah have any more agency than the Black Georgians immortalised on canvas in the previous century? We also learn that four of her sixteen bridesmaids were 'ladies of colour', though it is unclear who they were or what relationship they had with Sarah, given how little control she would presumably have had over her nuptials. Sarah and her husband moved to Freetown and then Lagos. Sadly, Sarah died at the age of 37, having had four children. Their first daughter was named after her royal godmother and the two met several times, with the Queen writing in 1873 that she was 'wonderfully like her mother'. Victoria paid for her goddaughter's education at Cheltenham Ladies' College.

The story of Sarah is of course not typical of Black Victorian women, shown by the fact that she was certainly a source of intrigue to the British press at the time, who were particularly interested in her intellectual abilities as well as her status, with many referring to her as an 'African princess'. A *Daily News* article about her wedding from 1862 states that 'she is far in advance of any white child of her age in aptness of learning'. The article goes on to say that her head is an excellent 'phrenological specimen', reminding us that regardless of the privileges of accommodation and education that she enjoyed, she was still very much othered by those in society at the time, and she was seen through the lens of the Victorian civilising mission. Though we have little insight into Sarah's own thoughts, we do have a series of photographs of her taken by the renowned French photographer Camille Silvy, now part of the collection at the National Portrait Gallery.

There are clear parallels to be drawn between the story of Sarah and another young girl, whose face was immortalised in a marble bust that Victoria gave to Albert for his birthday in 1856. The girl in question was Princess Gouramma, the daughter of the deposed Maharajah of Coorg, whose land had been annexed via the East India Company's infamous doctrine of lapse. Like Duleep Singh, she was brought to Britain at the age of eleven. Queen Victoria agreed to be her sponsor and godmother, with her father's consent. She was baptised by the Archbishop of Canterbury in the chapel in Buckingham Palace and named, you've guessed it, Victoria. She was looked after by various families with connections to India, and she eventually married John Campbell, a lieutenant 30 years her senior.

Gouramma sadly died at the age of 23, having given birth to her daughter Edith just three years earlier. She is buried at Brompton Cemetery. Both of the key images we have of Gouramma that are closely associated with the Queen emphasise two elements in particular: the fact that she was of Indian heritage but also a Christian. The statuette was painted in watercolour to emphasise her ethnicity and she is shown with a prominent crucifix around her neck. A portrait of her by Franz Xaver Winterhalter shows her holding a Bible while dressed in a beautiful sari, complete with a full set of jewellery including a belt, bangles and headpiece.

Just like Sarah, Gouramma's voice is absent from the narrative; what we know of her is through the eyes of others. Queen Victoria had in fact hoped Gouramma and another converted Indian royal under her care, Duleep Singh, would couple up, though this was not meant to be. Victoria was keen to spread Christianity to India; what a coup it would have been to have her two Indian wards betrothed to each other. Queen Victoria had, in fact, also given Albert a bust of Duleep Singh on that same birthday. And while Gouramma and Singh did not unite in real life, their busts sit side by side to this day at Osborne House, alongside an 1890 portrait of Abdul Karim, the whole room reminding us of how close the ties between India and Victoria were. I wonder what they'd be saying to each other if these depictions could talk.

Meanwhile, elsewhere: the Europeans scramble for Africa

Between 1870 and 1900, Britain added sixteen colonies from Africa to its empire. This was part of the European-wide 'scramble for Africa', which resulted in European nations controlling 90 per cent of Africa's land mass in 1900, a huge increase from the 10 per cent control they'd had three decades earlier. This rapid empire building was encouraged by men like David Livingstone, a Scottish physician and missionary whose expeditions across central and southern Africa vastly expanded European understanding of the continent.

Enslaved people were no longer a source of revenue for cities like Liverpool after the 1833 Slavery Abolition Act. However, they soon found a 'legitimate' alternative to this. Palm oil was an increasingly important commodity in industrial Britain, as it was used in machinery lubricant and was a major ingredient in soap and candles. In 1807, 102 tonnes were exported by Britain – by 1895 this has risen to approximately 635,000. It's estimated that at least three quarters of Britain's palm oil imports went through Liverpool. Other resources that piqued the interest of Europeans included rubber, coffee, diamonds, gold and ivory.

As new forms of trade were emerging between West Africa and Britain, British missionaries began spreading the gospel too. Sierra Leone was an initial base for missionary work. In 1827 the Church Missionary Society set up a training facility in Freetown, Sierra Leone, to train Africans how to teach and preach Christianity to their own people. Its most famous student was Samuel Adjai Crowther, who was to be the first African Anglican bishop. He had, in fact, been saved from a life of enslavement by a British Navy West Africa squadron that had been patrolling the coast after the abolition of the slave trade. It's estimated that over 200,000 African men, women and children were similarly released as a result.

One of the motivating factors behind educating African people in the ways of the Church was also down to survival; there was a high mortality rate among European missionaries. Europeans stood little chance against diseases like malaria and yellow fever, hence Africa was often referred to during this time as 'the white man's grave'. It is no coincidence that this rapid colonisation of Africa coincided with an increase in treatments to combat such diseases. One of the most infamous was quinine powder, sourced from the bark of cinchona trees. Though it was effective in preventing malaria, its bitter taste meant British soldiers in India combined their quinine powder with sugar, lime and their gin rations. A new drink had been invented that not only offered key medicinal properties but was also delicious: the gin and tonic. No wonder Winston Churchill is alleged to have said, 'The gin and tonic has saved more Englishmen's lives and minds than all the doctors in the Empire.'

The French and Belgians colonised much of western Africa, while Germany and the British focused on the east and south. One of the aims of the 1884 Berlin Conference was to prevent war erupting between the Europeans over African land. As decisions were made without any real attempt to understand the diversity, traditions and cultures of the land they were dividing between them, resistance from indigenous people inevitably occurred, none so famous as the 1879 Anglo–Zulu War. Despite the eventual success of the British, the Battle of Isandlwana sent shockwaves across Europe as Britain's first invasion attempt was a decisive defeat, despite their abundance of rifles and machine guns. Zululand was partitioned into thirteen chiefdoms after this, a tactic used across the empire to guarantee compliance and limit rebellion.

The golden stool that triggered a war

Meanwhile, in another part of the continent, in what is now Ghana, there was a war brewing. The people native to this area were an Akan-speaking community known as the Asante. The Golden Stool is the royal and divine throne of the kings of the Asante people and their ultimate symbol of power. According to legend, Okomfo Anokye (the High Priest) caused the stool to descend from the sky and land on the lap of the first Asante king, Osei Tutu. The Golden Stool is believed to house the spirit of the Asante nation – the living, the dead and yet to be born. The protection of the stool was very important, as the Asante people believed that if the Golden Stool was ever to be destroyed or captured by their enemies, the whole kingdom would descend into chaos. The Golden Stool had a lot of rules and ceremonies surrounding it: the stool was never to touch the ground and instead was placed on a blanket. During an inauguration, a new king was raised and lowered over the stool without touching it. No person would be a legitimate ruler if it was not present. The war chiefs usually consulted the stool before going into battle. The strong links between power and the stool are clear when the language used in Akan culture is considered: when a chief is inaugurated they are 'enstooled', and when they die 'the stool has fallen'.

The Asante were the most powerful community in West Africa, and the British were determined to control them because of the raw materials within the region – gold, cocoa and rubber. The British had already fought two wars against the Asante, and the Asante king turned down an unofficial offer to become a British 'protectorate' in 1891. The British were determined to take over by force, then, particularly as France and Germany were beginning to show interest in the area. They forced the Asante king Prempeh to sign a treaty. He was then exiled alongside the rest of the leaders.

Sir Frederick Mitchell Hodgson, a British governor, declared that since the Asante king was exiled and the Ashanti lands were ruled by the Queen of England, the Golden Stool should now belong to Britain. You can probably guess what he asked next: as he was the representative of Britain, he believed he should be able to sit on the stool. It appears to have been somewhat of an obsession for him, with Lloyd George later stating in Parliament: 'The fact was that the quest of the Golden Stool was something like the quest of the Holy Grail. Sir F. Hodgson said that if he could only get possession of the Golden Stool he would be able to govern the country for all time.'

This was a step too far for the Asante. They hid the Golden Stool in the forest and the Queen Mother Yaa Asantewaa summoned her people to revolt. Even though she was 60, she was at the heart of the war, providing advice and organising supplies. It's even alleged that she fired the first shot against the British. The Asante used tactics like blocking food supplies and cutting telegraph wires so the British could not communicate with each other. Approximately 2,000 Ashanti warriors and 1,000 British troops died in the 1900 War of the Golden Stool, another clear example of how intertwined the histories of Africa and Britain are.

The war lasted for six months. The British eventually defeated the Asante, and Yaa Asantewaa was captured and banished to the Seychelles, the second woman we've met in this chapter who commanded arms against the British Empire. When the war ended, Ashanti was annexed into the British Empire, although the Asante still had some say over decisions. The Brits continued to search for the stool for the next two decades. It was eventually found accidentally by a group of labourers, who divided up the golden ornaments of the stool. Since then the gold has been replaced and there are many replicas around the world. The original remains in Ghana, and it is kept safe in the Ashanti Royal Palace in the city of Kumasi.

Loot from Benin

Objects that did not have as much luck in escaping the clutches of European colonists were the Benin bronzes, a collection of thousands of pieces of statues and plaques that had decorated the palace of the Oba or King of Benin, alongside ceremonial and decorative items like engraved ivory tusks. The Benin bronzes have a misleading name, as they are in fact primarily made of brass, as well as other materials like wood and ivory. It was during an 1897 British military expedition to Benin City (now southern Nigeria) that they were looted and brought back to Britain. While some were kept in private collections, many were sold to museums, and the spoils of the expedition are now scattered across over 160 museums around the world, although primarily in Europe. It's estimated that between 3,000 and 5,000 items were plundered from the Royal Palace and other ceremonial sites, though some estimates expand to as many as 10,000.

The Benin bronzes that adorned the palace walls are also a form of historical record. The plaques, mainly dating from the 16th and 17th centuries, were often commissioned by the new Oba to reflect the legacy of their predecessor. The plaques are a visual archive of the history and beliefs within the Kingdom of Benin. For example, some scenes reflect the fact that the Oba was believed to be a god, with his coral-beaded regalia representing the belief that an ancient king of Benin once defeated the sea god Olokun in a wrestling match on the beach and successfully prised a coral necklace from him. Leopards are seen across the plaques; their sacrifice was a ritual act aimed at strengthening the Oba's mystical powers. Other animals can be seen across the plaques, such as mudfish, thought to represent the human and divine nature of the Oba, as they lived both on the land and in the sea.

Anyone who suggested that the Oba participated in mortal acts such as eating, washing and sleeping risked facing capital punishment. The whole of the Oba's family was believed to have such divine powers, which is why the Queen Mother (Iyoba) was not allowed to see her son after they became Oba, as she could use her powers to control him. A pair of beautiful ivory masks of a 16th-century queen mother called Idia were commissioned by her son Oba Esigie. She is alleged to have raised an army of her own to support her son, as well as using magic to help defeat his enemies. One of the masks now resides in the British Museum, while the other is across the Atlantic in the Metropolitan Museum of Art.

A series of carved heads that had been arranged on ancestral shrines were also seized, one for each Oba since Ewuare I, who had reigned in 1440. He laid the foundation for the Kingdom of Benin to become an empire that stretched from the riverbank of the Niger in the west to the Lagos Lagoon in the east by introducing key administrative and military reforms. Other items reflect the connections between Benin City and Europe, such as brass figures of Portuguese soldiers, which were kept on the roof of the Royal Palace. Trade between the two countries had flourished since the Portuguese arrived in the 15th century, with huge exports of pepper, textiles and ivory. The Portuguese were the first Europeans to marvel at Benin City; it would have been uncouth not to have been impressed by its fractal design and the defensive walls that surrounded the city, thought to have been a man-made structure comparable in length to the Great Wall of China.

Another important facet to acknowledge is that, despite initial resistance, items like the brass manillas were not just traded with Europeans for cloth, but people were soon enslaved as part of this exchange. The slave trade is therefore tied to the spoils of the Benin expedition. The existence of these objects also tells us something incredibly important – that craftsmanship was a real source of pride within Benin; it was well-organised too, with guilds created for different types of work, including ivory carving. Today such skills are still passed on from father to son, in much the same way that they were centuries ago. While we may primarily associate 'golden ages' to have occurred within Europe, the level of craftsmanship within the Kingdom of Benin clearly demonstrates that these periods of prolific achievement happened far beyond its borders.

The story repeated in museums and galleries across the world is that a British official in the Niger Coast Protectorate called Captain John Phillips led an unarmed trading expedition to Benin City in January 1897, despite knowing the Oba would not be receiving foreign visitors due to a religious festival. Upon approaching the city they were viewed as an invading force and were ambushed, resulting in the death of seven British officials (including Phillips) and approximately 200 African porters. A punitive expedition was then set in motion, with the aim of capturing Benin. Houses, ceremonial buildings and palaces were destroyed. Across ten days, villages were razed and thousands of civilians were killed. Newspapers from the time sought to justify these actions by emphasising the barbarity at play within the kingdom, via the enslavement of people as well as the use of human sacrifice, which the Oba almost certainly accelerated in a futile attempt to get the gods on his side. What is unclear, however, is how many deaths each side was responsible for, which is data we will likely never know.

Primary material from the time suggests a slightly different angle to the tale. Captain Phillips wrote a letter a year before the expedition (1896), where he makes his plan crystal clear, using a reference familiar to us from the Asante kingdom: 'I have reason to hope that sufficient ivory may be found in the King's house to pay the expenses incurred in removing the King [of Benin] from his Stool.'

Evidently, British actions in Benin were motivated by economic enterprise, far beyond the scope of a punitive expedition. Whatever the motivation, Phillips's wishes did, of course, come true, shown perfectly in two photographs taken at the time. One is of several carved tusks lined up on a street of Benin with the simplest handwritten caption of 'loot'. Another shows the Oba Ovonramwen surrounded by soldiers and his feet shackled together. He was exiled by the British. Benin City would be under the colonial rule of the British for the succeeding six decades, until Nigeria gained independence in 1960.

The photographer of the first image was Captain Herbert Sutherland Walker, whose grandson Mark Walker remembers seeing a brass bell being used as a doorstop during his childhood. Unbeknown to him, this bell and a brass 'bird of prophesy' were in fact looted items from the Royal Court of Benin. In 2014, Walker, now a retired doctor, personally returned the two items directly to the current Oba in Benin City, despite attempts made by the government to thwart his act of restitution by intercepting the bronzes at the airport.

Queen Victoria was gifted two carved ivory leopards from the Benin expedition, which are now housed in the British Museum, once again reminding us how abundant these traces of empire are. Many of the bronzes are now being repatriated to Nigeria, including items from German, American and Dutch collections, although the single largest collection remains in the British Museum.

This chapter has deliberately focused on the Victorians through an imperial lens, as it was during this time that the empire reached its peak, amassing swathes of territory and plenty of loot. It was also a time of resistance to colonial rule, something else that is too often ignored, just as it was largely dismissed by Victorians at the time.

THE SUFFRAGETTES 5

It's May 1909 and you're standing in front of the Prince's Skating Rink in Knightsbridge. If you've not got ice skates, don't worry – you won't be needing them! You notice that there's a lot of purple, white and green, whether adorning the exterior of the building or covering the many women you see heading for the entrance. Suddenly you hear a marching band. They are heading in your direction. The Women's Drum and Fife Band, led by honorary drum-major Mary Leigh, have in fact been playing for a while, having been through central London already, including along Oxford Street. The crowds around them in some places swelled so large that they stopped traffic. As you head through the entrance you're offered a *Votes for Women* newspaper and a ballot paper.

Welcome to the Women's Exhibition. Organised by the Women's Social and Political Union (WSPU, known as the suffragettes), the aim of this two-week event was to fundraise as well as prove just how much women deserved the vote. The exhibition was a huge undertaking, and each morning there was the opportunity to 'vote' on an issue, the result of which was declared at the end of each day. On 25 May the issue was 'Should women be policemen?' There were also two replica prison cells, one for male political prisoners and the other a 'suffragette' cell. Visitors would be given a tour by ex-prisoners, who would, of course, emphasise the squalid conditions the suffragettes faced while incarcerated. By now almost 400 women had been imprisoned for protesting for women's suffrage. For some more light-hearted entertainment, there were plays, concerts and even a suffragette opera. If you noticed a large crowd craning their necks to view something rather exhilarating, it was probably a suffrajitsu demonstration. More on that later! If you needed a refreshment at any point there were plenty of options, including Perrier mineral water and ice-cream sodas. Photographer Christina Broom captured all the comings and goings. The *Manchester Guardian* reviewed the exhibition by concluding, 'It is suffrage with its very best frock on.'

What do you expect to see at a suffragette display in a museum? At the Museum of London you'll find the usual suspects: banners, pins, medals and pamphlets, all covered in purple, white and green. There is also a curious object, and as you peer closer you realise your eyes are not deceiving you: it's an old bread roll.

Roughly a year before the Women's Exhibition, on 30 June 1908, former teachers Mary Leigh and Edith New became the first suffragette 'window smashers' when they broke two windows at 10 Downing Street. They were arrested and sentenced to two months in prison with hard labour. Emmeline Pankhurst, leader of the WSPU, visited them in prison to reassure them that they had official approval for such militant tactics. During their sentencing, the women made it clear they had no intention of giving up on their activism. Mary and Edith had both been involved in suffragette activity prior to their arrest, giving up their teaching careers to commit fully to the campaign. Edith, for example, had previously chained herself to some railings outside Downing Street.

Upon their release a parade was held in their honour. They were greeted by a huge delegation, including members of the Pankhurst family, presented with huge purple, white and green bouquets and were provided with a carriage to travel in style. Edith and Mary were each triumphantly brandishing something they'd smuggled out of Holloway prison as something of an unconventional trophy. You've guessed it – bread. Countless suffragettes subsequently did the same. It was a symbol of their survival, which became even more powerful once hunger striking was adopted en masse the following year. Mary was, in fact, one of the first suffragettes to be force-fed.

When Mary and Edith were arrested in 1908 they had no idea that it would take two further decades for them to get the same voting rights as men. While 8.4 million women got the vote a decade after their arrest, there were limitations: they had to be over 30 and either meet the property qualification (an annual rent of £5) or the education qualification (to have graduated from a British university).

Women like Edith and Mary were two of many thousands of women who decided to take militant action to shake the government of the day into giving 'votes for women'. There were many working-class women, as well as men, who contributed to this. There were also groups created specifically to vehemently oppose the notion of extending suffrage beyond those who already had it in the early 20th century.

The suffragettes weren't the first to demand rights for women

Firstly, it's important to understand who could vote at the turn of the 20th century, as well as who had already been fighting to extend the franchise. Mary Wollstonecraft's *A Vindication of the Rights of Woman* was published in 1792, and as a result she is seen as a predecessor to the suffragette activists. She was a firm believer that education was key to the advancement of women within society. Her advocacy for gender equality was radical at a time when, for example, married women had no rights when it came to their children, property or money. (You can only imagine what the situation was like for single women.)

After her untimely death at the age of 38 following complications from the birth of her second daughter (and future author) Mary Shelley, her reputation was besmirched by her grieving husband William Godwin, whose biography included acknowledgement of Wollstonecraft having a child out of wedlock, the kind of salacious details her critics needed to essentially 'cancel' her. Although not celebrated during her lifetime, or indeed just after it, she is now honoured as being one of the first authors to put forward feminist arguments. The resurgence of appreciation for her work was actually spearheaded by the prominent suffrage campaigner Millicent Fawcett, whose introduction to the centenary edition of *A Vindication of the Rights of Woman* included the acknowledgment that 'the battle in which Mary Wollstonecraft took a leading part is still being waged'.

In 1819, around 60,000 people gathered in St Peter's Field in Manchester to hear radical speakers like Henry Hunt address the need for parliamentary reform. Changes to the electoral system were needed, epitomised by the existence of potwalloper boroughs, which were areas where men had the vote based on having a fireplace and a lockable door. This qualification could be confirmed simply by the man rattling his keys in a large cooking pot. Borough boundaries did not reflect how much the country had changed since industrialisation began. Huge, bustling areas like Birmingham had no MPs to represent the interests of the growing population there, in contrast to 'rotten' boroughs, which were areas with MPs but few constituents. Corruption was also rife during election season, as voters were subject to bribery.

Known as the 'Orator', Hunt advocated for reforms like universal suffrage at a time when no women had the vote and only approximately 10 per cent of men did. Shortly after the meeting began the local magistrate ordered Hunt's arrest. In the violence that followed, eighteen were killed and hundreds injured. The Peterloo Massacre resulted in a government crackdown on what they perceived to be 'radical' politics. The passing of the Six Acts meant it was now an act of treason to hold a meeting of more than 50 people without the consent of a magistrate.

The year after Peterloo, a group of political radicals took a slightly different approach when they decided that the only way to force political reform was to assassinate the prime minister, Lord Liverpool, and his key supporters. The plan had been to kidnap and then decapitate some of the Cabinet before displaying their heads on Westminster Bridge. A radical revolution would then follow.

The conspirators were, however, betrayed by their second in command, who was a government spy. The group were arrested at their hideout in Cato Street, London. In the end five members of the group were transported to Australia for life, while five of the ringleaders were convicted of treason and hanged before being decapitated, including William Davidson, who was the son of the former attorney general of Jamaica. He maintained his innocence throughout his trial, telling the jury, 'You may suppose that because I am a man of colour I am without any understanding or feeling and would act the brute; I am not one of that sort.' Davidson's involvement highlights the diversity of those involved in the calls for political reform.

The 1832 Great Reform Act addressed some of the voting issues of the time, such as the removal of rotten boroughs; however, the annual earnings qualifications meant that only one in seven men could vote, leading to working-class organisations like the Chartists. The demands on their People's Charter included votes for all men, wages for MPs, for voting to be in secret, the abolishment of property qualifications, equal-sized constituencies and annual elections.

There were disputes over tactics, with William Lovett advocating for methods like petitions, while Feargus O'Connor called for violent action. The 1839 Newport Rising resulted in the death of twenty Chartists after a violent altercation between the police and protestors. One of their last mass protests was in April 1848 at Kennington Common. The Chartist leaders claimed this petition they planned to present to Westminster had over five million signatures, but many were proven to be falsified. At this point there was a genuine fear that violent revolution was imminent; Queen Victoria was moved to the Isle of Wight for her own safety and the British Museum was given 50 muskets and 100 cutlasses in the event that a defence of the building needed to be mounted. The march to the House of Commons was called off at the last minute, however, much to the disgust of one Chartist in particular.

William Cuffay was a tailor whose father had been enslaved in St Kitts before finding himself to be a free Black man in England, having worked as a cook on a warship. In the summer of 1848, Cuffay was arrested, accused of plotting to violently overthrow the government. He's alleged to have planned which police stations he was going to set fire to, to signal the start of the insurrection. He was convicted of high treason and transported to Tasmania. Despite being pardoned three years later, Cuffay opted to remain there and continued with his political activities by supporting indigenous people through work with trade unions. He died in 1870.

Despite William Lovett supporting women's suffrage privately, it was decided that declaring this as a Chartist aim publicly might hinder their chances of success. In 1847, Anne Knight published what is believed to be the first ever leaflet on women's suffrage. In a letter to the *Brighton Herald* in 1850, she attacked the Chartists for not campaigning for universal suffrage. The following year Knight is believed to have established the Association for Female Franchise, and their first meeting was held in Sheffield in 1851. She also presented the first petition to demand female suffrage to the House of Lords, although as with Henry Hunt's bill in 1830, this was ignored by the government of the day.

In 1867 the philosopher and MP John Stewart Mill proposed that the Second Reform Bill should include female suffrage, arguing that as women paid taxes they should also have the vote, but 196 MPs voted against the bill with 73 votes in favour. One supporter was the MP for Brighton, Henry Fawcett. He had recently been married to Millicent Garrett, who would go on to become the leader of the National Union of Suffrage Societies (NUWSS – known as the suffragists), formed in 1897 as a federation of seventeen local suffrage societies across the country, a reflection of the appetite for this cause.

Born in 1847, Millicent had been an activist from a young age, speaking at the first women's suffrage meeting at the age of 22. She was active in supporting women within many spheres, from co-founding Newnham College, the second women's college at Cambridge, to campaigning to raise the age of consent.

The suffragettes vs the suffragists

The NUWSS (suffragists) had 54,000 official members by 1914, a huge number in comparison to their rivals the WSPU (suffragettes), who had approximately 5,000. One of the key reasons for the dominance of the WSPU within the popular narrative is because of the militant and violent methods their supporters adopted. In contrast, one of the NUWSS's key principles was the use of peaceful campaign methods such as petitions, as well as operating the organisation democratically so that all societies within the federation had a say. Their differences are epitomised by written correspondence between the two leaders from 1909, wherein Emmeline Pankhurst wrote 'deeds speak louder than words' to Millicent Fawcett.

The NUWSS believed that working alongside politicians was the key to success, which is part of the reason why almost every year between 1870 and 1914 there was a bill presented to the House of Commons in favour of women's suffrage. One reason why the ruling parties were unwilling to pass such a bill was because they feared women would vote for the opposition. It was Fawcett and the NUWSS who were directly involved in the process behind the legislation that eventually passed in 1918, giving some women the vote. Their decision to align with the Labour Party from 1912 was key here, as well as their increasingly popular and (crucially) peaceful activism, which proved there was strong public support for women's suffrage, in contrast to the increasing violence of the suffragettes.

The WSPU was formed in 1903 by Emmeline Pankhurst in her Manchester home, with the aim of securing for 'women the Parliamentary vote as it is or may be granted to men'. The family had an extensive history of political involvement. Before his death in 1898, Emmeline's husband Richard had been a founding member of the Manchester Society for Women's Suffrage. The Pankhursts had also worked closely with the Independent Labour Party and had close ties to Keir Hardie, the first working man elected as an MP.

Emmeline had been a member of the NUWSS, but favoured more direct and militant action as a means of pressuring the government to concede to women's suffrage. The *Daily Mail* coined the term 'suffragette' in 1906, intended as an insult (it was meant to indicate that these women were sham campaigners), but it was ironically embraced by the WSPU. The militant stance of the WSPU had kicked off in 1905, when Annie Kenney and Christabel Pankhurst, daughter of Emmeline, were the first suffragettes to be arrested.

Annie grew up in Oldham and was the fifth of eleven children. From the age of ten she worked in a cotton mill. In 1905 she was inspired to join the WSPU after hearing Christabel speak passionately about women's suffrage. She and Christabel attended a political rally at the Free Trade Hall in Manchester in October 1905, where they asked Winston Churchill, 'If you are elected, will you do your best to make women's suffrage a government measure?' They were ignored and thrown out of the meeting, but not before they unfurled a banner and repeated the slogan emblazoned upon it: 'Votes for Women.' Both of them were arrested and charged; Annie with obstruction and Christabel with assaulting a policeman. Christabel later justified her decision to spit at the policeman by explaining that she had no other choice, as her arms were pinned down and she could think of no other means, as, 'So long as we have no votes, we have to be disorderly.' They were taken to Strangeways prison.

Annie was sent to prison twelve more times; she went on hunger strike during many of her imprisonments and was force-fed several times. It is thought that the lifelong health problems she suffered from were a by-product of this brutal treatment. She was one of the only working-class activists among the WSPU's senior leadership and her prominence within the organisation is shown by the front cover of *The Suffragette* from October 1913, which is dominated by a photo of her with the headline 'The Brutal Arrest of Miss Annie Kenney'. At one point she was even in charge of the London wing. She organised meetings with leading politicians and explained the terrible pay and working conditions that working-class women suffered and how the vote would enable them to challenge their status quo.

After the WSPU ramped up their protests in 1912, many of the militant strategies, including their postbox-destroying and window-smashing campaigns, were organised from her flat. Annie's own words give us an insight into what this campaigning meant to her: 'It is most beautiful to see the true comradeship, the loyalty, the devotion that this movement has brought about between women.'

Annie's belief in celebrating the sisterhood physically manifested via Annie's Arboretum. This was a garden that was part of the grounds of Eagle House, a property owned by suffragette Emily Blathwayt and her husband Colonel Linley. Their home was used as a refuge for suffragettes who had been imprisoned, and between 1909 and 1911, some 47 trees were planted on the grounds, one for each visiting suffragette who had been imprisoned. Whenever suffragettes came to visit, Colonel Linley took photographs of the women standing next to their respective planted trees and accompanying small plaque. Holly was planted to celebrate those fighting for women's suffrage, while conifers were planted for the most militant women.

In the 1960s, Annie's Arboretum – also known as 'suffragette's wood' – was bulldozed over, leaving only one tree: a pine planted for Rose Lamartine Yates, who was secretary of the Wimbledon WSPU and was arrested in 1909 for obstruction. The Walking Forest project are aiming to recreate Annie's Arboretum by 2028 to mark the centenary of the Equal Franchise Act, which granted equal voting rights to men and women, using seeds from the pine tree planted for Yates.

Emily and Linley Blathwayt's daughter Mary kept diaries during this period, which highlight that Annie had at least ten intimate relationships with fellow suffragettes, including Christabel Pankhurst. Mary and Annie kept in touch long after the movement, and a letter from Mary to Annie written in 1951 included a cheque with the instruction, 'Please buy yourself a very late Christmas present from me.' Mary also included clippings from four of the trees of what she calls 'the Suffragette Plantation'.

One of them was from a tree planted by Lady Constance Lytton, the daughter of a former viceroy of India, who joined the WSPU in 1909 at the age of 37. The political connections of her family made her quite the propaganda coup for the WSPU, but for Constance this was a huge burden. During her first stint in Holloway prison she spent most of her month-long sentence in the hospital wing, partly due to her heart condition, but also because the government wished to avoid any further publicity – her arrest had already caused enough. Frustrated with this preferential treatment, Constance decided to carve the words

'Votes for Women' on her body, starting from her chest and with the intention that the last letter would reach her cheek. She managed to carve the 'V' over her heart using a sharpened piece of enamel (she had tried to use a darning needle at first), before alerting a guard upon realising that she could be subjecting herself to blood poisoning.

Constance was arrested for a second time in October 1909 at the Battle of Newcastle. Chancellor Lloyd George was due to make a speech, so the local WSPU gathered its forces to protest at the government's tactic of force-feeding in prisons. The local post office was pelted with stones and one suffragette tried to fight her way through the police barricade using a hatchet she'd concealed in a bouquet of chrysanthemums.

Working-class suffragettes were treated the most harshly in prison

The artist Marion Wallace Dunlop was the first suffragette to go on hunger strike, after being arrested for stencilling a passage from the Bill of Rights on a wall of the House of Commons. This was her own initiative, but it was then adopted by other suffragettes. Marion was released after her initial 91-hour strike on the grounds of ill health. She stated that she would not eat until she was treated as a political prisoner, which was how suffragettes wanted to be categorised on principle, rather than being labelled as common criminals. Common criminals were subjected to a harsh prison routine, limited contact with the outside world and prison uniforms, whereas political criminals were afforded privileges like food parcels.

The provision of sanitary towels for suffragettes was also an issue at Holloway. It's no wonder that the WSPU bought a house that backed onto it; not only for released prisoners to recuperate in, but also so they could sing supportively to those incarcerated. By September 1909, prisons were opting to force-feed suffragette prisoners rather than release them, a practice regularly used on those deemed to be mentally ill.

Selina Martin was a working-class suffragette who was one of the first to be force-fed. She was imprisoned in Liverpool in 1910 for disguising herself as an orange seller and hurling an empty ginger-beer bottle at the Prime Minister's car. She was treated brutally after she went on hunger strike. She was seized in her cell, forced onto the floor face-down and was then dragged out of the cell with her arms behind her while her head was held by the hair by another warden. This was known as being 'frog marched', for obvious reasons. She was then dragged up the stairs, her head banging onto the stone stairs on the way, before being force-fed and flung down the stairs back into her cell. A report into her mistreatment found no wrongdoing on the part of the prison and absolved the prison staff of any responsibility. For example, point four of the report stated, 'If her head was bumped at any time, which we are not satisfied was the case, it was done during the struggle.'

In January 1910, a signed letter from 116 doctors was sent to the Prime Minister in protest at the force-feeding practices in Birmingham jail. It included the statement, 'In our opinion this action is unwise and inhumane. We therefore earnestly beg that you will interfere to prevent the continuance of this practice.' For now, however, this fell on deaf ears and force-feeding practices continued.

The actress and militant suffragette Kitty Marion was subjected to 232 instances of force-feeding. The prisoners would usually be pinned down by several wardens while a doctor forced a rubber tube through a nostril or the mouth. Considerable force and violence was used, resulting in bruised shoulders, bleeding gums and broken teeth. Prisoners would often choke on the liquid mixture of milk and eggs, and vomiting was common, particularly if the liquid was made from fatty meat or Bovril, leading many suffragettes to declare themselves vegetarians when they were inducted into prison. Countless suffragettes suffered lifelong medical issues as a result. The suffragettes obviously used force-feeding in their propaganda as well as literally a badge of honour. Hunger Strike medals were designed by Sylvia Pankhurst and engraved with the words 'For Valour', to echo the Victoria Cross. They were presented at breakfast receptions.

Constance Lytton was arrested for a second time in 1909, for throwing a rock at Lloyd George's car. She'd wrapped it with a note which said, 'To Lloyd-George, Rebellion Against Tyranny is Obedience to God. Deeds, not Words.' Constance found her aristocratic position saved her once again, and she was released after a few days. She was more determined than ever to prove that working-class suffragettes were being subjected to far more brutal treatment.

Constance decided that her only option was to become unrecognisable, having noticed that 'prisoners of unprepossessing appearance obtained least favour'. She assumed the identity of a working-class seamstress called Jane Wharton, had her hair cut short, bought glasses and an outfit that included a tweed hat and a green coat. She thought she had considered every detail, removing her initials from her underclothes, but much to her dismay she did not have time to sew 'JW' onto them. She had, however, forgotten to check her pockets, and when she was sent to Walton jail in Liverpool after protesting against Selina Martin's treatment, she realised she'd left a clean handkerchief with the initials 'CL' in her pocket. Thankfully, she was able to toss it on a fire stove before anyone noticed.

After a four-day hunger strike Constance's jaw was forced open using a steel gag. A four-foot-long stomach tube was forced down her throat, with the doctor later commenting that he'd never witnessed such a bad case of force-feeding. She wrote about her experience, stating 'the horror of it was more than I can describe'. Unlike her experience as Lady Constance Lytton, the working-class seamstress Jane Wharton was not subjected to a thorough medical examination when she was first admitted to prison, which would have picked up on her heart condition. Constance achieved exactly what she'd set out to do; her prison experience exposed how working-class suffragettes were being treated, which was hugely embarrassing for the government.

It was testimonies like hers that led to the 1913 Prisoners Temporary Discharge of Ill Health Act, which put an end to force-feeding. More commonly known as the Cat and Mouse Act, it meant prisoners on hunger strike would be temporarily released before being re-arrested once they'd recuperated. Of course, the suffragettes tried hard to evade arrest, with Scottish suffragette Dr Dorothea Chalmers Smith escaping from her house, which was under surveillance, by donning her younger sister's school uniform.

Constance suffered a heart attack in 1910, and in 1912 she had a stroke, which paralysed her on the right side. She taught herself how to write with her left hand and wrote about her experience in prison as Jane. She died in 1923 at the age of 54, the cause of which was undoubtedly linked to the force-feeding she experienced.

Black Friday, November 1910

There were other deaths that were attributed to suffragette protests. Henria Leech Williams is thought to have died as a result of underlying health issues, which were exacerbated by injuries sustained at the hands of the police at the infamous Black Friday protest in 1910. Annie Kenney planted a tree in memorial to Henria in the weeks following her death.

The Black Friday protest occurred because Prime Minister Asquith had refused to debate the Conciliation Bill, which would have given women the vote. A procession to the House of Commons from Caxton Hall was promptly organised, and was the ninth deputation of this kind. They set out peacefully, and as they neared the House they were met by approximately 6,000 policemen, who were a mixture of plain-clothed and uniformed officers who had been drafted in from the East End, rather than the usual men who guarded the Commons.

As the women tried to go forward they were pushed and beaten, thrown to the ground and trampled, had bones broken and dislocated; some were even dragged down side streets. Twenty-nine indecent assaults were attempted and at least 150 women were assaulted. Suffragette Jessie Murray and one of the founders of the Men's League for Women's Suffrage, Henry Brailsford, compiled eyewitness accounts from the day.

Brailsford was truly committed to his beliefs, resigning from his position as a journalist from the *Daily News* when they made it clear they supported the policy of force-feeding. The final report was called 'The Treatment of Women's Deputations by the Metropolitan Police' and recommended that an inquiry should follow. Unsurprisingly, the police commissioner reacted to their report with indignation, responding to accusations that the police had battered women with their helmets by saying he had weighed a police helmet and found it to only be 'three and a half ounces heavier than an ordinary silk hat'.

One of the women present reported that 'my skirt was lifted up as high as possible, and the constable attempted to lift me off the ground. This he could not do, so he threw me into the crowd and incited the men to treat me as they wished'. Insidiously, some of these attackers had come to the protest wearing Men's League for Women's Suffrage badges to present themselves falsely as allies to the WSPU. Ada Wright was thrown to the ground and unknowingly photographed as she lay there in a daze. The next day the photograph appeared on the front page of the *Daily Mirror*.

The papers neglected to report the sexual assaults the women had faced. The government ordered the negatives to be destroyed, a clear reflection of how damaging they knew such images were. Despite the evidence, the home secretary, Winston Churchill, did not pursue an inquiry.

Not all suffragettes were able-bodied

One of the women present at Black Friday was Rosa May Billinghurst. Rosa was born in 1875, and had polio as a child, resulting in her having to use a tricycle wheelchair. Rosa was committed to supporting those in need and spent her time doing social work as well as teaching at a Sunday school. During her time as a suffragette she was involved in all the familiar militant tactics you would have learned about at school. She founded the Greenwich branch of the WSPU and was arrested in March 1912 for participating in a co-ordinated window-smashing campaign.

Suffragettes were allocated different parts of the West End of London and were told what time to start their attack. Targets included unsympathetic newspapers, like the offices of the *Daily Mail* and *Daily Express*. They were told how to avoid being harmed by falling glass and were offered an 'implement' if they did not have their own. Lilian Bell was given a hammer to hide up her sleeve with 'Better broken windows than broken promises' written on it. They used 'toffee hammers', which were small (and so easily concealable) and were originally used to break up sheets of toffee by confectioners, but proved just as useful in breaking sheets of glass. Suffragettes participated in this campaign knowing that there was huge risk of arrest. Not all members had the means to be able to do this, such as school teacher 'Miss Avery', who informed Constance Lytton that she could not get involved in window smashing as her imprisonment would mean the sacrifice of her economic independence and would throw her onto her family for support.

Many suffragettes would be bailed out by the wealthy Pethick-Lawrences, Frederick and Emmeline, who had bankrolled the WSPU from its inception. Suffragettes were under strict instruction to say nothing when they were arrested in case it was used in evidence against them later. Over 200 suffragettes were arrested for window smashing between 1911 and 1912. Rosa was arrested for smashing a window on Henrietta Street in Covent Garden and was sentenced to a month's hard labour at Holloway, although the prison authorities limited this, presumably due to her disability. In December 1912, Rosa was charged with damaging postboxes in Deptford, another classic militant technique. Just as Edith New and Mary Leigh were the first window smashers, Emily Davison took it upon herself to try this new tactic based on her judgement that 'the next step to window breaking was incendiarism'.

When questioned about this in court, she confessed that she had sought a new militant tactic in protest at how working-class suffragettes were being treated more harshly, using her friend Mary Leigh's recent charge of two months in comparison to Lady Constance Lytton's two-week imprisonment, saying, 'The injustice of the snobbery was so great.' The tactic was embraced by the WSPU, and by the end of 1912, some 5,000 letters had been damaged by such attacks.

Pillar boxes represented the ruling class, particularly the political gatekeepers who were denying women the vote. They would be attacked by either pouring black varnish or tar into them, or setting a kerosene-soaked piece of cotton alight before dropping it inside. Postman Arthur Stockwell testified that he couldn't work for a fortnight because his hands were severely burnt after collecting letters from a pillar box in Chelsea that had been soaked in sulphuric acid.

Suffragettes had protested against Royal Mail before: on 23 March 1909, Daisy Solomon and Elspeth McClelland decided to post themselves to 10 Downing Street. A new service offered by the post office meant that people could be delivered to an address by an 'express messenger'. Daisy and Elspeth thought it was about time they had a chat with Prime Minister Asquith, so, armed with placards and having paid threepence for the service, they were escorted to Downing Street by a messenger. Unfortunately, the police refused them entry to the residence, and despite their protestations, they were eventually returned to sender, at WSPU HQ.

Many suffragettes launched official complaints against the police regarding their conduct on Black Friday, including Rosa May. Due to her disability, Rosa May arrived at Westminster on her tricycle, which she often decorated in suffragette-themed ribbons. At one point she was thrown out of her tricycle by a policeman. Later, when back in the tricycle, she was forced down a side road and was completely debilitated, as the police removed the valves from her wheels so she could not escape the crowd she'd been left in the middle of. She was so roughly handled by the police that she was bedridden for the days following Black Friday. Rosa did not let it deter her from the cause, however.

She was an extraordinary woman and clearly someone who should be at the centre of our understanding of this campaign. I'd therefore like to end Rosa's story with her own words to give her as much agency as possible. In 1913, when she was on trial at the Old Bailey for unlawfully pouring a 'deleterious' fluid into a pillar box in Blackheath, she stated the following to the jury:

> The government may further maim my crippled body by the torture of forcible feeding, as they are torturing women in prison today. They may even kill me in the process, for I am not strong, but they cannot take away my freedom of spirit or my determination to fight this good fight to the end.

Not all suffragettes were women

By the end of Black Friday, 118 women had been arrested on various charges. After this, many suffragettes and their allies were ready to use extreme militancy against what they saw as state violence. One man in particular decided to take matters into his own hands, quite literally. The groups for men, or 'suffragettes in trousers', mirrored the divisions between women's groups, with organisations like the Men's League for Women's Suffrage opting for a more NUWSS-style approach of lobbying and petitioning, while the Men's Political Union for Women's Enfranchisement favoured 'vigorous agitation'. Hugh Franklin, a member of the Men's Political Union, had abandoned his engineering degree at Cambridge to commit to the cause of women's suffrage full-time.

Born into a Jewish family in 1889, Hugh became involved in classic actions like chalking pavements and selling suffragette newspapers. He was present at Black Friday and witnessed first-hand the brutal treatment the female protestors faced at the hands of the police. As many others did, Hugh believed Winston Churchill should face retribution for the events. He eventually came face to face with the home secretary on a train headed to King's Cross from Bradford. Hugh was fully prepared for the moment: he pulled a dog whip out of his jacket and took aim at him, yelling, 'Take this, you cur, for the treatment of the suffragettes.' Hugh was arrested at King's Cross station and imprisoned for six weeks.

Hugh's militancy continued, and in 1912 he was imprisoned for the third time, for setting fire to an empty train carriage at Harrow station. It was during this stint at Wormwood Scrubs that he was force-fed 114 times. Hugh was, in fact, one of the first to be temporarily discharged from prison via the 1913 Cat and Mouse Act.

While he was in prison he received letters of support as well as hate-mail. One letter addressed him as 'HA Franklin (Lunatic)' and ended on the line, 'You are a dirty tyke and a dangerous madman.' Hugh's story also reminds us that some men were willing to go to the same lengths as their most infamous female counterparts.

However, while some men were allies in the fight for suffrage, it is also the case that some were active in anti-suffrage campaigning. One of the largest anti-suffrage organisations was the National League for Opposing Women's Suffrage, the result of a merger in 1910 between the separate women's and men's organisations. They too amassed petitions, created propaganda and founded local branches, of which there were over a hundred across the country. The arguments of the so-called 'antis' were clearly summarised by the National League's president, Lord Curzon, who often referenced his '15 reasons'. These included that many women did not want the vote, were not of 'balanced mind', should not vote as they could not be soldiers, sailors or policemen and also that giving women the vote would cause upset across the empire, particularly in India.

Curzon's resistance to political change was steeped in the fact that it would mean upsetting the status quo. Such attitudes are reflected in the propaganda created by his and other groups, which often emphasised how giving women the vote would negatively impact their families in particular. Images showing women asleep mid-cleaning while their children were left to their own devices in a home in general disarray were common, as were even simpler images of a screaming baby below the statement, 'Mummy's a Suffragette.' Other postcards emphasised how 'ugly' the cause made women, often depicting them as old maids with exaggerated teeth, red faces and in a constant state of frenzy. The image 'A Woman's Mind Magnified' made it clear that women couldn't possibly handle the vote when their minds were filled with thoughts of dresses, dogs, men and ... chocolate.

Not all the suffragettes were white

I was honoured to attend the unveiling of a blue plaque in May 2023 at the home of this next suffragette, having been one of a small group who applied for this honour on her behalf to English Heritage. Princess Sophia Duleep Singh was born in 1876, and her royal lineage stemmed from her father's side of the family, with her grandfather Maharaja Ranjit Singh known as the Lion of Punjab. Her father, Duleep Singh, as we already know from Chapter 4, was deposed by the British and exiled, before Queen Victoria took a keen interest in him. He married Bamba Müller, the illegitimate daughter of a German merchant and his Abyssinian mistress. They brought their six children up in Elveden Hall in Suffolk, which Duleep Singh renovated to reflect his family heritage, the interior filled with intricate staircases and arches fit to rival any Mughal palace back home in India. The family only lived there till 1886 on account of the huge debts Duleep Singh racked up.

Following the death of both her parents, Sophia's godmother Queen Victoria granted her a 'grace and favour' apartment called Faraday House, which was situated opposite Hampton Court. In the year following the death of her father, Sophia found herself as an accidental Victorian 'influencer' of sorts. Following her 'coming out' (Sophia and her sisters Bamba and Catherine had been debutantes) in 1895, Sophia was often included on the guest list of important social events of the day, including balls and banquets. Her fashionable clothes accessorised with Indian jewellery were commented on in the newspapers, as was her penchant for cycling, something some Victorians weren't quite sure was appropriate for women.

It was a visit to India in 1906 that was a real turning point for Sophia. She met influential Indian nationalist leaders like Lala Lajpat Rai, and upon her return to London she sought something more fulfilling to spend her days doing. A chance meeting with Una Dugdale in 1908 changed everything. Una was a member of the WSPU and spoke so passionately about the cause that Sophia signed up that afternoon. In 1912 Una would cause quite a stir when she married Victor Duval, the brother-in-law of Hugh Franklin. Newspapers ran the story of their wedding under the headline 'The Bride Who Would Not Promise to Obey', as Una did not repeat the word 'obey' during her vows. She's thought to be the first woman to do this.

Sophia was involved in a variety of suffragette activity, often using her wealth and status to contribute financially to the WSPU – on average £30 a year (approximately £2,340 today). Not only would she donate money, but she would also purchase goods to help fundraising efforts, such as festive produce to sell at the 1912 suffragette Christmas fair. Sophia was photographed outside Hampton Court Palace selling *The Suffragette* newspaper, much to the annoyance of King George V.

Sophia was also present at Black Friday alongside key members of the movement, including the Pankhursts. During the ensuing violence, Sophia placed herself between a suffragette and a policeman who had been repeatedly assaulting her. Sophia memorised his badge number and launched a series of complaints. Churchill's response was clear, 'Send no further reply to her,' and the case was closed. Sophia's arrest on Black Friday did not result in any jail time. Neither did the occasion in 1911 when she slammed a 'Votes for Women' pamphlet against Prime Minister Asquith's car. The embarrassment of arresting Queen Victoria's goddaughter likely saved her from the prison cells so many of her peers found themselves in.

Sophia was also named 'an active tax resistor' by the Women's Tax Resistance League (WTRL), with her celebrity status contributing to the notoriety of the organisation. The group was inspired by the American War of Independence, whose infamous slogan of 'No taxation without representation' was used in court by many members who found themselves before a judge for their direct but non-violent activities. Members refused to pay taxes in all forms: animal, income, property, servant insurance and other types of licence fees, for items like carriages, for example. Their slogan was 'No Vote, No Tax'. Refusal to pay taxes could lead to fines and even imprisonment. Often the offender's goods would be impounded by bailiffs and then sold by public auction in order to recover the sums due. These auctions were great publicity for the WTRL, as members would often support and purchase the goods offered at auction, triumphantly returning them to the owner.

In 1911, Sophia stood accused of owing the courts 6 shillings (approximately £23 today). As a result, her seven-stone diamond ring was impounded and sold at auction, although it was purchased by a fellow suffragette, Jopling Rowe, who returned it to her immediately. In December 1913, Sophia refused to pay licences for two dogs, one carriage and a manservant. She was summoned to Feltham Police Court and stated, 'If I am not a fit person for the purpose of representation, why should I be a fit person for taxation?'

Sophia was very active in both the WSPU and WTRL, placing herself in potentially dangerous situations for the cause of women's suffrage. Her proximity to the royal family no doubt saved her from the cells at Holloway. Learning her story thanks to the brilliant work of Anita Anand had a profound impact on me and kickstarted my interest in 'hidden histories'.

Sophia's existence as a descendant of Indian royalty at the centre of events like Black Friday, and her role as the chair of local WSPU meetings, highlights once again the importance of widening the lens of familiar contexts like the suffragettes. You never know what gems, or indeed diamonds, are hidden in plain sight.

The most surprising portmanteau: suffra-jitsu

The sort of violence that Sophia witnessed on Black Friday meant the WSPU were keen to find a more effective means of protecting their members. Attaching cardboard to their ribs was no longer going to cut it. Edith Garrud was a member of the Women's Freedom League and therefore already an advocate for female suffrage. She was the first

Western woman to teach the ancient Japanese martial art of jiu-jitsu, and therefore of great interest to the WSPU. Such was the novelty of her abilities that in 1907 she'd even been the star of a British Pathé film called *Jiujitsu Brings Down the Footpads*, which featured her chasing a thief all across London before she very literally brings him down with her impressive moves, despite the fact that she was only four-foot-ten. Edith was already involved in publicly supporting the cause; in 1910 she led the 'Athletes' section of the June 1910 Women's Suffrage Procession.

Edith and her husband William were first introduced to jiu-jitsu in 1899. They soon took over a jiu-jitsu school in Soho, with Edith running classes for women and children. Edith was approached by the WSPU, which then gave her a bigger platform to share not only her moves, but also her belief in the importance of 'providing a necessary safeguard for the woman who has to defend herself through life'.

In her 1910 article for *Votes for Women* entitled 'The World We Live in: Self Defence', she writes, 'In this art all are equal, little or big, heavy or light, strong or weak; it is science and agility that win the victory. Is not this a forecast of the future? Science, quickness, vitality and brains are surely equal to brute strength, in politics as well as in fights.'

The *Daily Mail* sent a reporter to one of her classes later that year under the headline 'The Suffragette Athlete Jiu-jitsu Test: The Little Woman and a Big Policeman'. The first policeman to face Edith opted for a classic boxing-style face-off, smirking while commenting on her height: 'Why, you're only a little dot of a woman.'

Confident and unperturbed by the thirteen-stone man in front of her, Edith simply said, 'I think I'll throw you.' It was game on. They tussled briefly before Edith kicked him in the diaphragm and promptly did as she'd promised – she threw him over her head! He somersaulted in the air and landed on his back. Having no choice but to admit defeat, he generously said, 'If that had happened on the pavement instead of these mats, the police force would be one man short.'

Edith and William were soon demonstrating their moves everywhere, and the WSPU approached Edith to take on events like the Women's Exhibition, which encouraged more women to sign up for 'suffrajitsu' lessons. The classes took place in Kensington at 7pm each Tuesday and Thursday, and cost 5s, 6d per month (now approximately £21.50). Due to increasing demand, the classes moved to a dance school in Argyll Street in central London, before having to change locations regularly in order to avoid detection. The studio also doubled as a useful hideout for suffragettes in London, who would use the central location to evade the police. Officers would arrive at the building only to find 'innocent' women participating in an exercise class, the hammers and stones the women had just been using on Oxford Street hidden under the mats.

Edith's self-defence club was open to all suffragettes, but there was a secret dedicated unit from late 1913 to protect the leaders of the movement that was given extra training. Known as the Bodyguard, it consisted of around 30 women, all of whom were willing to undertake the most dangerous tasks that needed to be executed. They were headed by Gertrude Harding, who had famously broken into Kew Gardens with fellow militant Lilian Lenton and attacked three orchid houses, much to the confusion of the press, who couldn't fathom how two women had been able to scale the walls.

The Bodyguard were essentially there to protect Emmeline Pankhurst at all costs. They also knew how to use inconspicuous items to defend themselves – for example hatpins, which were soon barred from prisons as a result, and barbed wire hidden in bouquets. They were also trained to use Indian clubs, which they concealed in the bustles of their long dresses. They were encouraged to use the clubs to knock policemen's helmets off, because policemen were required to pay for any lost equipment out of their own wages. If you knocked their helmet off they'd often stop to retrieve it – giving the suffragette a chance to get away. Membership of the Bodyguard was discreet, but we do know that Kitty Marshall was a member, an obvious choice given her first arrest in 1910 was for throwing a potato at Churchill's residence.

The Bodyguard once successfully got Emmeline Pankhurst out of a building and into a taxi by swinging their clubs in formation to protect her from attempts by police to seize her. They were also trained in tricking their opponents. A great example is from 1914, when Pankhurst gave a speech from a balcony in Camden Square. When she emerged from the house in a veil, escorted by members of the Bodyguard, the police swooped in. Despite a fierce fight, she was knocked to the ground and dragged away unconscious. But she wasn't taken into custody. When the police triumphantly unveiled her, they realised that she was a decoy. The real Pankhurst had been smuggled out in the commotion.

Edith died in 1971 at the age of 99, and a green plaque now marks her house in Islington. Edith used her passion for jiu-jitsu to fight, quite literally, for social and political reform. She undoubtedly empowered countless women with her knowledge of martial arts at a time when such opportunities were not usually available to them.

The suffragettes made police surveillance as tricky as possible

On 4 April 1913, a distinct 'cracking of glass' was heard inside the Manchester Art Gallery. By the time Lillian Forrester, Annie Briggs and Evelyn Manesta were done, thirteen paintings had been damaged. All three pleaded guilty and used the opportunity in court to state their case. I particularly like what Briggs had to say: 'I have a degree in History and my knowledge of history has spurred me to this fight for women's freedom.'

Manseta, a 25-year-old governess, used the courtroom to make clear her disgust at how unfairly women were treated within the realm of divorce law. The women served a month in prison, but the police knew this was unlikely to deter them from vandalising other galleries and museums when they were released. The police therefore wanted to send their photographs to cultural institutions. However, the suffragettes were not going to make this easy for them. The imprisoned suffragettes made faces and moved around so much while prison wardens tried to take photos of them that the government had to find other means.

Professional photographers in special vans were therefore hired by Scotland Yard. They were authorised by the home secretary,

Reginald McKenna, to take photos of the suffragettes in the prison courtyards using eleven-inch lenses. These images were likely the first modern-day 'surveillance' photos in Britain, which were then distributed via Criminal Records Office memos alongside descriptions of the women, including their height and eye colour. Museums and galleries were on high alert, and there was even discussion of banning women from admittance altogether. That didn't happen, but women now had to check in bags, muffs and umbrellas in case they had weapons concealed within them. The British Museum continued to allow women to visit, but only if they were accompanied by or had a letter of recommendation from a 'respectable' man.

Despite the high-tech surveillance, the police did not manage to discreetly take a suitable enough photo of Manesta. They decided to get a warden to restrain her while they took a photo and then simply edited him out. She did what she could not to cooperate, placing her hands in her pockets and scrunching her eyes tight. She's also smiling defiantly. The doctored image was indeed sent to galleries, alongside the following description:

> Evelyn Manesta, age 26, height 5ft, 2 inches, complexion pale, hair fair, eyes grey. Was convicted with Lillian Forrester of damaging, with a hammer, pictures in the Manchester Art Gallery.

Sylvia Pankhurst leaves the family group chat

Criminal damage was not for everyone. In 1912, Emmeline Pankhurst addressed crowds at the Royal Albert Hall and famously said, 'I incite this meeting to rebellion.' Emily Blathwayt, who had opened her home and indeed her garden to the WSPU, left the organisation, as she disagreed with the rise in violent militancy. Splits had happened before, with concerns about Emmeline and Christabel's control over the WSPU leading to an initial group of 70 members leaving to form the Women's Freedom League (WFL). They were still willing to break the law, but wanted members to be consulted over strategy as well as ensuring they did not use violence.

In 1908, Australian-born Muriel Matters and Helen Fox chained themselves to the grille of the Ladies' Gallery in the Commons, something which obscured women's view of parliamentary debates and was therefore seen as a symbol of oppression. When Matters was removed from the scene, with the grille still attached to her, she technically made the first speech by a woman in the Commons. In 1909 she chose the state opening of Parliament for her unusual protest. She hired an airship, and on one side emblazoned it with 'Women's Freedom League', and on the other 'Votes for Women'. She intended to scatter WFL pamphlets all over the King's procession on his way to Westminster. Unfortunately, the windy weather meant she left Hendon and flew over parts of west London before landing in Croydon 90 minutes later.

A few years later, Muriel spent time working with somebody else who'd parted ways with the WSPU: Sylvia Pankhurst. Born in 1882, Sylvia was the middle sister, with Christabel the eldest and Adela the youngest. Sylvia was an incredibly talented artist and trained at the Royal College of Art. In 1907 she toured northern England and Scotland and documented the lives of working women, painting them, as well as writing about the conditions they worked in and recording their levels of low pay. She began working for the WSPU full time from when she was 23 and used her talents to shape the iconography of their campaign. The aesthetic of the suffragette movement was very much spearheaded by Sylvia, with the 'angel of freedom' blowing a trumpet replicated across banners, flyers and badges. She channelled her creativity into direct action, depicting women sowing the seeds of emancipation and stepping over broken chains.

In that same year she was arrested for the first time for protesting in the lobby of the Commons. She would be arrested fifteen times for protesting in favour of women's suffrage, and like many others would endure force-feeding as a result of hunger strikes. But Sylvia's politics grew further apart from Emmeline and Christabel's, who became increasingly annoyed at Sylvia's insistence that the WSPU should work with the Labour Party. Syliva had also become despondent at the autocratic nature of the organisation, as well as the emphasis on middle-class women rather than centring the plight of marginalised working-class women, criticisms that had resulted in the breakaway Women's Franchise League. Her friendship with George Lansbury meant she moved to Bow in 1912, setting up a WSPU branch there. Lansbury had resigned from his seat in the Commons in protest at the treatment of suffragette prisoners. He stood for re-election in 1912 on a 'Votes for Women' platform, but was sadly defeated.

In 1913, Sylvia, with the help of people like Keir Hardie, leader of the Labour Party, with whom she had a very close relationship, set up the East London Federation of Suffragettes (ELFS). Though at this point they were still affiliated with the WSPU, a formal break would come soon enough. The ELFS combined socialist ideals with the demand for women's suffrage. Their aims were for all women over 21 to have the vote, to raise the economic status of women and improve the social and economic organisation of the community. These aims are particularly telling given that her mother was increasingly in favour of fighting for votes for middle-class women rather than for all.

She also began a weekly paper for working-class women called *The Women's Dreadnought*. Many of the contributors were working women who shared their personal experiences of things like wages and housing conditions. As with many high-profile suffragettes, Sylvia often found creative means to evade the police. After addressing crowds at Bromley Town Hall, she urged the audience to protect her from arrest. The doors were flung open and a fire hose promptly plunged water at the police, creating a clear path for Sylvia to flee the scene unharmed.

Sylvia was arrested and sent to prison eight times between 1913 and 1914 and was force-fed every time. She would also go on thirst strikes, meaning she would be in a constant cycle of fainting in prison, experiencing constant buzzing in her ears and pain in her heart. Her sleep strikes had a similar effect, as she would force herself to walk around her cell to stay awake until she collapsed.

Sylvia spoke at a London meeting alongside Irish trade unionists, which was too much for her older sister; the ELF were formally expelled from the WSPU in 1914. Sylvia's relationship with Emmeline also deteriorated significantly. When Sylvia later had a child out of wedlock, Emmeline refused to see her, severing their ties for good.

When the First World War broke out, Sylvia helped form the Women's Peace Army, an organisation of pacifists who demanded an end to the war. This was again in stark contrast to her older sister and mother, who vehemently supported it. Sylvia was acutely aware of the pressures her east London neighbours faced from the very start of the war. She helped open several mother-and-baby centres, which initially provided free milk for babies, but gradually extended to include eggs, barley and maternity clothes, as well as services like baby weighing and home visits from nurses. The ELFS also supported working mothers during the war, creating nurseries where women could drop off their children while they did factory work. They even created a small toy-making factory, which Sylvia convinced Selfridges to stock the products of. She employed only women, but paid them a man's wage. 'Cost-price' restaurants were also founded, providing cheap two-course meals for children and adults, and free meals for expectant and nursing mothers.

What Sylvia's suffragette story tells us is that despite what you may have assumed, the Pankhursts, like so many families, did not align in their politics at all. They were not all fighting for the same cause, with Sylvia's views moving further left as her family's moved right, reflected starkly in both Christabel and Emmeline's failed attempts to become Conservative MPs after the war. Sylvia's commitment to prioritising the plight of working-class women became more intersectional throughout the rest of her life, when she dedicated her time to the anti-racist and internationalist cause. The emergence of the ELFS after other groups like the WFL also highlights that the story of votes for women was not solely down to the WSPU.

Emily Davison spends the night in a broom cupboard

Born in Blackheath in 1872, Emily Davison joined the WSPU in 1906 and soon became one of their most notorious members. We already know she had a penchant for vandalising pillar boxes. In 1909, while in Strangeways jail, she barricaded herself in her cell in an attempt to avoid being force-fed again. She used her bed planks, a stool, her leather shoes and a hairbrush to do so. To get her out, the authorities used a ladder to climb up to her window and placed a fire hose into her cell. By the time they managed to break in, she was six inches deep in water. She was forcibly fed through the nose shortly afterwards.

She made an official statement of complaint, asking for £100 in damages. She also said, 'I think it is necessary to state that after the hose-pipe incident, the menstruation process began. No enquiries had been made before the turning of the hose to ascertain my condition. The risks were taken.' She was awarded 40 shillings in damages, worth roughly £156 today. By June 1912 she'd been forcibly fed 49 times, and on 30 November 1912 she was arrested for assaulting a Baptist minister whom she thought was David Lloyd George.

Emily's infamous decision to stage a protest at the Epsom Derby was shared with no one. From near the Tattenham Corner end of the racecourse, Emily ducked under the railings, timing it perfectly to meet the King's horse, Anmer. Her intentions are still debated to this day, but a 2013 documentary for Channel 4 digitally restored the footage of the race, revealing that Emily was holding a WSPU scarf as Anmer approached her, which she was presumably trying to attach to him.

Photos of the King's horse draped in a WSPU insignia would have been quite the triumph, but, of course, the headlines could not have been further from this. The speed of the horse inevitably meant a collision, resulting in Emily dying four days later as a result of a fractured skull. At her funeral on 14 June, some 5,000 suffragettes formed the funeral procession from Victoria to King Cross, organised by the WSPU. They divided into groups, with each group given a specific instruction. Those in section G were to wear purple dresses and carry peonies. Everyone wore a two-inch black band on their left arm. A crowd of 50,000 people lined the streets and wreaths were sent from all over the world. Not everyone was there to show their respects, however, with some in the crowd jeering, while one person threw a brick at the coffin.

Irrespective of her intentions and her prior relationship with the WSPU, she was held up as a martyr for her 'heroic protest', with *The Suffragette* newspaper declaring that 'She Died for Women' and that 'she has taught the world that there are women who care so passionately for the vote and all it means that they are willing to die for it'. Today, Emily Davison's name is as synonymous with the suffragettes as Emmeline Pankhurst's.

If you learned about the suffragettes at school then you almost certainly covered Davison's protest at the Epsom Derby, which, irrespective of the intention, ended in absolute tragedy. But did you know that, before she wrote herself into the history books for ever, Davison had attempted another unusual protest?'

On 2 April 1911, census takers were sent out to collect the details of all households across the country. The householder was asked to list everyone in the house. Little did they know that the Women's Freedom League had in fact organised a boycott of this government census. Some spoiled the form by either refusing to provide any information at all, while others scribbled comments in protest. Sophia Duleep Singh spoiled hers and wrote: 'No Vote, No Census, as women do not count, they refuse to be counted. I have a conscientious objection to filling up this form.' A Miss Davies from Birkenhead wrote the name of a manservant followed sarcastically by, 'No other persons, but many women.' Some women hid or kept moving from place to place throughout the night to avoid being recorded. In London, some gathered for a midnight picnic on Wimbledon Common. On the menu was roast fowl, ham, pasties and, of course, an abundance of tea and coffee. Others went to Trafalgar Square, where they spent the night talking and singing. Protests were held in cities nationwide.

The award for best census-boycott attempt goes to Davison, who hid in a broom cupboard in the Houses of Parliament for 46 hours so that she could record the Palace of Westminster as her place of residence. Discovered by a cleaner, she was arrested and then released without charge. Davison was recorded in the 1911 census with her address being given as 'found hiding in the Crypt of Westminster Hall, Westminster'. Ironically, her landlady at her rented home in Coram

Street also included her on the census form, and so she was actually recorded twice. If you're wondering how she survived for 48 hours without food, don't worry. She'd packed some snacks: lime juice and meat lozenges.

The NUWSS walk their way to victory

Four days after Davison's funeral, the NUWSS started the largest and most ambitious peaceful protest yet: the Great Pilgrimage. This had been in the works for only two months, which is remarkable considering the scope of the event. The Great Pilgrimage was the idea of Katherine Harley, a leading suffragist, and the aim of it was clear: 'To tell all England why women want the vote.'

The pilgrimage would be a strictly 'law-abiding' affair and would provide a chance to show people all over the country that the WSPU were not the only women who wanted the vote: 'The Pilgrimage gives us our chance. Coming from the ends of the country to its capital, without either bombs or paraffin oil, with no other appeal than that of reason and order, risking what there may be of violence used against us, but using none ourselves, we shall have the opportunity of a lifetime of stating our case.' In a tone similar to that in enlistment propaganda posters during the First World War, the NUWSS asked, 'Who will be absent from our Pilgrimage now, or who fail to help? Or who say, "Great deeds were done ... and I was not there"?'

This would be a grand gesture to capture the public imagination. Although the name of the event had religious connotations, its intention was to emphasise peace and unity among the sisterhood. The pilgrimage was 'an act of devotion', intended to show just how seriously these 'thousands of law-abiding women' wanted the vote. Clearly this was a deliberate and calculated attempt by the suffragists to counter what they saw as the negative publicity associated with the suffragettes. They would hold meetings and pass resolutions all across the country, with the intention of presenting the results to the government to prove just how much popular support there really was for women's suffrage. They wanted to educate the public and show them 'a new understanding of the meaning of the suffrage movement'.

This was a military operation, comprising of six principal routes with multiple starting points. You could join from any point and attend for however long you could. The march would culminate in a mass meeting in Hyde Park on 26 July, after six weeks on the road. Each person who signed up was given clear instructions, including a village by village itinerary, with important details like where the nearest ladies toilets were. It was recommended to bring only one piece of luggage alongside your special NUWSS haversack, and although most people walked, other options included going on horseback or bike. Other details of the event remind me of school trips, with morning roll calls and a clear daily itinerary to ensure every day ran as smoothly as possible.

Swan & Edgar department store on Regent Street advertised a special 'For the Pilgrimage' collection, which included a fetching 'manilla straw hat trimmed with band and bow of ribbon of National Union colours', which were white, leaf green and berry red. People of all classes joined the pilgrimage, from Lady Rochdale, who marched from Carlisle to London, to Emily Murgatroyd, a mill weaver and crucially the breadwinner in her family. She saved up meticulously in order to support her family while attending the pilgrimage for its entire six-week journey.

The 'antis' were on a mission to ruin the pilgrimage, using the maps printed in *The Common Cause* to arrive in towns and villages the day before the pilgrims to spread rumours that they were, in fact, dangerous suffragettes in disguise. The group from Land's End were pelted with compost when they reached Falmouth. Bags of soot, rotten vegetables and even rats were thrown at the pilgrims by members of the public who had been riled up by false rhetoric. Alice New and Jane Colquitt were almost knocked off their bicycles by a woman brandishing a spade. In Thame, a crowd of men attempted to set a caravan of four pilgrims on fire, until thankfully a local doctor raised the alarm with the police before any serious harm was done. In Cornwall, however, the police refused to get involved in any issues relating to the pilgrimage, perhaps due to the controversy surrounding the police during Black Friday.

But while the pilgrims did face pockets of violence, they also found themselves being supported, like in Durham, where a group of miners created a cordon around the speakers to deter the rowdy students who'd arrived to disrupt the meeting. Some of the students even found themselves thrown into the local river by these mining allies. In Leeds the suffragists were waved off by cheering and supportive crowds, while in the Lake District a local vicar was so inspired that he led his congregation in a suffrage sermon. A Mr Bark, who had prior to the pilgrimage been an anti, even invited some pilgrims for a home-cooked meal. As planned, the Hyde Park meeting happened at the end of six weeks and involved nineteen speakers' platforms scattered across the entire park.

Politicians from both sides of the aisle praised the success of the pilgrimage, with Prime Minister Asquith even agreeing to receive a deputation of suffragists on 8 August, though he was unwilling to support a women's suffrage bill, despite the increasing number of MPs in favour of it. By 1916, however, circumstances had changed. In the next chapter we'll delve into the work women did during the war, and there's no doubt that this tipped the balance for men like Asquith, who declared in the Commons, 'How could we have carried on the war without them?'

But, while the war was a turning point in persuading the majority of men in both Houses to give (some) women the vote, there was more to it than that. Lloyd George was prime minister from December 1916 and was aware that the war meant the voting system would need amending anyway, with so many men who had given so much in the trenches currently excluded. He was also leading a coalition government of politicians who were, by and large, sympathetic to the cause.

Millicent Fawcett in particular acknowledged this, and she pushed for women's suffrage to be included. She was key in lowering the suggested women's age qualification from 35 to 30. It seemed the moment was within grasp, and on 29 March 1917 the NUWSS organised a spectacular deputation of women's organisations, with representatives from over 40 different occupations and over 20 suffrage societies. Three months later the Representation of the People Act was passed by a majority of 330 in the Commons, in January 1918 it was passed by the Lords, and on 6 February 1918 it received royal assent. It enfranchised 8.4 million women. Nancy Astor became the first woman to take her seat as an MP, although technically Constance Markiewicz was first, she but declined to accept in line with the Sinn Fein party line of the time.

In the following decade, the WSPU was dissolved in favour of the short-lived Women's Party. The NUWSS rebranded as the National Union of Societies for Equal Citizenship, now led by Eleanor Rathbone, as Fawcett was now retired. They campaigned for equal franchise as well as equal opportunities for women in the workplace and education. In 1928 the Equal Franchise Act was passed, giving men and women over 21 the vote.

After 1918, the WSPU leadership largely framed the fight for women's suffrage as their fight and theirs alone. I hope what this chapter has shown is that this was not quite the case. The existence and significance of groups like the NUWSS, for example, shows that this victory was not just won by WSPU's suffragettes. And even that story, dominated so often by Emmeline, is also not reflective of the many voices that have been amplified throughout this chapter, from Sophia Duleep Singh to Edith Garrud and Rosa May Billinghurst. As ever, it has not been possible to tell you the story of every single person who contributed to women in Britain getting the vote, but hopefully you've now got a sense of some of those whose stories were perhaps not part of the ones you learned at school. While those clad in purple, white and green fought incredibly hard for women's suffrage, so did those in white, leaf green and berry red.

THE GREAT WAR AND BEYOND 6

In 1920, four unknown British servicemen's bodies were exhumed, one from each of the key battlefronts on the Western Front: the Aisne, the Somme, Arras and Ypres. There are many contested versions of what happened next, but one of the four bodies, each draped in a Union flag, was selected at random. This was to be the Unknown Warrior. While the other bodies were reburied, this one was placed in a coffin partly made from oak grown in the Hampton Court Palace garden. A 16th-century sword from the Tower of London collection was placed in the coffin.

The coffin was buried in Westminster Abbey 'among the kings', and the grave contains soil from France and is covered in a slab of black Belgian marble. Crowds lined the streets and stood in silence as the coffin travelled by horse and carriage. Part of the funeral procession included the official unveiling of the Cenotaph, engraved with the words 'The Glorious Dead', which now replaced the temporary plaster and wooden version that had been constructed the year before. The guests of honour were approximately a hundred women, all of whom had lost their husbands and all of their sons in this war. This was a nation in mourning, with over 1.5 million people queuing to visit the grave by the end of the month. When the future George VI married Lady Bowes-Lyon, whose brother was killed in action in 1915, she laid her wedding bouquet at the grave, a tradition carried on by many royal brides ever since. Many of the individuals whose stories feature in this chapter represent groups who were not adequately represented at such remembrance events at the time, or since.

Seeing the term the First World War for some may conjure up images of trench foot that you were exposed to in your history classroom, which may still haunt you to this day. Other than that, what are the three things you most associate with the First World War? Poppies, trenches and Christmas football? Or perhaps it's tanks, gas attacks and shell shock. We'll explore all of these elements in this chapter, as well as the unexpected links they have with some of the lesser-known elements of this devastating war.

The first shot by the British army was fired in Africa

The German plan had been to attack France through neutral Belgium, with the hope of taking over France before the Russians were ready to help their Western ally. Much to the German army's surprise, the British Expeditionary Force were dispatched to defend Belgium. Twenty-year-old Ernest Edward Thomas fired the first shot by a British soldier in Europe when facing the Germans in the Belgian village of Casteau, where a memorial plaque now marks the spot. Later in the war he was mentioned in a dispatch for distributing German boots he'd stolen from an enemy trench among his friends.

The first shot fired by the British army had, in fact, happened ten days earlier, when Alhaji Grunshi of the West African Frontier Force moved into the German colony of Togoland from Britain's Gold Coast colony. Their goal was to infiltrate German territory and take the Kamina transmitter station, which was key to German communication across their imperial assets. One of the key motivators behind German Emperor Kaiser Wilhelm II's decision to go to war with Britain was because of his desire to expand Germany's empire, which was rather paltry compared to Britain's. The fact that he and King George V of Britain were first cousins added an awkward family dynamic to the entire affair.

Both Thomas and Grunshi survived 1918, and both received military medals for their service. Grunshi's shot in Africa reminds us how intertwined empires were in this war.

Peer pressure played a key role in recruiting soldiers

The war was meant to be 'over by Christmas'. However, the decision by the Germans to 'dig in' after the Battle of the Marne in September kickstarted the building of trenches, which would eventually mean there was a 475-mile scar of parallel trenches stretching from the Channel to the Alps. Life on the Western Front would have been challenging beyond imagination, but perhaps might have been eased by the familiarity of some of the faces soldiers shared their trenches with.

Pals battalions were a way to readily recruit large groups of men who enlisted under the promise that they would serve side by side. The first of these groups was the 'Stockbrokers' battalion, where over 1,500 City workers signed up at the Tower of London. This had a devastating impact on the communities they left behind, where in some areas, entire generations of young men were wiped out. In 2001, the remains of twenty British soldiers were found buried near Arras in a fifteen-metre-long pit. They'd been carefully laid down, with their hands crossed in front of them so they were buried 'shoulder to shoulder'. These were twenty men from the 'Grimsby Chums', a stark reminder that so many who'd joined up together also fell together.

One man recruited in the 1st Football Battalion of the Middlesex Regiment was Walter Tull. He was born in Kent in 1888 to a Jamaican father and white English mother. He eventually played for Tottenham Hotspur and became the second person of African-Caribbean heritage to play in top division football. He served on the Western Front, experiencing the monotony and terror of trench life. He was hospitalised with shell shock in 1915, yet returned to action in 1916. By 1917 he was the first man of mixed heritage to become an infantry officer, despite the restrictions at the time which meant promotions were only available to 'British subjects of pure European descent'. He was killed during the second Battle of the Somme in France, having shown enormous bravery throughout the war, such as leading his men to attack enemy soldiers while pushing across a vast river on the Italian Front. Despite attempts by his comrades to retrieve his body, they were unsuccessful. He is therefore one of thousands of men who fell in this war with no known grave.

An unlikely addition to the 15th West Yorkshire Regiment, unofficially known as the Leeds Pals Battalion, was Jogendra Sen. Known as 'Jon' to his fellow soldiers, Jogendra was born in Bengal and moved to England in 1910, where he studied electrical engineering at Leeds University. When war broke out he enlisted, becoming the only non-white member of the regiment. He was well respected by his peers, with some noting the discriminatory policies which held him back from promotion. Details of his story would not have been uncovered had it not been for historian Santanu Das seeing his broken glasses on display in a museum in India. He is thought to be the first Bengali to have died during the First World War when he was killed during a heavy bombardment at the Somme in May 1916. Among other items in Jogendra's possession was a booklet entitled *Poems about Friendship*, signed by 'Cis', now thought to be Mary Cecily Newton, a friend he likely made during choir practice. Jogendra's story is unique in that he was an Indian who fell not within the Indian Army on behalf of Britain, but as an unlikely pal and Indian soldier within the British Army.

Aside from pals battalions, other recruitment methods included rallies and posters, the most iconic of which remains the 'Your Country Needs You' poster featuring Secretary of State Lord Kitchener pointing directly at you. Posters appealed to a variety of ages, as the army welcomed men between 19 and 41, so long as you were over five-foot-three and had a chest size of at least 34 inches. Posters for younger men emphasised the 'fun' of enlisting, with posters of soldiers playing cricket and football, while those aimed at fathers featured children asking questions like, 'Daddy, what did you do in the Great War?'

And it wasn't just the British 'Tommy' at home who was the target of these campaigns. 'Young women' were addressed in posters that didn't mince their words, hoping the sentiment would strongarm them into convincing their sweethearts to enlist: 'If your young man neglects his duty to his King and Country, the time may come when he will NEGLECT YOU. Think it over – then ask him to join the army today.' Others encouraged women to join the war effort themselves, in a variety of jobs from munitions factories to the Land Army.

Men from across the empire did not escape such propaganda, either. In Australia they were enticed with posters claiming enlisting was essentially a 'free trip to Europe', while the 'young men of the Bahamas' were being asked to 'come forward to fight' to save the empire that ruled over them.

When volunteers from the Caribbean arrived from 1915, many found they were not welcome, and instead were entirely rejected from recruitment offices. It was only the intervention of George V and pleas from the Colonial Office to avoid any uprisings back home that the British West Indies Regiment was formed. Some 16,000 men would eventually serve within the BWIR, although in Europe they were deliberately segregated from white soldiers and limited to labour work, such as digging trenches, felling trees and loading ammunition. This work was crucial and dangerous, but they were not given the combat roles some of them had sold their belongings for. Three battalions were sent to Egypt (where they could serve as infantry), while others worked exclusively as labourers on the Western Front.

This is not to say they didn't fight at all, though. George Blackman described his own experience of hand-to-hand fighting with the Germans in the trenches using his bayonet. There were Allied Labour Corps units from a huge swathe of colonised nations from the British and French empires, including those from Burma, Egypt, South Africa, India and Indochina. Some 550,000 recruits to the various units of Indian Labour Corps were enticed with promises that they'd never have to pay housing tax again.

Life in the trenches was treacherous

Life in the trenches was testing, but as the Grimsby Chums' final resting positions show, there was also an inevitably strong sense of comradery. Soldiers spent so much time together that 'trench slang' soon developed as a means to communicate this unusual way of life. Classic Brits abroad, 'vin blanc' regressed to 'plonk', a word still used today to describe a bottle of wine. French infantrymen were given 500ml of red wine a day, whereas men fighting for Britain's army received a daily rum ration of 28ml. Bread, cheese and vegetables were the foundation of a classic front-line menu, alongside meat like bully beef or corned beef packed into oblong tins, along with condensed milk, jam and, of course, tea. However, as everything was usually made in one or two of the same vats, the tea often tasted like whatever vegetable soup had been previously prepared. As the war continued daily rations dwindled, as resources became scarcer. In 1916 a flour shortage meant that bread had to be made from ground-up turnips (which induced diarrhoea), and soups and stews now contained nettles and weeds. Sometimes soldiers would have to boil water found in shell holes, which would often lead to outbreaks of dysentery. Parcels from loved ones provided much-needed comfort in the form of tinned sardines and chocolate.

A great distraction from the dubious rations was the *Wipers Times*, a newspaper born from the discovery of an abandoned printing press. The paper was named after the way in which British soldiers pronounced the town of Ypres, and its publication was an extraordinary feat considering the constant artillery bombardment the soldiers were under, in addition to the limited availability of 'y' and 'e' letters for typesetting. My favourite element of the newspaper is the satirical adverts that litter the pages, which reflect the good humour these men maintained. Ads include fake films like 'The Empty Jar, A Rum Tragedy.'

The *Wipers Times*' weather reports included mention of there being an 8:1 chance of chlorine. The British first used chlorine gas at the Battle of Loos in 1915, although the weather meant the wind blew the gas back over the Allied trenches, injuring 2,600 British men. As gas masks were developed, so too did the type of chemicals that were deployed. Chlorine, with its distinctive colour and smell (a mix of pineapple and pepper), was soon relegated in favour of odourless mustard gas, which caused painful chemical burns and blisters. As impure forms of mustard gas were used, they did in fact have both a colour (mustard, unsurprisingly) and a smell (garlic).

An 'exaspirator' was trench slang for a box respirator, which we would identify as an early form of gas mask. The Germans first used chlorine gas at Ypres in April 1915. As they released the taps attached to their gas cannisters, a greenish-yellow smoke moved towards the French and their North African colonial troops (largely from Morocco and Algeria). Not knowing what approached them, the troops stood firm and met this mysterious mist head on, which soon showed its true colours. Chlorine gas affected soldiers in a myriad of ways, from causing temporary blindness to coughing and vomiting, and in large enough doses it would attack your lungs, causing you to essentially drown internally. Reports from the attack describe how understandably terrified the French North African troops were, unable to articulate their distress in a language understood by those who'd brought them here.

Other 'trench speak' included going 'over the top', which meant climbing out of your front-line trench and charging across no man's land towards the enemy. Sometimes that could be a few kilometres or as little as 30 metres. Being told to go 'over the top' was preceded by heavy artillery bombardment so that, in theory, you could get across no man's land unscathed. However, the reality was that you'd still face masses of barbed wire, snipers and the possibility of being mowed down by enemy machine-gun fire.

Infamously, the week-long bombardment of enemy trenches before the Battle of the Somme in 1916 had, in fact, left the German defences intact, despite the 1.5 million shells that had been launched upon them. The War Office had been so confident this would be a glorious victory that they permitted two filmmakers to record it for recruitment purposes. Twenty million Brits packed cinemas within six weeks of its release.

Over 57,000 British soldiers were injured on the first day of the battle, and almost 20,000 lost their lives, making it the bloodiest day in British military history. Up to 30 per cent of the shells had been 'duds', another trench slang word, and the Germans had concrete dugouts that withstood the shells that did detonate. Thirty-seven sets of brothers are known to have been killed on that first day, at the price of three square miles. Over the course of those 141 days, the British forces consisted of troops from Britain, Canada, Australia, New Zealand, India, Newfoundland, South Africa, Bermuda and Southern Rhodesia. The role of 'non-combatant' Labour Corps units cannot be forgotten, such as the Indochinese, who were deployed as military drivers.

A combination of the cold weather, waterlogged trenches and tight boots causing restricted blood circulation meant immersion foot syndrome affected over 20,000 Allied troops in the first year of the war. Soldiers' feet would start to swell and even decay. In extreme cases it could lead to amputation. Clean socks and whale oil were issued to troops, which thankfully worked to combat this unfortunate consequence of trench life.

Lice were also a huge problem in the trenches, as they lay eggs in the seams of one's uniform. Sometimes this could lead to trench fever, which affected armies across all theatres of war, and recovery could take up to a month. Most soldiers found themselves in a constant cycle of sore rashes as a result of how itchy and irritated their skin would get.

The *Wipers Times* included a huge number of sport references, such as an alternative to the Olympics 'under the patronage of most of the crowned heads of Europe', presumably a reference to the fact that the Tsar of Russia, King of England and Kaiser of Germany were all cousins whose rivalry was at the heart of this war. And sport featured heavily across the Western Front. The Imperial War Museum holds a collection of photos entitled 'British Empire Troops on the Western Front 1914–18'. This includes images taken in June 1917 of members of the South African Native Labour Corps performing a 'Zulu warrior dance' in 'native' dress. There are images of them preparing and performing, as well as shots of the audience and one of the men, Muti, being presented to General Maxwell afterwards. These images were taken during a sports day at Dannes in France, and no doubt the day included events such as wheelbarrow racing and tug of war. This 'warrior' dance, however, was performed by men whom the audience didn't view as worthy enough to engage in combat. As we've learned during this chapter, Labour Corps units did crucial and dangerous work, but they were largely denied the chance, on racial grounds, to fight alongside their white counterparts. It begs the question, how much agency did they have when performing in front of such crowds? Their presence in this context also reminds me of the Black Georgian children featured in paintings, or indeed the story of Sarah Forbes Bonetta.

There are, however, examples where cultures and traditions were celebrated by indigenous people privately, and on their own terms. For example, the Maori of New Zealand performed their famous haka to scare the Turks they faced down in Gallipoli. George Strangling Wolf passed the medical examination required of the Canadian Overseas Expeditionary Force in June 1916, ensuring he packed his elk-teeth earrings. Before the Battle of Cambrai, George and a few others from the Kainai Nation (or Blood Tribe) prayed together, during which he cut a piece of flesh from his knee and buried it as an offering to the Sun Spirit. Similarly, after the war, Mike Mountain Horse, another member of the Blood Tribe, chose to enshrine his experiences on the Western Front on a piece of calfskin. Despite receiving a Distinguished Conduct Medal, he used traditional symbols, in keeping with the customs of his ancestors, to commemorate the war in his own way, including depicting the four days he spent buried in a bomb shelter.

There were chapatis in the trenches

I wear a small marigold pin on my work lanyard (alongside my poppy pin) and am often asked what this small orange flower represents. My response usually includes the fact that there's little acknowledgment of the 1.3 million Indian soldiers who served in the First World War, and that I wear the remembrance flower chosen by India to remember the forgotten fallen.

Indian soldiers were some of the first imperial soldiers to appear on the Western Front in late September 1914. Many were ill-informed and ill-equipped for what lay ahead, with their thin summer uniforms and sandals grossly inappropriate for life in the trenches.

Men across India had faced recruitment posters with a variety of sentiments, some emphasising soldiers' pay and the regular meals they would receive, while others stated, 'The best way to help your family is to join the army.' Such posters were printed in a variety of languages, included Punjabi, Urdu and Hindi. It's worth noting, however, that many of the recruits from India would not have been literate, though this did not stop the Germans from bombarding Indian soldiers with propaganda leaflets during the war in an attempt to encourage them to defect and ally themselves with the Turks in the name of holy war. Indian soldiers were recruited in a similar way to the pals battalions, with men from the same villages targeted to sign up together, and new recruits were shown regimental trophies to reiterate the message that loyalty to the British Army would bring great honour to the community. Indian soldiers were restricted from promotion within the army, with the most senior position available to them being below the most junior of English officers.

Following the fiasco of the gun cartridges – covered in grease derived from pork and beef fat – which had sparked the 1857 Great Rebellion in India, and a misunderstanding over tinned mutton at the start of the war, separate slaughter stations were provided so that the goats and sheep brought over from southern Europe could be prepared in accordance with the appropriate religious customs. This more enlightened approach can be seen elsewhere, such as the three marquees set up in a field in Flanders which acted as a temporary mosque, gurdwara and temple. Religious festivals like Eid and Vaisakhi were celebrated on the Western Front. It was during one of our many school trips to the First World War battlefields in France that a colleague and I began to wonder how Indian soldiers had been buried, given their different religious customs. It turns out that appropriate burial rites were adhered to as much as possible, with a burning ghat or cremation site built at the Hardelot hospital for Indian soldiers in north-east France.

Indian soldiers were provided with atta, a flour essential for making chapattis, and lentils, which meant they could make daal. Having said that, Horlicks Malted Milk became a firm favourite among them. Extra home comforts like Indian tobacco, pickles and papad were sometimes provided as a goodwill gesture from the Indian Soldiers' Fund, which relied on donations. The suppliers of Vaseline in London donated 50,000 small tins of petroleum jelly in answer to a request from Sikh soldiers for coconut oil for their hair. An entrepreneurial Frenchwoman called Mrs Beasley opened a canteen for Indian soldiers and was provided with 60-gallon tea boilers to help her services. Similarly, the West Indian Contingent Committee drew up a list of gifts that the troops would appreciate most, which included cocoa, ginger, guava jelly and hot sauces.

These soldiers were, of course, impacted by rationing issues as the war went on, such as the Indian Expeditionary Force who faced the Ottoman army in Kut (modern-day Iraq). As many as five men a day died from chronic starvation when subsisting on a paltry amount of horsemeat and only five ounces of mouldy atta. Eating in the trenches was difficult enough as it was, with flies often covering food, as well as rats pilfering any saved rations. No wonder some of them grew 'as big as ordinary cats', with Private Thomas McIndoe writing, 'Rats! Oh Crikey! If they were put in a harness they could have done a milk round, honest.' Many of these conditions were exacerbated in Gallipoli (Turkey) in 1915, where swarms of flies, blistering summer heat and frostbite-inducing winters combined with low water supplies, causing over 150,000 casualties. The aim of this campaign in April 1915 was to capture Constantinople and knock the Ottoman Empire out of the war. However, by December the decision was made to withdraw due to lack of adequate progress. This campaign was typical in terms of the diversity of those involved; the million soldiers involved included men from Britain, France, Australia, New Zealand, Canada, Egypt, Palestine and India.

Trench slang also highlights the influence Indian soldiers had on the vernacular of the time, with 'Blighty' adapted from the Urdu word 'bilayati', meaning foreign. The *Birmingham Daily Mail* was absolutely right when in 1915 they wrote, 'The wars of the past have invariably coloured the language of returned soldiers, and this worldwide war will be no exception to the rule.' A 'cushy' trench might well be one that wasn't waterlogged and full of rats, stemming from the Hindi word 'khush', meaning pleasure. Soldiers would often sit in groups while splitting their time between talking and killing lice with candles or their fingernails. The Hindi word for parasite was 'chat', hence these informal gatherings became known as 'chatting'.

The Indian Army endured gas attacks, though they had been moderately prepared, as they'd been told to soak the cloths attached to their turbans in chloride of lime or urine to protect themselves. One such turbaned soldier was Mir Dast, a veteran who had served with the British Indian Army since 1894. In 1908 he'd been awarded the Indian Order of Merit, a reflection of his excellence. The gas attack caused Dast to briefly pass out. When he came to, in the absence of any British officers, he expertly led as many men as he could to safety. After dark he was determined to save those still alive on the battlefield, eventually ensuring eight more men were brought back behind British lines, despite facing heavy enemy fire. He was awarded the Victoria Cross for his bravery.

Dast's situation contrasted significantly with his brother, Mir Mast. A few weeks earlier, and mere days after he'd been awarded the Indian Distinguished Service Medal, he climbed out of his trench near Neuve-Chapelle with fourteen others and deserted to the Germans. His hope was that this risky move would get him back home to India as quickly as possible. Mast revealed intel to the Germans about the Khyber Pass in order to prove his worth, so much so that a detailed map was drawn of this area between India and Afghanistan, either by Mast himself or as a result of the information he gave. Mast was transferred to a special prisoner of war camp, which even had a purpose-built mosque. It was here that he was chosen for a diplomatic mission to Afghanistan. The aim? To persuade the Emir of Kabul to join the Germans. Travelling alongside diplomats from Germany and Turkey, they reached Kabul in May 1915, having lost half of the initial group along the way due to defection and exhaustion. Though the Emir could not be persuaded, Mast was granted leave and, as far as we know, was back home by June. What we'll likely never know is whether these two brothers were ever eventually reunited, their story surely crying out for a Bollywood reimagining.

The first Indian soldier to receive the distinguished Victoria Cross medal was Khudadad Khan, and it was well deserved. Khan's unit had endured terrible conditions and were outnumbered five to one when the Germans attacked on 30 October 1914. Many Indian soldiers were killed or wounded but Khan's machine gun crew, along with one other, carried on fighting until they were overrun by Germans and everyone was bayoneted or shot. Khan was the only survivor. He played dead and then managed to crawl back to his regiment under the cover of darkness. The bravery of Khan and his fellow soldiers gave the Allies enough time for British and Indian reinforcements to arrive and stop the German Army from reaching the vital ports. Khan received his VC medal from King George V at Buckingham Palace. Prior to this he was treated for his wounds at a hospital in a place you might not expect.

As we already know, some of the first soldiers from the British Empire to fight on the Western Front were Indian soldiers. Within three months of fighting, nearly one in four of the sepoys who'd passed through Marseilles were injured. Soon, hospitals across the south-east of England were prepared to welcome these injured soldiers, the most famous of which was the former royal palace in Brighton, the Royal Pavilion. Having visited there myself, it's no wonder the Indian soldiers who stayed there were in awe of the architecture, both inside and out. The grandeur of the Indian-inspired domes, towers and minarets on the outside scarcely prepare you for the décor inside, which includes Chinese wallpaper and glass-painted chandeliers shaped like exotic plants, which you can see looming over the Indian soldiers in their hospital beds in photographs from the time.

Just like it was in the trenches, separate facilities were set up for Hindu, Muslim and Sikh places of worship. Food was prepared separately according to religious customs, and those who died were given funeral rites in accordance with their beliefs. Fifty-three Hindus and Sikhs were cremated at Patcham Down, where a cremation memorial now lies. Adjacent to this is the Chattri Memorial, unveiled by the Prince of Wales in 1921. Part of its inscription reads, 'Erected on the site of the funeral pyre where the Hindus and Sikhs who died in hospital at Brighton, passed through the fire, is in grateful admiration and brotherly affection dedicated.'

Muslims were buried in a special graveyard built in Horsell Common, near the Woking mosque. One of the most powerful images from the home front is a photograph of Muslim soldiers praying outside this mosque. The graves were relocated to Brookwood Military Cemetery in 1969 due to vandalism. In 2015 a memorial peace garden was opened on the original site, with 27 Himalayan birch trees planted to represent each of their original burials.

The facilities at Brighton Pavilion were highly publicised by the War Office, with visits by the royal family and photographs and paintings of recuperating soldiers splashed over a myriad of publications. In fact, it was here that King George presented Mir Dast with his Victoria Cross. Princess Sophia Duleep Singh regularly visited the soldiers here, something they wrote about enthusiastically in the letters they sent back home. However, the reality behind these paternalistic images was quite different. While religious customs were strongly adhered to, beneath the propaganda it was upholding colonial values that was key. Moreover, it's possible the Germans were spreading rumours that religious customs were not being followed, hence the volume of publicity that sprung from the Pavilion. For example, despite what some of the photographs may imply, wherever possible, white British nurses were prohibited from taking care of Indian soldiers and were only to be present on wards if they were in a supervisory role. It was thought this was best practice in order to avoid 'scandals' involving relationships between nurses and sepoys.

There was also strict security at Brighton and other hospitals, including police and military guards. In the larger military hospital in Brighton, the Kitchener Indian Hospital, Colonel Bruce Seton introduced a series of rules that included banning all women from the hospital, even the doctors' wives, and all Indian personnel were essentially limited to the hospital area at all times. One patient grew so frustrated at this confinement that he actually tried to shoot Colonel Seton. The rules were relaxed as a result, undoubtedly linked to the sentiment of the commissioner of the hospitals who said in 1915, 'I never lose an opportunity of impressing on all who are working in these hospitals that great political issues are involved in making the stay of these Indians as agreeable as possible.'

There is a small memorial to Indian soldiers in Ypres, which I now visit annually to lay a wreath. There are also 412 Indian soldiers' names etched on the incredible Menin Gate Memorial to the Missing, including Hari Singh, of the 34th Sikh Pioneers, and Bugler Zaman Ali. If you see anyone else wearing a marigold pin, now you know why. Lest we forget.

The Chinese Labour Corps worked tirelessly behind the scenes

Prior to the Somme, the British had rebuffed several offers from the Chinese government to provide troops to support the Allies. The Chinese were keen to signal their place as an emerging modern nation, but the British favoured help from Japan, whose forces fought beside British and Indian troops at the Siege of Tsingtao in 1914, the scene of the first air attack launched from a ship. After the Somme's casualties, British attitudes changed, and by April 1917 the first of the Chinese Labour Corps were in France, having signed their deliberately vague contracts with their thumbprints. Trade unions expressed concerns about this, worrying that Chinese labourers would be employed in Britain and would undermine British workers' wages.

The Chinese were first used as trench-diggers, but many were soon identified as being highly skilled, with the Corps preparing 476 tanks for the Battle of Cambrai in 1917, using their ingenuity to create mechanisms to ensure these enormous machines could be transported into battle, as well as maintained and repaired. The Chinese Labour

Corps faced many challenges, such as a lack of adequate interpreters and violence from other troops, who viewed them with suspicion.

One incident in 1917 between a group of drunk Australian troops and the Chinese Labour Corps resulted in three Chinese men being executed. Living mostly on rations of rice, the Chinese were segregated into camps that resembled prisons, complete with barbed-wire enclosures. Their movements were restricted and there was tight security around the camp to ensure this. The Noyelles-sur-Mer Chinese Memorial and Cemetery near the Somme commemorates the sacrifice of these forgotten contributors to the First World War. The inscription carved above the entrance translates as: 'This site commemorates the sacrifice paid by 1900 Chinese workers who lost their lives during the 1914–18 war.' These men continued to work after the war ended, with 50,000 still working for the British in 1919, mostly helping to clear the battlefields and gather the dead.

Shot at dawn

A year after the start of the Somme, going over the top at Passchendaele came with its own very specific problems. Unusually heavy rain in the summer of 1917 meant this part of the Western Front was now a swampy bog. Bombardier J.W. Palmer wrote of the impact the scenes had on him: 'Every shell-hole was a sea of filthy oozing mud. I suppose there's a limit to everything, but the mud of Passchendaele – to see men sinking into the slime, dying in the slime – I think it absolutely finished me off.'

Arthur Roberts, a young mixed-race Glasgow resident of part Trinidadian heritage who survived the battle and kept a diary throughout the war, reminds us that mud wasn't the only obstacle: 'One fellow in front of me had his head blew off.' For some, such experiences were altogether too much. Seeing friends killed before you, the constant bombardment and the constant threat of maiming and death meant thousands of men were understandably diagnosed with 'shell shock', which we would now call post-traumatic stress disorder.

Doctors were inexperienced with dealing with this type of trauma, and this meant responses ranged from electric-shock treatment to the dismissal that this was simply 'cowardice'. Pioneering doctor W.H.R. Rivers used his understanding of psychology to support men like Wilfred Owen, one of the great poets of the war, who suffered from shell shock and penned 'Dulce et Decorum Est'. In most cases however, men were simply sent back the trenches.

Abraham Bevistein was born to a Jewish family in Poland in 1898. They moved to England when he was a young boy, and Abe signed up at sixteen after changing his surname to Harris. He was physically wounded and suffered from shell shock after the trench he was stationed in exploded as a result of German underground siege mining. Letters to his mother highlight his distress, and despite his attempts to seek help, he was ordered to remain on the front line once he was deemed fit enough. After his trench was under attack from German grenades, he was arrested for walking back from the front lines.

In the last letter his family received, he wrote, 'Dear mother, I'm in the trenches and I was ill so I went out, and they took me to the prison and I'm in a bit of trouble now.' He pleaded not guilty, but was charged with 'deserting His Majesty's service'. He was 'to suffer death by being shot'. Abe was only seventeen and he was one of 306 British soldiers executed during this war. In 2001 the Shot at Dawn Memorial was unveiled in Staffordshire. The statue is surrounded by a wooden post for each serviceman who was executed, including Abraham Bevistein, a physical reminder of the psychological trauma these men suffered.

Pilots of the Caribbean, and beyond

Wars have the not entirely unexpected consequence of leading to medical advancements. Despite the limitations in treatment for shell shock, processes like blood transfusions and the use of blood banks were pioneered during this time. The use of X-rays became commonplace, with mobile X-ray machines utilised near the battlefields to quickly identify where pieces of shrapnel and bullets were lodged. Skin grafts were also used for the first time, the first step in developing plastic surgery. If you watch hospital dramas then you'll be familiar with the term 'triage'. This was a process that was standardised during this war, due to the huge influx of casualties medical staff would be faced with. It involved dividing cases into those who were slightly injured (and could be treated quickly and sent back to the front), those who needed to be transported to a field hospital, and lastly those who were made as comfortable as possible, but were seen as being beyond realistically saving.

Another witness to the muddy nightmare of Passchendaele was Norman Manley. He was born in Jamaica in 1893 to parents of African, Caribbean and Irish descent. He was talented physically and academically, winning sports championships and earning a Rhodes Scholarship to read Law at Oxford. Despite his clear talents, Norman was rejected from the Officer Training Corps on the grounds that he was not of 'pure European descent'. Norman and his brother Douglas enlisted as infantrymen instead and were sent to the Western Front.

Douglas was killed at Ypres in 1917 in a shell attack as he was helping to carry a wounded soldier to the dressing station. Norman helped bury Douglas and wrote a letter to his family, highlighting one of the many other challenges that those on the front line faced – having to push back your grief and literally soldier on. At the end of his letter he writes: 'One had to face this sort of thing and carry on ... neither of us joined the army without fully expecting everything. God knows I shall miss him. But as he would have it, one must just stick it and we've got to win.'

While Norman experienced comradery in his early days in the trenches, when he was promoted to corporal the racial prejudice he experienced began to intensify. He therefore joined a new regiment and reverted to the lesser position of gunner, a job he did for the rest of the war. Norman survived the war and received a military medal for his bravery. He went on to practice law, was an advocate of universal suffrage and eventually became the Premier of Jamaica.

In the skies above Passchendaele was Hardit Singh Malik, the first of four Indians to join the Royal Flying Corps (later known as the

RAF) and one of two to survive the war. A History student at Oxford, he initially joined the war as an ambulance driver, but Malik soon convinced the RFC to take him on. It was lucky they did, as he took his first solo flight after only three hours of training. He came to be known as the Flying Hobgoblin, due to the special helmet he wore over his turban. He made his first kill less than a fortnight before he found himself in a dogfight on 26 October in which the Germans shot both Malik's fuel tank and his leg. Forty miles away from his base, he managed to fend off several German aircraft before landing and miraculously surviving, despite his plane showing evidence of being hit over 400 times. Malik's two kills meant he was three short of being known as a 'flying ace', another term coined during this war.

Indra Lal 'Laddie' Roy filled those shoes, though not without complication. He was almost rejected for not passing the eye exam, and after being shot down in December 1917 and presumed dead, he regained consciousness and found himself lying in a French morgue. Roy was unfortunately killed for real by a German fighter pilot in July 1918. He was nineteen years old and had fully earned his status as India's first 'flying ace', having shot down nine German planes in less than a fortnight. He's buried in France, his grave inscribed with the words, 'He died for the ideals he loved.' He was posthumously awarded the Distinguished Flying Cross.

One of the first Black pilots to qualify and fly for Britain was Sergeant William Robinson Clarke from Kingston, Jamaica, over the Western Front in the summer of 1917. He was on a reconnaissance mission over Ypres when he was shot down by the Germans. Thankfully he survived his crash landing, and lived till he was 88.

The Saxe-Coburg-Gothas changed their name

Meanwhile, at home, anti-German sentiment was high, with fake news stories circulating in all the major papers of the day that the Germans were 'extracting oils, fats and pig food' in factories using the corpses of dead soldiers. In May 1915 there were anti-German riots in east

London and other parts of the country. This was prompted by the sinking of the *Lusitania* off the coast of Ireland, a passenger liner that was torpedoed by German submarines killing 1,191 people. It has since been confirmed that the *Lusitania* had been carrying weapons for the Allied war effort.

Rumours, such as the idea that German bakers were putting arsenic into their bread, had been circulating since the war began. Shops and homes were ransacked, with rioters entering homes and throwing furniture out of the windows. In Liverpool, 200 businesses were destroyed. At one point a German piano found itself out on the street, with crowds gathering round it to sing patriotic songs. Some families with German-sounding names started changing their surnames, including the Saxe-Coburg-Gothas, who changed theirs to Windsor. The royal family have been known by that name ever since.

A woman's place is on the factory floor

While rioters were out on the streets in May 1915, Prime Minister Asquith's government faced mounting pressure. The disastrous Gallipoli campaign was bad enough – but then reports leaked from the Western Front that the British Army was facing a weapons shortage, particularly shells and bullets. Asquith was backed into a political corner and was forced to create a coalition government with the Conservatives. A new Cabinet position was created, and David Lloyd George was now Minister of Munitions. Lloyd George knew that the only way to solve the 'shell crisis' was to employ women.

The Pankhursts had been patriotically supporting the war since the summer of 1914, so it did not take much persuading to get the WSPU to organise a Women's Right to Serve demonstration through central London on 17 July. Unlike suffragette demonstrations, they ditched their usual purple, white and green for patriotic red, white and blue. One woman walked the streets dressed as Belgium. Thousands of women signed up via the Women's War Register.

This did not mean, however, that women were welcomed into factories with open arms. Trade unions were reluctant to support this, arguing that women workers would 'dilute' men's pay, so they had to be reassured that women would only work until sufficient male labour became available. The government led by example, setting up over 200 national factories that employed largely women. Women worked in all sorts of jobs during this war. Half a million women replaced men in office jobs, and 200,000 more women started working in various government departments. Approximately two million women replaced jobs that had previously been done by men, from welding to grave digging, and from bus drivers to postal workers. Some 260,000 women worked in agriculture, including the Women's Land Army, which was set up in 1917.

By far the most visible female workers became known as 'munitionettes', who produced 80 per cent of the weapons used by the British Army. In 1917, 76 million shells were produced, 150 times the amount produced in 1914. This was incredibly dangerous work. There were no health and safety regulations, meaning you could spot munitionettes a mile off due to the yellow glow their skin and clothes now had, thanks to the chemicals they were exposed to and their lack of safety wear and poor ventilation. Metal items were prohibited in factories (such as hairpins) and workers wore wooden clogs to minimise any reactions, but such measures only mitigated the dangers.

Lottie Meade was a 25-year-old mother of four who had been a laundress before the war. In 1916 she was incredibly proud to be working as a munitionette, so much so that she had a photograph taken of her posing in her factory overalls. Her husband Frederick had been a greengrocer, but was now fighting in France. In October 1916, Lottie died in Kensington Infirmary due to liver, heart and kidney failure caused by her exposure to TNT. The post-mortem in 1916 concluded a verdict of 'death by misadventure'.

Another 'canary' was seventeen-year-old Mabel Lethbridge, who lied about her age, passed the medical examination and was now an official employee at the National Filling Station in Hayes. At the height of its production the factory employed 10,000 women and 2,000 men.

Her first role was cleaning detonators, where she saw a sign asking for volunteers to work in the 'danger zone'. This job involved filling shells with amatol, a deadly mixture of ammonium nitrate and TNT. Every afternoon a trolley of milk would come round for the workers, as it was thought to minimise the effects these chemicals had on them. Shortly after the milk had been distributed, one of the shells exploded. Mabel's injuries included a fractured skull, a burst eardrum, burnt hands and lung damage. She also lost her left leg. It was only her ninth day working in Hayes. She became the youngest person at the time to be awarded an MBE, and she endured a lifetime of operations as a result of her injuries.

One of the largest factory explosions happened in London's East End in 1917, leaving 73 dead and up to 400 injured. And in 2005 a memorial was unveiled to remember the 'Barnbow lasses', the 35 women who were killed in a factory explosion in Leeds in 1916. Knowledge of explosions like these were censored at the time, with such deaths explained as 'accidents', with no further details.

This censorship came under the Defence of the Realm Act (DORA), which essentially authorised the government to pass laws deemed necessary to protect the country and support the war effort. Pub opening hours were shortened and alcohol was watered down in an effort to keep workers as sober as possible. The 'no treating' order made it illegal to buy a round – you could now only purchase a drink for yourself. Loitering near bridges and tunnels was banned, as was whistling, as it could be mistaken for an air-raid warning. DORA also led to the inception of British Summer Time, and the clocks first went forward in the spring of 1916 in order to maximise daylight working hours.

Exercise was encouraged for those working in factories, leading to the creation of women's football teams. Lily Parr was the star player of the football team associated with the Dick, Kerr & Co. factory in Preston, which produced munitions, locomotives and aircraft. She was striking in more ways than one. At five-foot-ten she was a formidable player, despite being a chain smoker, and she scored over a hundred goals in her first year. The women continued to play after the war, in front of crowds of up to 46,000. But despite the clear popularity of women's football, in 1921 the Football Association declared that football was 'unsuitable' for women and banned its clubs from hosting their games. This ban wasn't lifted till 1971, which begs the question: how much more progress would have been made in women's football had this ban not taken place?

This setback did not deter Lily and her teammates, however. They pioneered international competition and toured North America, playing games there instead. Lily was also openly gay and had a partner, Mary. Lily trained as a nurse and continued playing football well into her forties. She was the first woman inducted into the English Football Hall of Fame and is the first female footballer in the UK to be commemorated with a statue.

Of course, the First World War's most obvious football connection is the infamous Christmas truce of 1914, when both the Germans and Allied soldiers met to sing carols, share cigarettes and play a friendly game of football. Not every soldier on the Western Front experienced this in 1914, but there are enough personal testimonies and photographs to prove that many did. Private Williams of the London Regiment had quite the experience and had to help escort a drunken singing German soldier back across No Man's Land before fighting resumed.

A nurse, an aspiring journalist and a female commanding officer walk into the First World War

What is often forgotten is that there were women across all the fronts, working in various roles. Women provided crucial support behind the lines, from driving ambulances to nursing soldiers under a myriad of conditions. Edith Cavell was in England when the war broke out, but Belgium was familiar territory to her, having spent time there before the war training nurses. She'd even found the time to set up a medical journal (*L'Infirmiere*) in 1910. She returned to Brussels during the war, where her clinic and nursing school had been taken over by the Red Cross.

That winter, Edith and her nurses began harbouring soldiers caught in German-occupied Belgium. The escapees would stay in Cavell's clinic before they were given documents and guides to be able to flee into neutral Holland. She may well have aided almost 200 soldiers and civilians over the subsequent eleven months. But on 5 August, Edith and Sister Elizabeth Wilkins were betrayed and arrested. Edith was placed in solitary confinement. She admitted her guilt and was shot by a firing squad on 12 October 1915, despite pleas from neutral America and Spain. Her execution caused outrage and her image became a symbol for the Allies. After the war her body was exhumed and a memorial was held at Westminster Abbey, before she was reburied at Norwich Cathedral.

Dorothy Lawrence had dreams of becoming a war correspondent when war broke out, but her age (eighteen) and her gender meant she was not taken seriously by any of the London newspaper offices she visited, whom she implored to give her a chance. She decided to travel to France and forge her own path, stating, 'I'll see what an ordinary English girl, without credentials or money can accomplish.' She travelled to Paris and convinced two British soldiers to support her mission of posing as a soldier. They agreed to sneak her pieces of uniform disguised as washing, which meant that within a week she had the right boots, trousers, braces, jacket, cap and shirt. Upon trying the uniform on she realised she did not look like a convincing enough man and needed to 'discover some means of reducing my robust figure to masculine slimness'. This meant swaddling herself in bandages, 'like a mummy', and then creating a corset out of sacking and wool.

The soldiers helped her forge a pass to grant her access to Bethune, where she would then be able to access the trenches. She chose the alias Denis Smith and created a cover story, ensuring she would be able to convincingly answer questions about her 'regiment'. She also managed to convince a military policeman to cut her hair 'in true outline of a British private' and covered her face in disinfectant to try to cover her 'girlish colouring' as well as to 'appear conspicuously unattractive'. She discarded all her petticoats, not wishing to let such obvious female undergarments give her away.

She travelled towards the Front by bicycle, and found herself recruiting yet another British soldier to help her, in the shape of a former coal miner, Lancastrian sapper Tom Dunn. He convinced her to hide, finding her shelter in a dugout full of fleas. She eventually moved to an abandoned cottage and slept on a soggy mattress. That first night Dunn sneaked away from the trenches and brought her a feast in the shape of bully beef stew, bread and classic trench biscuits.

Dunn eventually agreed to let Dorothy accompany him on a night shift in the trenches. After ten days Dorothy experienced fits of fainting and became increasingly paranoid that her 'khaki accomplices' would be found out. She turned herself in to a sergeant and was soon arrested and taken to various military headquarters, where she had to convince her interrogators that she was neither a spy nor a 'camp-follower', although Dorothy did not realise that this meant a sex worker, which caused a lot of confusion.

Eventually, she was allowed to board a ship for Britain, where she actually met Emmeline Pankhurst, who wanted Dorothy to tell her story at a suffragette meeting. The Defence of the Realm Act's censorship, however, prevented her from doing so and indeed from writing about her experiences, which of course had been the whole point of her adventure.

All the quotes I've used to tell Dorothy's story are from the book she wrote in April 1918, giving her as much agency as possible. This book was not the commercial success Dorothy had been hoping for, though. The remainder of Dorothy's life was truly tragic, as her mental health deteriorated and she was institutionalised from 39 years in what was then a 'lunatic asylum', before her death in 1964. Dorothy labelled herself as the 'Only English Woman Soldier in the Royal Engineers 51st Division', though news of her compelling adventure remains limited. Hopefully it's clear why it was one I wanted to share as widely as possible using words she penned herself about her impressive stint adjacent to, but not quite on the front line.

Another remarkable woman who reached the front line also wrote about her story. Dorothy's story contrasts sharply with that of Flora Sandes, who was the only British woman to officially serve in an Allied army during the First World War. While Dorothy was silenced by the British, Flora was celebrated by the Serbians she served with. Originally volunteering as a St John Ambulance driver, Flora was posted to Serbia and eventually became the first woman to be commissioned as an officer in the Serbian Army. She experienced exactly the same conditions that the average soldier did, from the lice, which she described as 'a certain kind of livestock', to finding ways to pass the time, such as trying to teach bridge to a group of people 'in a language your knowledge of which is so slight that you can only ask for the simplest things in the fewest possible words. You'll find the result is a very queer and original game.'

She also wrote extremely fondly of the Serbians she encountered, ensuring they were supplied with items like sugar, and noting customs she came to love, such as when you visit someone's house you're offered a spoonful of jam to eat before you take your water. She once met an old Serbian lady but was unsure, due to the language barrier, whether the lady was enthusiastically talking to Flora about her husband or cat. Flora's writing also reveals her innermost thoughts, such as noting how good-looking the Serbian military policemen tended to be. In 1916, the year of her fortieth birthday, Flora was badly injured by a grenade while fighting in Macedonia. She returned to England and wrote *An English Woman-Sergeant in the Serbian Army*, which is where all these quotes are from. She wrote the book to raise awareness and funds for the Serbians. She was given the highest honour in the Serbian military and promoted to a sergeant-major. She died at the age of 80, and is known to the Serbian people as Nashi Engelskina, meaning 'our Englishwoman'. Thankfully, unlike so many of the people (particularly women) we have encountered, both Flora and Dorothy left us with their unique experiences from the First World War, written in their own words.

In 1917, the Russians were eventually convinced by Maria Bochkareva to allow her to form the first all-female battalion, and some eventually saw combat in Austria. The decision to approve their creation, however, was partly out of wanting to shame men into signing up. In Britain a different tactic was used: white feathers would be handed out to men (in public) who had not enlisted, or at least looked like they hadn't. Seen as a symbol of cowardice, the hope was that men would be embarrassed and emasculated by the gesture, which would encourage them to join.

One group of men who refused to give in to this pressure were conscientious objectors. The No-Conscription Fellowship was created in 1914, and one member was William Harrison, a lifelong pacifist and vegetarian, who was court-martialled and sentenced to a year of hard labour at Wormwood Scrubs for refusing to join the army. Some 16,000 men were recognised as conscientious objectors: 7,000 of those did serve in the army, but in non-combatant roles; 3,000 volunteered to do work of 'national importance', such as farming; while 6,000 went to prison; 41 were illegally sent to France to endure Field Punishment Number One, which meant they were tied to a fixed object for up to two hours a day.

Of the sixteen conscientious objectors detained at Richmond Castle, many of them left graffiti on the prison walls, a permanent record of the values they'd been detained for. One example is by Richard Lewis Barry, who refused to fight on the grounds of his socialist views. He wrote, 'You might just as well try to dry a floor by throwing water on it, as try to end this war by fighting.' They were sent to France in 1916 and were told they were not on active service. All of them refused to obey the order to move supplies at the nearby docks, so they were sentenced to death by firing squad, before it was hastily amended to ten years of hard labour.

The road to armistice

In February 1917, the new Ministry of Food introduced guidelines for voluntary rationing, as flour stocks were running dangerously low thanks to U-boat sinkings. These guidelines were largely ignored, and by October the first sugar-ration cards were introduced. Measures like introducing the Women's Land Army were made to support food production. In December, *The Times* ran stories about queues for margarine around the country, with some as large as 3,000 people long. It was also now a criminal offence to throw rice at weddings. Panic-buying ensued, leading to a programme of national rationing by January, which included meat and butter. We have meat-free Mondays in our school canteen today, a tradition actually started in the First World War (minus the alliteration) when, from March 1918, the Ministry of Food promoted the idea of 'meatless Wednesdays'.

While the German U-boats were sinking our merchant ships and disrupting food supplies in Britain, the British naval blockade had far more dire consequences on the German home front. The infamous Turnip Winter of 1916–17 caused by poor harvests and exacerbated by Allied blockades meant that meals centred around turnips, a particularly bitter pill to swallow, as this was seen as food only good enough for cattle. It's no wonder that 300,000 German civilians died from malnutrition.

This year, 1917, was a real turning point in the war, as Britain lost an ally and gained another, with America joining the war and the Russian Revolution leading to the new Communist government withdrawing from it. The Germans gave it one last shot with their Ludendorff Offensive, but failed to make much progress from May 1918. By August the Allied armoured units were smashing through German trenches. German naval mutinies and civil unrest meant that Kaiser Wilhelm II fled Germany and abdicated the throne. It was down to German envoy Matthias Erzberger to sign the terms of peace, which he did at 5am on 11 November 1918. The guns fell silent six hours later. War was over.

Post-war violence – from Liverpool to Punjab

One of the lesser-known consequences of the First World War was the 1919 race riots, which started with an outbreak of violence in Glasgow in January. Race riots happened around the UK until late in the summer, including in Liverpool, Hull, Cardiff, Salford, Newport, London and South Shields. In Liverpool, for example, the Black population had grown dramatically during the First World War in order to fill the labour shortage created when white British workers joined the army.

After the armistice, the city's population increased further when Black servicemen were demobilised and Black sailors were discharged to Liverpool. Many white servicemen returned from the front lines, hoping to continue their pre-war lives, but found that there were fewer jobs and too much competition from workers from Africa, the Caribbean, China, the Middle East and South Asia. Racial tensions around Liverpool's ports ran high – and on 4 June a West Indian man, John Johnson, was brutally stabbed in the face by two Scandinavian sailors because he refused to give them a cigarette. The following night, violence erupted.

Charles Wotten, a 24-year-old Black sailor originally from Bermuda, who was not involved in the fighting, was pursued by two policemen and a crowd of around 300. They chased him to the Queens Dock and surrounded him at the water's edge. Bricks and stones were thrown at him, driving Wotton into the water. Some reports say that members of the crowd at that point shouted, 'Let him drown,' as Wotten perished. His corpse was later recovered, but no arrests were made.

Despite the death of Charles Wotten, the violence continued. Crowds several-thousand strong attacked Black-occupied homes and hostels. Within a week the police, unable to cope, detained over 700 Black residents in police stations for their own protection. In the end, several navy ships were called in to support the police in Liverpool. This unfortunately echoes the experience of many African American soldiers when they returned home. Some were actually stripped of their army uniforms at railroad stations by those who were incensed at the sight of them in American army uniforms, and nineteen African American veterans were killed by lynch mobs.

For Indian soldiers who returned home, 1919 was also a year of tragedy. The 1919 Rowlatt Act effectively imposed martial law on India, including imprisonment without trial. This was particularly frustrating given India's human and financial contributions to the First World War, on top of which hardships were still being endured, such as food and fuel shortages. A series of strikes were organised and pockets of rioting occurred, resulting in the deaths of Indians and Brits. The governor of Punjab, Michael O'Dwyer, ordered Brigadier-General Rex Dyer to act as he saw fit. On 13 April, Dyer sent a thousand troops and two armoured cars to the Jallianwala Bagh, where many were gathered to celebrate Vaisakhi, a religious festival. A peaceful political meeting was also taking place, asking for the Rowlatt Act to be repealed. Dyer and his troops arrived through the narrow passageways at one end of the Bagh. They fired repeatedly at the unarmed crowd (men, women and children) – 1,650 rounds of ammunition were fired in ten minutes, and approximately 400 were killed and 1,500 wounded. Among them 120 perished in 'the martyr's well', in a futile attempt to find safety. Dyer admitted later that he would have used the armoured cars if they'd been able to fit through the gates.

After the massacre Dyer imposed additional laws, such as cutting off water and electricity to Indian quarters and flogging any Indian who refused to bow to a European that they passed. The crawling order was also introduced, meaning Indians who wanted to pass through the Kucha Kurrichhan street were expected to crawl across it in retribution for an attack that had taken place there on missionary Marcella Sherwood. She survived after being saved by a group of locals.

An investigation was made into the Jallianwala Bagh massacre, and the British Hunter Committee concluded that there was no proof of a conspiracy to overthrow the Raj in the Punjab. Dyer was censured and asked to resign. The *Morning Post*, however, raised a £26,000 fund for him and presented him with a sword of honour.

The Jallianwala Bagh Massacre was a turning point in the story of Indian nationalism; Nobel laureate Rabindranath Tagore returned his knighthood in protest and Gandhi organised his first mass protests in its wake. Churchill described the massacre as 'monstrous', showing that even some of the most stringent defenders of empire were appalled by Dyer's actions.

A month later, the infamous Treaty of Versailles was signed. Divided into fifteen parts, with a total of 440 articles, the treaty reconfigured Germany in several ways. Germany's borders were reduced, its colonies seized and armed forces limited. They were banned from having an air force altogether and had to agree to pay reparations that amounted at the time to £6.6 billion. Article 231 forced Germany to accept responsibility for starting the First World War. Despite protesting against this 'war guilt clause', they had little choice but to accept, as the Allies threatened to return to war if the terms were not accepted. The German people called it 'diktat', meaning a dictated peace.

The Empire Exhibition which made a loss of £1.5 million

Where in the world in 1924 could you find the first Jaffa oranges for sale in England, an elephant called Saucy, a Buddhist shrine and a life-size butter sculpture of the Prince of Wales? The answer: Wembley, obviously.

Seventeen million people visited the 1924 Empire Exhibition, held at a specially built stadium, the site of which now hosts all manner of events, from FA Cup finals to Harry Styles concerts. Plans for the event started in 1913, but a world war then got in the way. The roads that lead down to the stadium today are reminders of its original purpose, from Exhibition Way to Empire Way. It was the biggest concrete building on earth at the time, and the publicity maps of the event make it look like a Victorian imperial Disneyland. For those in need of a cocktail, the place to be was the Jamaican Planter's Punch Bar. King George V's speech on the opening day was the first time a monarch had been broadcast on the radio.

There was a huge variety of entertainment, including the Pears' Palace of Beauty, featuring ten models dressed as beautiful women from history, including Mary, Queen of Scots, Helen of Troy and Cleopatra. There was also a miniature train within the Treasure Island section, and various stage shows like *The Defences of London*. This took place in the British Government pavilion, and the opening scene was a dramatic bombing of Westminster by an unnamed enemy, eerily predicting what London would go through in the Blitz less than a decade later. Intended to emphasise the strength of the RAF, the show's later scenes involved British pilots successfully defending the capital. Audiences could also watch a re-enactment of the Great Fire of London, which ended with a model of St Paul's Cathedral being set aflame.

There were national 'pavilions' for every colony, built in the architectural style of each place. The Nigeria section included replicas of the mud walls of Kano and were advertised as 'the most realistic show of the Exhibition. It is as though you are actually in Nigeria'. Just like in the Great Exhibition of 1851, people were brought over from different colonies as living, breathing exhibits, such as 'Tibetan dancers', 'Indian Jugglers' and 'Leather craftsman' from Sierra Leone, as races in residence. Such displays were meant to reinforce paternalistic views of the imperial mission, adding support to the notion that 'civilising' the colonies was working, shown by the brochure's description of the Indian pavilion, which would show how much Britain had helped in the 'victorious fight against ignorance, famine, flood and pestilence'.

West African students in London lodged complaints that these pavilions were reductive in that they perpetuated stereotypes of a 'primitive' lifestyle rather than reflecting how increasingly urbanised the continent was becoming. Indian nationalists called for the exhibition to be boycotted, reflecting how differently the colonised and colonisers viewed the empire at this time. A workers' strike, the aim of which was to have their union representatives recognised, had in fact threatened the opening of the exhibition, with the Australian press reporting that a 'mob' of workers met outside the Burma section and threw 'missiles' ranging from bricks to tools. Five hundred policemen had to be drafted in as a result. Other things about the exhibition were also not as they seemed. Despite visitors being able to take luncheon at the India exhibit, overall the exhibition made a loss of approximately £1.5 million. Financial issues plagued the empire in the years succeeding the exhibition too.

Nigerian women sit on the British while Gandhi steals their salt

Nigeria was advertised in the brochure as 'Our Youngest Colony', Britain having formally ruled it since 1914. In 1925, a new tax linked to the census was soon levied upon all men, and rumours started that this would soon be extended to women too. Many women were already contributing to these taxes, so when an Igbo woman called Nwanyeruwa was approached by a census taker, she was incensed, with some accounts suggesting he tried to grab her throat in disgust, in response to which she simply grabbed his.

She recounted her experience to her local women's network, and she, alongside three other women (Ikonnia, Mwannedia and Nwugo), organised an anti-tax campaign. They sent palm leaves to neighbouring villages, a symbol of invitation for their planned protest; when you received a palm leaf you knew to pass it on. This worked, and soon over 10,000 women were demanding that the tax extension be abolished. The British-appointed warrant chief soon made it clear that he did not support their demands. In response, groups of women gathered outside his house (and the houses of other colonial administrators) and started singing, dancing and playing music so that he could not ignore them. This tactic aimed to humiliate and shame, and was known as 'sitting on a man'. As news of the protest spread, so did their demands. Now the women wanted an official guarantee that they would not be taxed.

This collective action became known as the Women's War. They would dress in warrior clothing and have their heads wrapped in ferns, a symbol of war and rebellion. Sticks would be carried wrapped in young palm leaves to gain blessings from their ancestors. Most of their activity played out through song, dance and music, but in some areas, district offices and court buildings were burned down, which alarmed the British. On two occasions Britain directed the security forces to break up the protests, and at least thirty women were killed as a result. This was the first major anti-colonial revolt by women in West Africa. In 1930 the system of warrant chieftains was abolished and women were appointed within the court system. In 2018 the UN recognised the activism of these women as having officially contributed towards Nigerian independence.

Similarly, Mahatma Gandhi led a protest against the salt tax in 1930 in an attempt to unite the masses against a common cause. The

Salt March attracted thousands of Indians to walk towards the coast to make their own salt in defiance of the tax. It was seen as a propaganda victory for Indian nationalists, with international press attention focusing on the elderly Indian man wearing a dhoti who dared to take on the British Empire in such a simple, peaceful way.

That's not to say there wasn't violence, of course. At the Dharasana Salt Works, two were killed and hundreds injured as peaceful protestors were clubbed with lathis by police. This was witnessed by American journalist Webb Miller, who broke the story globally. This echoed events in Lahore two years earlier, when peaceful protestors met to show their disdain for the Simon Commission, an endeavour of the British to decide upon the future of India, which had no Indian voices within the delegation. Beloved nationalist Lala Lajpat Rai died from head injuries sustained at the hands of another police lathi charge. A young writer vowed to avenge his death, although he mistakenly shot the wrong policeman and was then arrested when later attempting to bomb the Central Legislative Assembly in Delhi.

Bhagat Singh spent 116 days on hunger strike, for the same reason as the suffragettes: he wished to be treated as a political prisoner and not a common criminal. He was executed at the age of 23 in March 1931. Clearly, stability within the empire was not quite as the 1925 exhibition had conveyed it, though the empire would once again be relied upon in a huge way from 1939.

THE SECOND WORLD WAR 7

The early 1930s were a tumultuous time for Europe, with America's Wall Street Crash wreaking havoc across the continent. It hit Germany particularly hard, as America had provided loans in the wake of their inevitable inability to pay the huge reparations forced upon them by the Treaty of Versailles. Industry collapsed and over six million became unemployed as a result, equating to one in three Germans.

In times of hardship, many turned to more extreme solutions. While Adolf Hitler had tried and failed to take Munich by force in 1923, the recession of the early 1930s provided the conditions his Nazi party had been waiting for. The arguments they had been making for years were now received more receptively, with promises to rid Germany of communist influence music to middle-class ears, while workers were lured by promises of 'work and bread', a simple slogan that resonated almost universally with a Germany on the brink of collapse. Hitler became chancellor of Germany, second only to the president, because of the electoral success of the Nazis. After the death of President Hindenburg, Hitler assumed the title of Führer, having already consolidated his power through nefarious means, such as the infamous Night of the Long Knives, which involved assassinations of the Nazis' opponents under the codename Operation Hummingbird. If your name appeared on the Reich List of Unwanted Persons, you likely did not make it beyond 2 July 1934. Some were shot as soon as they opened their front doors, while others were hacked to death in secluded woods. These murders were carried out largely by the SS (Schutzstaffel). Instantly recognisable in their black military uniform, they were an organisation which started out as Hitler's personal bodyguards, and membership was contingent on proving one's Aryan heritage dating back at least a century. They would eventually possess huge military and police powers, and carry out devastating crimes during the war.

The rise of the Nazis during the interwar years is probably one of the most familiar contexts from secondary school history. As a result, you can possibly name more Nazi government ministers than politicians from any other time or place. Reich Minister of Propaganda Joseph Goebbels was responsible for spearheading the indoctrination of the population. This involved a wide programme of censorship, such as the infamous book burnings of any works seen as 'un-German', such as those by Jewish authors, pacifists and communists.

Art the Nazis disapproved of was displayed and mocked via the touring Degenerate Art exhibition of 1937. The way the Nazis dealt with objects such as 'degenerate' art paralleled the actions they took against people they deemed to be 'undesirable'. Captions around the pieces sought to remind the 20,000 daily visitors that this art represented 'insanity, insolence and incompetence'. Some confiscated art was seized and sold by the Nazis, while some was kept by top officials like Hermann Göring, Hitler's second in command, who amassed a huge collection of works, from Van Gogh to Monet, many of which were taken from Jewish owners and kept in his country home near Berlin.

In March 1939, some 5,000 artworks were burned in the courtyard of the Berlin fire department, but some art was hidden, with 6,500 pieces, including works by Michelangelo and Rembrandt, held in an Austrian salt mine for the duration of the war. Artists themselves were persecuted too, with German avant-garde painter Elfriede Lohse-Wächtler (who had been diagnosed with schizophrenia) forcibly sterilised and eventually gassed to death under the T4 euthanasia programme in 1940.

The Nazi propaganda machine goes on overdrive

Propaganda infiltrated every aspect of civilian life, with all media taken over by the Nazis, from cinema to newspapers and radio. Some films aimed to glorify the Nazis, such as *Triumph of the Will*, essentially a documentary of the 1934 Nuremburg rally which opens with Hitler arriving to adoring crowds via aeroplane, no doubt a snub to the Treaty of Versailles, while others inspired hatred and division, like *Jud Süss*, the 1940 anti-Semitic period drama, which was seen by twenty million people in Germany alone and sparked such prejudice that it was screened to the guards at Auschwitz. Social policies aimed to indoctrinate different groups under the guise of the 'Volksgemeinschaft', or 'People's community', where everyone had their specific roles under the same goal – to do whatever the regime asked of you.

Workers were depicted as the central figures across propaganda posters and were 'rewarded' via the KdF (Kraft durch Freude), or Strength Through Joy programme, which provided theatre trips, sports days and even cruises, which shipped 130,000 passengers to places like Madeira and the Norwegian fjords. These 'rewards', of course, had another political purpose: to keep workers busy so they didn't agitate the state. That's why there were always members of the secret police onboard to check for any rebellious behaviour. You definitely didn't want to refer to Goebbels as 'Mahatma Propagandhi' within earshot of an informer disguised as a fellow holidaymaker. The secret police, or Gestapo, were a key instrument of terror in Nazi Germany. Using surveillance tactics like wiretapping and a huge network of informers, they were able to accumulate information on anyone they deemed to pose a threat to the state, including political opponents and gay people.

The 'sphere' of women was epitomised by the Three Ks – Kinder, Küche, Kirche, meaning children, kitchen and church. The rather directly named Law for the Encouragement of Marriage reflected exactly what women were meant to do: have as many children as possible. Newly married couples were given a loan of a thousand marks (nine months of an average wage), which did not have to be repaid if said couple eventually had four children. In 1934 alone, 250,000 loans were issued. Styled after army distinctions and categorised like Olympic medals, the Honour Cross of the German Mother ceremonies would take place on Hitler's mother's birthday (12 August). By 1944, 4.7 million birth medals had been awarded. A bronze for four children, a silver for six and a gold for eight.

This obsession with increasing birth rates was coupled with other policies, like restrictions on access to contraception and abortions. The Nazis envisioned a new world order that involved huge German territorial expansion, and in which the Reich would need as many Aryans as possible to occupy these lands. Maternity homes were created for the wives of SS officers so they could be as comfortable as possible in the later stages of pregnancy.

Despite the emphasis on the importance of traditional family values, from 1935 the Lebensborn programme sought to accelerate the desire for more Nazi babies, successfully orchestrating the births of approximately 11,000 children by 1944. Women would apply to participate and could only be approved once they'd passed extensive health and 'racial purity' tests. They would be 'introduced' to SS men and, once pregnant, the women would stay in the maternity homes until they gave birth. Two weeks later they would leave, and their child would be adopted and raised by a suitable Aryan couple. During the war 'desirable' children were kidnapped from Nazi-occupied countries and either placed in German boarding schools or adopted.

Education was a key means by which the Nazis indoctrinated the younger generations. School subjects were twisted to maximise Nazi messaging in surprising ways. You might wonder, how could a subject like Maths be used to brainwash students? The Nazis used 'social arithmetic' to emphasise Nazi ideology, by, for example, asking students to work out the cost of keeping a mentally ill patient in an asylum, and then comparing that with how many marriage loans it equated to. History was used to place the blame for Germany's defeat in the First World War on Jewish people, while Biology was used to essentially teach eugenics, with students taught to 'identify' the features of non-Aryans. Such beliefs were influenced by writers like

Hans F.K. Günther, whose nickname 'Rassenpapst', meaning 'Race Pope', leaves little to the imagination. Aryans from northern and western Europe were seen as 'Übermenschen', meaning master or superior race. Gunther argued that Nordic Aryans with blond hair and blue eyes were the most supreme of all the Aryans, while Western Aryans, like Hitler, were still Aryans, but without the blond hair. Such race theories viewed non-Aryans as 'Untermenschen', or sub-human, including, but not exclusive to, Slavs (Eastern Europeans), Black people, Gypsies and Jewish people.

Of the 13 million people who were systematically murdered by the Nazis, the most prominent victims were Jewish people. Anti-Semitism was enshrined in Nazi political policy from the very start, starting with small changes like excluding Jewish people from jobs such as the civil service and participating in social activities like choirs and sports clubs. In 1935 the Nuremberg Laws formalised that Jewish people were no longer 'citizens' of Germany. Signs saying 'Jews not wanted here' became more frequent in public spaces, and Germans who chose to continue their relationships with Jewish people found themselves humiliated, sometimes having their heads shaved in public.

It wasn't just Jewish people who were punished for what the Nazis viewed as 'racial defilement'. Born in German East Africa, Bayume Mohamed Husen was the son a Sudanese soldier. Husen was a child soldier in the First World War and was living in Berlin by 1929, where he worked at the university alongside starring as an actor in over twenty German films. In 1941 he was imprisoned at Sachsenhausen concentration camp when it was discovered he was in a relationship with a German woman. He died three years later.

The leisure time of pupils was also controlled by the Nazis via the Hitler Youth, where children were divided into different groups according to age and gender. Despite initial enthusiasm, many grew tired of the military drills and strict discipline. For some it was specific events that were the last straw. Helmuth Hübener was born into a Mormon family based in Hamburg. He joined the Hitler Youth, but quit at the age of thirteen in the wake of the increasing anti-Semitism in 1938. In 1941 he discovered a radio his half-brother had brought back from

France and started listening to BBC broadcasts. He made leaflets based on the information he was hearing in the hope they would persuade the population at large to resist the Nazis. Unfortunately, Helmuth was arrested by the Gestapo on charges of treason. When asked if he had anything to say at the end of the trial, he looked squarely at the judges and simply said, 'Wait. Your time will come.' He was beheaded at the age of seventeen, becoming the youngest person to be sentenced to death and executed by the Nazis.

As well as enacting various domestic policies to try to control the nation, Hitler was aided by events on the international stage. The decision to allow Hitler to take the Sudetenland was negotiated under the Munich Agreement, epitomising the policy of appeasement that had allowed him to consistently and very publicly snub Versailles at the cost of avoiding another world war. It was hoped that this was where his ambitions ended. Hitler agreed not to take any further European territory, while Prime Minister Neville Chamberlain infamously landed amid cheering crowds. In parliament he declared that this was 'peace for our time'. Churchill, on the other hand, called it, 'A disaster of the first magnitude,' sharing his view that Hitler's ambitions would eventually look westwards to France and Britain, and ending his speech with the eerie warning that, 'This is only the beginning of the reckoning.'

The month following the Munich Agreement was when Kristallnacht – the Night of Broken Glass – took place. This pogrom took place across 10 and 11 November, not only in Germany but across territory the Nazis had occupied earlier that year, namely Austria and areas of the Sudetenland in Czechoslovakia. The Nazis had already reoccupied the Rhineland in 1936, also forbidden by the Treaty of Versailles. Similarly, fascist leader Mussolini had managed to gain control of Abyssinia (Ethiopia). Rioters attacked synagogues and other Jewish institutions, thousands of businesses were looted, and up to 30,000 Jewish men were rounded up and placed in local prisons and concentration camps. The German Jewish community were blamed for the pogrom and were fined a billion Reichsmark (at the time approximately $400 million) to cover the damages.

It's worth noting that it was incredibly difficult for Jewish people to emigrate from Germany under Nazi rule, with huge emigration taxes making it economically impossible for many. This became even more challenging from 1939, when they were prevented from taking any valuables with them. It's no coincidence that less than a month after Kristallnacht, the first 200 of what would eventually be 10,000 Jewish children travelled to Britain via the Kindertransport system.

One child who moved to Britain was sixteen-year-old Ernst Fraenkel, aboard a Kindertransport from Germany. He arrived via Holland and settled with the Forrester family in Lancashire, having lodged with another family prior to this. He attended the local grammar school, unsurprisingly winning the school German prize in his first year. Thankfully, Ernst was able to return to Germany after the war and be reunited with his mother, who insisted that he attend the ballroom dancing lessons he'd missed out on while in England. Ernst eventually settled in London, becoming an eminent international businessman. He stayed in touch with the Forresters, with his host mother insisting on frequently sending him home-knitted socks, long after he'd reached adulthood. Ernst never forgot their kindness and hospitality and bequeathed some money to them in his will. His two children and five grandchildren are still in touch with them, with history bonding these two families together well into the 21st century. I first heard about Ernst through his grandson Matt, who has worked alongside me in the History department for over a decade.

1939: The outbreak of war, again

On 3 September 1939, Neville Chamberlain announced on the BBC, 'This country is at war with Germany.' By June 1940 the Nazi flag was hoisted symbolically over the Palace of Versailles, the very place Germany had been punished so brutally after the First World War. Nazi soldiers also climbed up the Eiffel Tower, although the first flag they secured had to be replaced, as it blew away almost immediately. Unlike Britain and France, Germany had been fully prepared for war, hence their Blitzkrieg ('lightning war') tactics meant they easily swept through Poland, Denmark, Norway, the Netherlands, Belgium and eventually France using a combination of attacks on land and from the air.

In May 1940, soldiers from the British and French armies had been pushed to the port of Dunkirk, surrounded by the Nazis. Operation Dynamo was the codename given to the decision to try to evacuate these men from the beaches and bring them back to Britain. Some 338,226 soldiers were rescued from Dunkirk between 26 May and 3 June, and approximately 900 vessels were commandeered for the task, from passenger ships to hopper barges and fishing fleets. Weapons and equipment had to be left behind, many of which were then used by the Germans, including 64,000 vehicles.

Among those who were rescued was Jemadar Maula Dad Khan, who received the Indian Distinguished Service Medal because he 'showed magnificent courage, coolness and decision', while being shelled from the ground and bombed from the air, which resulted in his contingent losing no men or animals. Jemadar serves as an important reminder that there were soldiers from across the empire supporting British soldiers from the very start of this war, including approximately 615 Indian soldiers present on the beaches at Dunkirk. They would not have been the only brown faces at Dunkirk, given that the French Army included soldiers from Morocco, Tunisia and Algeria. Some 2.5 million Indians would go on to serve during the Second World War, the largest volunteer army in history, with 24,000 killed and 64,000 wounded.

Just like in the First World War, Indian soldiers' diets were accommodated, with halal meat, ghee and the rogue addition of marmite included in their rations. The music we associate most with this war is probably the songs of Vera Lynn, particularly 'We'll Meet Again'. However, there were other musical sounds to be heard across the different theatres of war. In France in 1940 the beats of a dhol would have rung out as Indian soldiers performed bhangra, a traditional dance originating in Punjab, in front of huge crowds. In June 1941, the sounds of the Maori performing the haka would have been heard at a training camp in Egypt as a welcome for visiting British royals. Altogether there were 3,600 Maori soldiers who fought in this war, and they became the most decorated of all the New Zealand battalions.

Operation Sealion is thwarted

As much as the rescues from Dunkirk were celebrated, it meant that the Nazis now occupied all of France. Hitler now looked across the Channel and started making plans. Don't be fooled by its cutesy name; Operation Sealion was now on, a full-scale invasion of Britain, but Hitler knew this would not be possible without removing the threat of Britain's RAF first. No one had successfully invaded Britain since William the Conqueror in 1066, making it even more poetic that the RAF pilots were referred to as 'knights on wings'.

In July 1940, the Battle of Britain began. Throughout that summer the skies were filled with British Hurricanes and Spitfires fighting against the Luftwaffe's Messerschmitts. The range of nations involved in the Allied fight against the Nazis is really epitomised by the pilots involved, with the RAF's 145 squadron including men from Argentina, Australia, Belgium, Canada, Czechoslovakia, Britain, New Zealand, Poland, South Africa – and, by the end of the war, Trinidad and the United States.

The first set of Polish pilots arrived here in December 1939, and their first priority was language lessons, as Polish and British officers trying to converse with each other in French just wasn't going to cut it! Wing Commander Antoni Glowacki fled from Warsaw in September 1939 and escaped to Romania after the collapse of Poland. He made his way to France and was soon in Britain training with the RAF. He shot down his first enemy plane on 15 August, and on 24 August he became the first 'one-day ace' after shooting down five German planes over Ramsgate.

Pilots like Antoni would not have been able to succeed in the air had it not been for a huge amount of support on the ground, or, more specifically, underground. Radar meant enemy aircraft could be located, and it was nicknamed the Dowding System. RAF Fighter Command set up a secret bunker at RAF Uxbridge to make the crucial decisions about which squadrons to send into the sky and when. Eighty per cent of the staff in the bunker were women who worked for the Women's Air Auxiliary Force (WAAF), and in total there were 180,300 women in the WAAF during the war.

Three members of the WAAF were awarded military medals in November 1940 for showing extraordinary bravery. Sergeant Joan Mortimer, Flight Officer Elspeth Henderson and Sergeant Helen Turner all carried on with their duties despite the fact that their RAF station in Biggin Hill was under attack by the Luftwaffe. Elspeth and Helen continued to keep in contact with RAF Uxbridge, understanding that without their continued correspondence the pilots in the air would be flying blind. Joan was in the armoury when it was hit by a bomb. Despite being surrounded by explosives, she continued to send messages to the defence posts around the airfields and even placed red flags to mark wherever she saw an unexploded bomb.

By 1943 there were seven million women working across all types of services, the least glamorous of which were those in the Women's Land Army who specialised in rat-catching. These anti-vermin squads were specially trained to also kill foxes, rabbits and moles, all of which were a threat to food supplies. One pair of 'land girls' apparently killed 12,00 rats in just one year.

Lilian Bader was born in Liverpool in 1917 to an Irish mother and a Barbadian father who had served in the First World War, and she subsequently faced discrimination throughout her life. When the Second World War broke out, Lilian took up employment with the Navy, Army and Air Force Institutes (NAAFI), at Catterick Camp, Yorkshire. When an official discovered her father's heritage, Lilian was asked to leave. Undeterred, Lilian heard of a group of West Indians who had been rejected by the army but accepted by the RAF. Lilian enlisted in the Women's Auxiliary Air Force (WAAF) in 1941, recounting that she was 'the only coloured person in this sea of white faces'. Lilian trained as an instrument repairer and, in December 1941, she became a Leading Aircraftwoman (LACW), soon gaining the rank of acting corporal.

It wasn't only women on Britain's home front who were contributing to the war effort. In India, women were drafted into similar auxiliary corps organisations, such as Second Officer Kalyani Sen, who joined the Women's Royal Indian Naval Service (WRINs). These women did very similar jobs to the WRNs in Britain, including clerical duties, decoding and military maintenance. The key difference lay in their uniform, with the WRINs in white or navy saris.

Just like the Brits, Indians had to get used to accommodating foreign soldiers as the war went on, with a Coca-Cola plant in Karachi in operation from 1942 to quench the thirst of American troops. In 1942, tea-planters were told that their labourers were now to be used for the war effort, and were set the task of building three major roads to link India and Burma. While some had pickaxes, others had to cut by hand. Most slept on the ground at night, praying they'd be safe from rockfalls. Despite it being made illegal in 1937, by the end of the war 22,517 Indian women worked underground in coal mines, something British women hadn't done since 1842. Fatal accidents cost the lives of over 900 women, and despite the British government receiving many letters in protest of using female labourers in such dangerous conditions, the practice continued, as coal was seen as being essential to the war effort. Pregnant women worked into their ninth month of pregnancy and often went back to work just four weeks after giving birth.

Radar technology and the increasing number of German losses meant Hitler paused on Operation Sealion, as it became increasingly clear the RAF were not to be defeated. On 16 August, Churchill famously said, 'Never in the field of human conflict was so much owed by so many to so few.' It's worth noting that those 'few' included approximately 3,000 pilots in Fighter Command who came from across fifteen different nations, including Poland, Czechoslovakia, Canada and New Zealand, as well as the countless women who contributed. Hitler decided a new tactic was needed: he was going to bomb Britain until they surrendered. Welcome to the Blitz.

The Blitz takes hold

The RAF had lost 800 pilots in the Battle of Britain, leading to a decision to seek out pilots from across the rest of the empire. In order to do this, the colour bar, which had prevented those not of 'European descent' from becoming officers, was lifted. Twenty-two-year-old Mahinder Singh Pujji saw an advert in an Indian newspaper and decided to respond, as flying was a childhood hobby of his, despite his parents' concerns for his safety. Mahinder became a trailblazer in more ways than one. He completed his fighter pilot training at Uxbridge and asked if he could fly while wearing his turban; as such he was granted the use of modified headgear. He kept a spare one with him, but he was so paranoid that he might end up being captured that he made a request for turbans to be parachuted behind enemy lines if he was taken prisoner.

During an interview he gave after the war he said his padded turban saved his life when his plane crash-landed near Dover. He served as a pilot in three major theatres of war, in France, North Africa and Burma, providing a stark reminder of how truly global this war was. In North Africa he was allowed to fly to Cairo every weekend so he could 'have a decent meal', as he was avoiding bully beef at all costs. He personalised his aircraft with the name Amrit, his fiancée, with whom he would go on to have three children after the war.

Ulric Cross from Trinidad joined the RAF in 1941 at the age of 24. After twelve days' travel across the Atlantic he started his training in Lincolnshire, noting that he'd 'never heard four-letter words used so frequently'. Ulric flew countless missions over Nazi Germany and occupied Europe. He was awarded the Distinguished Service Order in 1944 for his 'immense value', and he would go on to have a distinguished legal and political career.

You probably remember learning about the Blitz in primary school, and you may even have visited a shelter where you were no doubt played air-raid sirens. If you were really lucky, you might even have dressed up as an evacuee, with your own cardboard-and-string gas-mask box. London was infamously bombed every night (bar one) for an eleven-week period. Major cities across the country were targets, including Plymouth, Bristol, Swansea, Glasgow and Coventry, and 43,000 civilians were killed during the Blitz, with a further 139,000 injured. Millions built bomb shelters in their gardens, while thousands of Londoners sought refuge in the Underground stations, with tracks concreted over and bunks and toilets fitted across 79 stations. Special 'refreshment' trains would travel through the Underground filled with culinary delights like hot soup, meat pies, sausages and, of course, tea. But while there were snacks, concerts and film showings, life in the Underground was tough. 'Shelter throat' became a common ailment, due to a lack of adequate ventilation, and in 1940, 67 people were killed at Balham station when a bomb detonated above it, which then caused the roof of the underground tunnels to collapse. The resulting ruptured piping meant the platforms soon started filling with water and sewage.

In order to make it more difficult for enemy bombers to locate their targets, evening blackouts were now customary, meaning street lights were switched off. Unfortunately, this meant that the 88 bus did not see the huge crater now in the middle of Balham High Road, thus creating one of the most harrowing images on the Blitz. Thankfully, those passengers were able to climb out of the crater unharmed, but many underground were not. The youngest victim was four-year-old Michael Ravening, while the oldest was Roy Dibble, who was 97.

In 1943 disaster struck at Bethnal Green station, although this was not caused directly by bombs, but by the panic they generated. At 8.17pm on 3 March, an air-raid siren sounded. A human crush ensued as one person lost their footing, causing others to fall too, and 173 people were killed, including 62 children. Reports of the tragedy were censored at the time, and details were only publicly acknowledged 50 years later. The Bethnal Green Tube Disaster was the UK's largest single loss of civilian life during the Second World War.

The Blitz was over by May 1941, but this did not mean the bombing was over. From spring 1942 the Luftwaffe started bombing historic towns and cities across Britain, starting with Exeter. These attacks came to be known as the Baedeker raids, and were in retaliation for the RAF bombing of the historic German city of Lubeck. The Nazis allegedly chose their targets according to which buildings were given three stars in the Baedeker guide, the famous German guidebook first published in the 1850s. This incessant bombing meant the home front was affected at every level. Children were evacuated, along with some teachers, pregnant women and 7,000 blind and disabled people. Over 1.5 million men who weren't in the army joined the Home Guard on a part-time basis. Their job was to protect their local area from possible attacks. Famously, they weren't given weapons so had to improvise, using anything from golf clubs to knives attached to broomsticks.

The Auxiliary Ambulance Service also continued with their vital support across the home front. They actually had an 'Indian section', which was organised by Mr Dorai Ross, who managed to convince Indians from all over London to pitch in, including doctors and barristers. The image of two of the female volunteers dressed in saris was used as part of a series called 'On War Work in Britain', which sought to publicise how different people from across the empire were helping out on the home front. Other images included 'A Hindu Makes a Camera Gun', featuring Mr M. Kar, originally from Bengal, and 'A Volunteer from British Guiana', featuring Private Diana Williams wearing khaki overalls while retreading a tyre in a depot in the Midlands. Thankfully the two Indian ladies have tin hats on, unlike at the start of the war when some wardens had to don pudding basins as protective headgear.

Another crucial volunteer service was the 1.4 million-strong Air Raid Precautions (ARP). Volunteers had to attend lectures and were given textbooks about aerial warfare, as well as physical, practical training. One such warden was Ita Ekpenyon, a teacher from Nigeria who moved to London in 1928 to study law. During his time as a warden in Marylebone, he put out fires, rescued people and gave first aid. He also had to keep order in the shelters, and on occasion encountered racism and had to intervene, such as when a minority of shelters tried to prevent foreign nationals from entering, telling them instead to 'go back' to their own countries. His argument that 'friendliness, co-operation and comradeship' should take precedent when facing a common enemy showed that he had a way with words, something the BBC noticed too. He wrote and broadcast a series for them called *Calling West Africa*, which aimed to boost morale in that part of the empire via the BBC Empire Service.

Despite their very different backgrounds, Ita's story parallels that of Princess Indira Devi. She was born in India in 1912 to Paramjit Singh and Brinda Devi of Kapurthala. She moved to London in 1935, partly to avoid an arranged marriage, but mostly to realise her dream of becoming a movie star. Unlike in 1914, women on the home front from 1939 were conscripted into war work. Princess Devi worked as an ambulance driver, which as we've already seen from the 88 bus, was particularly dangerous during the Blitz. She was also a postal censor, ensuring sensitive information wasn't being communicated, as well as ensuring letters did not contain anything that could negatively impact morale. In 1942 she joined the BBC and, much like Ita, hosted a radio show aimed at Indian soldiers stationed in the Middle East and Mediterranean. There is a fabulous photograph of her posing with a BBC microphone while wearing a sari. She went on to work for the BBC until 1968.

The encouraging, authentic and morale-boosting voices of Ita and Princess Devi formed the foundation of what we now know as the BBC World Service. Jamaican-born Una Marston was part of this too, becoming the first Black woman to be employed by the BBC during the Second World War as a producer for *Calling the West Indies*, a programme that read out messages from soldiers to their families back home. Who knows, perhaps they crossed paths at the BBC and found solace in the fact that they were all far from home, but they got stuck in to protecting the British home front, embodying the Blitz spirit the nation remains so proud of.

Churchill's Secret Army

In 1940 the war was clearly not going well for Britain, so it was time for a different type of warfare – one that was 'ungentlemanly', secretive and dangerous. From two inconspicuous flats near Baker Street in London, the Special Operations Executive (SOE) was born. Sometimes referred to as Churchill's Secret Army, the SOE worked outside the regular parameters of the armed forces and intelligence services, aiming to use subversion and sabotage to undermine and infiltrate the Nazis and their Axis allies from within.

For example, in 1942 twelve agents were parachuted into Greece and teamed up with the Greek resistance to blow up the Gorgopotamos Bridge, which was vital to Nazi supply lines. This team included two New Zealanders (Captain Tom Barnes and Arthur Edmonds) and Lieutenant Inderjit Singh Gill, agents which reflected the make-up of the empire. Operation Harling saw the Greeks successfully distract the (mostly Italian) guards while the SOE agents laid down the explosives that were being carried by mules. The mission was a complete success, although it could easily have gone awry had one of the agents not stopped some local children from ingesting the explosives. They had mistaken them for fudge!

If you think this is all starting to sound a little bit James Bond then you're spot on. Ian Fleming was inspired to write about 007's international escapades based on his fascination with these incredible men and women. The scope of the SOE reflected the global nature of the war. Despite most agents serving in France (1,800 of them were dispatched there between May 1941 and September 1944), there were spies sent to every major theatre of war, from Burma to Ethiopia, across more than twenty countries. Recruits were from a huge variety of backgrounds: from those with military links, like Italian deserter and part-time champion skier Pierre Dareme, who made it to training in Britain via Cairo and Lagos, to French-born dress-maker Vera Leigh. Both agents were eventually captured and killed by the Nazis, which was sadly the fate for so many of the SOE.

This dangerous work required intensive training, which mostly took place in secluded country mansions commandeered by the SOE's head of training and operations, Colonel Colin Gubbins. It was in these rather grandiose properties that agents were taught key skills, like street fighting, how to derail a train and conduct 'silent kills', and how to get yourself out of handcuffs as quickly as possible. One key skill was making keys, something that came in handy for Robert Sheppard, who did so using a bar of soap, which allowed him to escape from Nazi-occupied France. There were gruelling physical tasks like assault courses, as well as mental challenges such as fake interrogations and memory recall. Keeping your cover story while under duress would have been particularly challenging if you'd been seized from your bed in the middle of the night.

Overall, 35 per cent of recruits didn't pass the training. Amazingly, Jacques Ledoux was not put off, despite being hospitalised in his fourth week of training, when he fell fifteen feet while failing to negotiate a particularly challenging obstacle. Jacques died at the age of 23 from the horrific injuries he sustained from being tortured by the Nazis. Prior to this, he somehow still mustered the strength to leap from a train in an attempt to escape his captors. Evidently the SOE was not for the faint of heart.

SOE agents were supported by an enormous network of different departments. Blending in was key, meaning the SOE sourced a huge amount of clothes from second-hand shops and refugees in order to make agents look as authentic as possible. By 1944, the SOE were dispensing 90,000 pieces of clothing a year. Everything from hair styles to make-up had to be adapted to fit in with the area the agents would be working in. Zips, stitches and collars used in different regions were researched, and SOE tailors and seamstresses would actually wear newly made clothes at work in order to make them look more worn, as a new suit would arouse suspicion in Nazi-occupied Europe. Sandpaper and Vaseline were also used to make clothes appear lived in, and dentists even replaced fillings with gold ones, as this was customary in France at the time.

If one of your childhood memories involves browsing through the Argos catalogue then you'll be pleased to know there was an SOE version called 'Special Devices and Supplies'. The items in the catalogue shed light on the vast range of activities these agents were involved in, as well as highlighting how inventive the personnel were behind the scenes. The ability to discreetly carry messages was crucial, which is why 'double shell' items were produced. While these may have looked like innocent tubes of toothpaste, shaving cream and lipstick, they would in fact be fitted with secret chambers to hold vital information. Silk maps were another feat of the SOE – not only could they tolerate rainy weather, but they could also be folded to be very compact and, vitally, did not make a noise when unfurled. Silk maps were smuggled into POW camps hidden in Monopoly game boxes. Full stops would be added to place names on the boards as clues for which POW needed it. Some 33,000 British, Commonwealth and US servicemen escaped from enemy territory, and many of them no doubt used these maps to show them how to get back into Allied territory.

Sabotage was a key part of life as an SOE agent, and there was a plethora of items available to help you get the job done. Some agents opted to carry a tube of popular German suntan lotion, which in fact contained a cream that could frost clear glass in five minutes, particularly useful when used on Gestapo agent windscreens. Some took sabotage to an intimate level, smuggling itching power to laundry-women working in German Army camps, or, even more cleverly, to sex workers in brothels frequented by German soldiers.

Explosives came in all shapes and sizes, from exploding excrement modelled on cow pats or camel dung, depending on the location, which would explode when driven over, to detonators hidden in bottles of red wine (Chianti, to be precise). Explosives were also hidden in rat carcasses, which would then be placed in German factories in the hope that they'd be swept into furnaces, causing both a literal explosion and a blow to the German war effort. It's unknown whether these rats did in fact lead to any explosions, but they were considered a success by the SOE, as the Germans then spent so much time trying to find them.

Agents were, of course, also given weapons that could kill, such as the self-explanatory sleeve gun with a range of three yards. Of course, the Gestapo had similar devices of their own. Jacques Ledoux had his identity assumed by a Gestapo officer who wanted to infiltrate the resistance. When challenged by an SOE agent, the fake Jacques shot him with a small gun disguised as a fountain pen.

More chillingly, L tablets, otherwise known as cyanide pills, were also distributed to agents. They could be concealed in a ring or even a tooth filling, and were often covered in a coating that led to no harm unless it was chewed. The distribution of these suicide pills to SOE agents reminds us of the courage and determination these men and women showed; they knew full well what was at risk and showed extraordinary bravery.

The first female agent to be sent to France was American Virginia Hall, though her cover name was Brigitte le Contre and her codename was Germaine. She posed as a journalist for the *New York Post*, and she was able to establish a network of resistance fighters and organise jailbreaks for captured agents. By late 1942 she sensed danger and opted to escape the Nazis by trekking through the Pyrenees. This would have been challenging enough for anyone, let alone someone with a prosthetic leg (called Cuthbert) caused by a hunting accident before the war. Before she left she sent a message to the SOE, saying that she hoped Cuthbert would not trouble her on the way. The SOE did not understand the reference and replied, 'If Cuthbert troublesome, eliminate him.' Hall then returned to London, and her work directly led to the liberation of large parts of France. She became the only civilian woman in the war to receive the Distinguished Service Cross for 'extraordinary heroism'.

Like many women who were recruited into the SOE, Noor Inayat Khan was essentially talent spotted while working for the WAAF. Born to a white American mother and an Indian father with family ties to Tipu Sultan, Noor's family had fled from France at the start of the war. An accomplished writer and fluent in French, English and Russian, Noor was also a talented wireless operator, skills the SOE desperately needed in the field. Noor began her training in Hampshire and was flown into France in June 1943 as the first female wireless operator, before her training was fully complete. This was despite one training report stating: 'It is very doubtful whether she is really suited to the work in the field.'

In 1943 an operator's life expectancy was six weeks. Her key role was to maintain links between the circuit in the field and London, sending and receiving messages about planned sabotage operations, for example. Under the codename Madeleine, she worked alongside the Prosper network, whom the Gestapo soon started closing in on. Eventually her radio became the only one still active, and she refused to leave Paris as advised, knowing that without her all communication would be lost. She was seized by the Gestapo, but like so many SOE agents, and in spite of what some thought of her back in the training camp, she fought back furiously, attempting two escapes, during one of which she ended up on the window ledge of a five-storey building, having demanded that the Nazis let her have a bath. Noor was deemed a 'dangerous' prisoner and was treated brutally by the Nazis, but she never gave away any intel.

She was held in solitary confinement and was eventually taken to Dachau, alongside three other female agents, Madeleine Damerment, Eliane Plewman and Yolande Beekman. All of them were executed before their bodies were cremated. Noor was just 30. An SS guard recorded that her last word was *'liberté'*, the French word for freedom. Noor was posthumously awarded the George Cross in 1949, and a French Croix de Guerre. There is also a bronze bust of her in Gordon Square, Bloomsbury, the first memorial in Britain to either a Muslim or Asian woman, somewhere I visit annually to lay flowers on behalf of my students. There is also now a blue plaque for Noor at 4 Taviton Street in Bloomsbury, where she stayed in 1942–3. Noor's story is one of courage and resilience; she was a true inspiration who gave her life for Britain, and she is someone I always think of on Remembrance Day.

The teenagers who stood up to Hitler

As the Blitz came to an end, the Nazis turned their attention to the USSR. Despite the Nazi–Soviet Pact, the two were not genuine allies, and the Nazis in particular saw this as a temporary peace to avoid a war on two fronts. With western Europe largely dealt with, on 22 June 1941, the Nazi invasion of the Soviet Union, known as Operation Barbarossa, began. Despite Germany's successes at the start of this new phase of the war, ultimately Operation Barbarossa failed. Lack of supplies, harsh conditions and fierce resistance all played their part. The Soviet counterattack in January 1942, as the Germans edged closer to Moscow, saw Germany's first land defeat of the war. Another crushing blow to the Germans on the Eastern Front was their defeat at Stalingrad in February 1943, the first time German field armies had surrendered during this war.

Meanwhile, back in Germany, some people had become uneasy with the war effort, particularly following the debacle on the Eastern Front. In Munich, a group of teenagers began distributing several sets of resistance leaflets in the hope that their fellow students would join them in rising up against the Nazis and sabotaging the war effort, as, 'We have grown up in a state of ruthless gagging of any free expression of opinion.' They managed to develop a network of supporters who helped them to spread their ideas across the country.

Unfortunately, while distributing the pamphlets at the University of Munich, they were spotted by a caretaker. Three of the White Rose group were arrested initially, with three other members arrested later. One of the resistors was Sophie Scholl, who insisted on joining the group once she discovered that her older brother Hans was already a member. When they were arrested he attempted to swallow the draft of the seventh leaflet he had on him. Sophie, Hans and Christopher Probst were put on trial but were not permitted to defend themselves. All three were beheaded. Sophie was just 21 years old. One of their leaflets was smuggled in to the UK after the trial, and the words of the White Rose were subsequently reprinted and dropped in their millions by the RAF all over Germany.

The tide was turning, but it came at a cost. The Nazis initially swept through the USSR having used 80 per cent of their army, and soon got to the USSR's second-largest city. The 872-day siege of Leningrad, which started in January 1941, led to the deaths of over a million people, the costliest siege in human history. The winter brought plunging temperatures of -30°C. The Nazis sought to cut off supplies to the city; with a meagre 125g daily ration of bread (equivalent to a bar of soap), residents had to resort to unfathomable means to feed themselves. Leather belts were boiled to make edible jelly, wallpaper paste was consumed for its potato content and you can only imagine the fate that awaited household pets like cats and dogs. The city police created an entire division to deal with cannibalism; no wonder parents did not let their children out at night. The term 'desperate times call for desperate measures' has never rung truer. The siege was lifted in 1944 when Soviet forces pushed the German Army away from the city.

Operation Overlord marked the beginning of the end for the Nazis

Meanwhile, in the West, an invasion plan was in the works, called Operation Overlord. The aim? To free occupied Europe from the Nazis. This was supported by troops from more than twelve countries, including the USA, who officially entered the war in December 1941 after the Japanese launched a surprise attack on the American naval base of Pearl Harbour, killing 2,235 American troops.

Over two million American servicemen would eventually pass through Britain during the Second World War. Subsequently, by June 1944, there were 130,000 Black GIs in Britain. These troops were segregated from their white counterparts. With no such rules in Britain, there were 44 violent incidents reported on British soil between white and African American troops between November 1943 and February 1944. One notorious incident was in a pub near Bamber Bridge in Lancashire, which led to the death of Black soldier Private William Crossland.

Brits opened up their homes to their American guests, possibly in the hope that they'd be rewarded with highly sought-after gifts from across the pond in the shape of Coca-Cola and nylon stockings. It's estimated that there were 90,000 marriages between British women and American, Canadian and Polish soldiers as a result of this wartime mingling. American troops in Britain were issued with a booklet called 'A Short Guide to Great Britain'. Tips included knowing that the British don't like showing off or hearing criticism of the king, but do enjoy drinking warm beer, as sacrilegious as that may seem. My favourite is: 'The British don't know how to make a good cup of coffee. You don't know how to make a good cup of tea. It's an even swap.'

The coastline of north-west Europe was heavily defended by the Atlantic Wall. Great care was taken by the architects of Operation Overlord to deceive the Germans into thinking the attack was going to take place at Calais. Such a ruse was supported by a huge intelligence operation (codename: Bodyguard) that allowed the real location of Normandy to be kept a secret.

The codebreakers of Bletchley Park in Buckinghamshire played a key role in this, as they'd broken Enigma, the German secret coding system. The mathematician Alan Turing had worked alongside Gordon Welchman to create a machine called the Bombe, alongside other decryption methods which provided crucial intel for the Allies. Turing and his colleagues cracked German naval signals, which meant Allied convoys could now be kept a safe distance from German submarines. Women played a huge role here, making up one in three of the workers at Bletchley. Much like the WAAFs at Uxbridge, many of the WRNS (Women's Royal Naval Service) worked on the Bombe machines in eight-hour shifts.

Turing's achievements went beyond this too; the 'universal Turing machine' was the forerunner to the modern computer, and in 1950 he developed a test for artificial intelligence. In 1952, Turing was arrested for homosexuality, which was illegal in Britain at the time. He accepted a punishment of chemical castration and died by suicide in 1954. The contribution he made to the war effort and the scientific community at large was not fully known until the 1990s. His conviction was posthumously overturned in 2013. Just like the work of the SOE, it's widely acknowledged that the work of code-breakers like Turing shortened the length of the war, thus saving countless lives.

The second facet of the D-Day deception was the double-cross system, which involved the British intelligence services feeding false information to the Nazis via double agents. These included Juan Pujol Garcia, who fed the Germans extensive information that was so convincing they awarded him the Iron Cross. Garcia played a critical role in convincing the Germans that the 150,000-strong First United States Army Group (FUSAG) were preparing to attack Calais. Also known as the 'ghost army' of the Second World War, it was completely fictitious. The Germans still believed FUSAG existed even several months after the D-Day landings. MI5 went to great lengths to support this fake news, including creating radio chatter and 'leaking' that the highly respected American General Patton was their commander. For all his efforts, Garcia was also awarded an MBE, making him the only person to have received such prestigious recognition from both Britain and Nazi Germany. After the war, Garcia was so concerned of German reprisals that he faked his own death and lived in relative anonymity in Venezuela till his death in 1988.

Another agent was Elvira Chaudoir, the daughter of a Peruvian diplomat, who was recruited by MI5 despite their concerns that she might be an easy target for blackmail due to her 'lesbian tendencies' and her excessive heiress party lifestyle. In the lead-up to D-Day, she fed information to the Nazis, via letters written in secret ink, that there was an American army in Kent preparing for an imminent assault on Calais. Alongside tales of the FUSAG, dummy landing craft and inflatable tanks were placed near Dover to further support the deception. Aluminium strips were dropped by Allied aircraft to dupe German radar into thinking there was a fleet on the move. Dummy paratroopers were dropped to distract the Germans from Normandy, supported by special forces equipped with sonographers, which even broadcast the sound of soldiers' voices.

All of this preparation meant that on 5 June 1944, 175,000 men, a fleet of 5,000 ships and landing craft, 50,000 vehicles, and 11,000 planes sat in southern England ready to attack Normandy, across the Channel. On 6 June, thousands of paratroopers landed behind enemy lines. By dawn, the Normandy coastline was the scene of five separate beach assaults, code-named Utah, Omaha, Gold, Juno and Sword. Soldiers had to run across the beaches under heavy fire while trying to avoid snipers, shells and mines. The beaches were secure by nightfall, at the cost of 4,000 Allied lives.

One of the soldiers who survived was Ramsay Bader, the husband of Lilian Bader, who joined the WAAF earlier in this chapter. He was of mixed English and Sierra Leonean heritage, and he had been motivated to fight when he saw Hitler's treatment of African American sprinter Jesse Owens at the 1936 Olympics. It was after D-Day that the 761st Tank Battalion, the first African American armoured unit entered combat; they were also known as the Black Panthers.

The Nazis tried desperately to continue with their Axis propaganda campaign, with some specifically aimed at African American troops. Mildred Gillars, also known as Axis Sally, was born in Ohio but moved to Germany in the 1930s. A career in radio led her to voice wartime broadcasts from Berlin, including *Home Sweet Home*, which deliberately aimed to make American troops paranoid by constantly talking about how their sweethearts back home could not be trusted. Some programmes deliberately targeted the 761st, with Sally imploring them to defect, as this was a white man's war, not theirs. After the war she was charged with treason against the American government and was served a thirteen-year prison sentence. The 761st took no mind of her broadcasts, though; they fought for 183 days straight across six countries in Europe. They achieved various accolades, including eleven Silver Stars, but it wasn't until 1978 that President Jimmy Carter belatedly recognised the Black Panthers' contribution by giving the 761st a Presidential Unit Citation for extraordinary heroism.

D-Day marked the beginning of the end of the war for the Nazis, as the Allies now had a foothold in Europe. Some Germans tried to quicken the end of the war through risky means. Colonel von Stauffenberg and his conspirators orchestrated an assassination attempt on Hitler as part of Operation Valkyrie. This got tantalisingly close to succeeding, but the briefcase containing the bomb was moved at the last minute, meaning a conference table leg shielded most people in the room when it detonated, including Hitler.

Meanwhile, in France, the Allies had taken back Paris in August 1944 and the Nazis struggled to cope with a war they now faced on two fronts, something they'd tried so hard to avoid. In April 1945 the Allies entered Berlin. Hitler died by suicide in his bunker in Berlin on 30 April. He had married his long-term partner Eva Braun the day before. At approximately 3.30pm, Hitler shot himself through the mouth while Braun had taken a suicide pill. As per Hitler's instructions, as he did not want his body strung to a lamppost like Mussolini, their bodies were burnt almost immediately. Goebbels and his wife Magda chose a similar fate, although not before they arranged for their six children to be poisoned in their beds.

The Holocaust

By the end of the Second World War in 1945, the Nazis had murdered approximately eleven million people, including Gypsies, gay people and communists. The Holocaust is the term given to remember the murder of the approximately six million Jewish men, women and children by the Nazis and their collaborators.

As we have already seen, prior to the outbreak of war, Jewish communities were severely persecuted within Nazi Germany and across every new territory they acquired. On 20 January 1942, fifteen high-ranking Nazis met at Wannsee House in Berlin to discuss the 'Jewish question'. One of the attendees was Adolf Eichmann, who had been in charge of organising deportations of Jewish people. He had estimated that there were now eleven million Jewish people in Europe. Previous suggestions had included forcibly moving Jewish people to Madagascar, which was abandoned in favour of concentrating Jewish people into ghettos. The largest ghetto in Nazi-occupied Poland was in Warsaw, and by March 1941 it had 445,000 inhabitants. Surrounded by a three-metre-high wall complete with barbed wire, the cramped and unsanitary conditions meant that 140,000 died in this ghetto in three years.

One of the reasons we know about the reality of life in the Warsaw ghetto is because of the secret archive created by Emanuel Ringelblum. Determined to create an accurate record, he collected everything from diaries, photos, art and newspapers to official decrees. He wrote in one of his diaries that 'we aspired to reveal the whole truth, as bitter as it may be'. The contents of the archive were hidden in milk churns, a third of which has still never been found. The archive reveals the terrible conditions as well as the determination of the archivists themselves to preserve this history. Despite escaping from a labour camp, their final hideout was discovered, and the Ringelblum family were murdered in March 1944.

Just as Emanuel wished to document life in the ghetto, the Nazis too wished to document the massacres they carried out. Faye Schulman was one of 26 Jewish people spared by the Nazis when they liquidated the Lenin ghetto in Belarus in 1942. Her skills as a photographer saved her; she was ordered by the Nazis to capture images, including of her family, now lying dead in a mass grave. She made secret copies for herself. Schulman eventually fled and joined the Molotova Brigade, who were mostly escaped Soviet POWs. She worked with them as a nurse, using saltwater as disinfectant and vodka as anaesthetic. She was even a surgeon at times, using an operating table made from branches. One particularly harrowing incident she recalled was when a fellow partisan was shot. She offered him drops of egg yolk to give him strength, but found that the yolk just ran out through the bullet hole in his neck.

She took hundreds of photographs of the resistance, often showing the partisans posing defiantly in the forest with their captured German weapons. She also captured events we have few records of, such as partisan funerals. She had to bury her camera to keep it safe, and she developed her photos under blankets. Faye survived the war, was reunited with her brother Moishe and married a fellow partisan, Morris. She passed away in 2021, at the age of 101. She's left us with a catalogue of incredible images of these resistance fighters. My favourite ones feature Faye herself in her matching leopard print coat and hat. There are many other examples, like those from April 1943 when 750 armed resistance fighters led by 23-year-old Mordecai Anielewicz started an uprising in the Warsaw ghetto, which held out for a month. Despite its eventual defeat, it inspired violent revolts in other ghettos.

Others resisted in other ways, like the amazing Irena Sendlerowa, a social worker who helped smuggle Jewish children out of the Warsaw ghetto and then placed them with Polish families or convents. She worked alongside the Zegota, an underground resistance network to support Polish Jews. Records show that she saved almost 2,500 children. She was arrested and tortured, but revealed nothing. On the day of her execution she was rescued by the Zegota, who had managed to bribe a Gestapo agent. She survived the war and died in 2008, at the age of 98.

It was after the start of Operation Barbarossa in June 1941 that the mass murder of Jewish people began in Eastern Europe, primarily carried out by the Einsatzgruppen, who were mobile killing units of SS men and local policemen. During the Nazi occupation of Ukraine in Kiev in September 1941, Jewish people were told to gather at the Babi Yar ravine under the instruction that they would be killed if they did not. Believing they were being resettled elsewhere, small groups were led into the ravine and shot. Some 33,771 people were massacred over the course of two days, and by the end of 1941, it's estimated that more than a million Jewish people had been murdered by these killing units.

The concern that mass shootings were having a negative psychological impact on those carrying them out led the Nazis to experiment with alternatives. They had already used poison gas to kill thousands of disabled children and adults, including 29-year-old Helene Melanie Lebel. She had been diagnosed with schizophrenia and was one of 9,772 people listed as being gassed at the Brandenburg centre in 1940.

In December 1941, mobile gas vans were first used near Chelmno in Poland. In January, Reinhard Heydrich led the discussions on how mass murder would be carried out moving forward. What followed was mass deportations to extermination camps in Nazi-occupied Poland. The name probably most associated with this horrific moment in history is Auschwitz. Originally built in October 1940 as a labour camp, it was here that experiments on prisoners were done using Zyklon B, a deadly rat poison. Later in 1941, the first site was overcrowded so a second site, Auschwitz-Birkenau, was built, this time intended to be an extermination camp. Gas chambers and crematoria were built within the complex, with the Nazis intending to use this as a main killing site due to its location and rail links. Ninety per cent of the 1.1 million people murdered here were Jewish. People from across Europe were transported here in cattle trucks via rail.

Once the unfortunate arrivals disembarked and were divided by gender, SS guards and doctors began selecting who was fit to work, while 75 per cent of those who arrived were informed that they were going for a shower. They were told to undress before being led into a large room designed to look like a large showering facility. Twenty minutes after the Zyklon B gas entered the room through the vents, everyone inside would be dead. Camp prisoners would remove the bodies so that they could then be burnt in the crematoria. Prior to this their hair, gold teeth and fillings would be removed.

Those selected by doctors may have been subjected to medical experimentation. Josef Mengele was the notorious doctor known as the 'Angel of Death'. He conducted lethal experiments, mostly on children, particularly Roma and Jewish twins. He also collected the eyes of his murdered victims. He was one of many Nazis who successfully fled to South America after the war, never to be brought to justice.

Those selected for forced labour had their heads shaved and clothes and belongings taken away. More than 100,000 pairs of shoes were found at Auschwitz when it was liberated, alongside 6,350 kilograms of human hair. Prisoners wore a striped uniform with an identification number and a coloured triangle to differentiate their status. For example, Jewish prisoners wore a variation of the yellow Star of David, while homosexual prisoners had a pink triangle and Romani Gypsies had a brown triangle.

Rudolf Brazda was the last-known concentration camp survivor to be specifically deported for being gay. In early 1930s Germany, Rudolf was open about his sexuality, living with his boyfriend Werner with the approval of his family. Once the Nazis were in power, they amended pre-existing laws, known as Paragraph 175, to persecute people for their sexual orientation. Fifty thousand gay men were sentenced to various prison terms, including Rudolf, who was imprisoned for six months before being deported to Czechoslovakia. Letters and poems he'd written to Werner were used against him at his trial.

In 1942, following his re-arrest, he was deported to Buchenwald concentration camp. Assigned the prison number 7952, he was there for 32 months. At one stage his teeth were knocked out during a particularly brutal beating. This was typical of the way homosexual prisoners were treated in these camps, as well as being given the most labour-intensive work – in cement plants, for example – under the assumption that this work might 'turn' them. It's estimated that 60 per cent of homosexual prisoners in these camps died.

It was at Buchenwald that Danish doctor Carl Vaernet conducted medical experiments on gay prisoners, which included injecting them with hormones. In some camps these prisoners were chosen by SS guards for a very specific purpose: the pink triangles on their striped shirts were used for target practice. Thankfully, Rudolf was hiding in a shed when the camp was liberated by American forces in 1945. Survivors like Rudolf, however, were not given the same support as his peers, such as state pensions, as the discrimination enshrined in paragraph 175 continued. There's no doubt that many men and women never talked about their experiences because of this. Rudolf did not reveal his story until 2008 (at the age of 95), when friends persuaded him to do so. He died three years later.

Forced labourers had a life expectancy of six months at Auschwitz. With the Soviet army approaching, Heinrich Himmler ordered the gas chambers to be destroyed. Surviving prisoners were taken on death marches, on which thousands died. Thankfully thousands of survivors were liberated by Allied troops, such as Bergen-Belsen, which the British took on 15 April 1945. Holocaust Memorial Day takes place on 27 January to mark the day that Auschwitz-Birkenau was liberated.

The war wasn't over during the first VE Day

In his last will and testament, Hitler appointed Admiral Karl Dönitz as head of state. On 7 May he ordered the signing of the German Instrument of Surrender. War was over, in Europe at least. King George VI gave a speech from Buckingham Palace and made eight appearances on the balcony alongside his family. Famously, that evening, Princess Margaret and Princess Elizabeth were anonymously allowed to enjoy the festivities out on the Mall. Licensing hours were extended and people danced, sang, lit bonfires and fireworks. Church services and parades were held and, of course, in classic British style, there were street parties. As butter and sugar were so hard to come by, sadly cake was unlikely to be on the menu. Think less Victoria sponge and more sandwiches, pies and beer (before it ran out at around 10.30pm). Photos of street parties in Reading feature Indian soldiers as well as African Americans, reminding us of the diversity of those celebrating. Churchill addressed the nation from Downing Street, saying, 'We may allow ourselves a brief period of rejoicing, but let us not forget for a moment the toils and efforts that lie ahead.'

What Churchill was referring to was the war still raging in Asia, and it was brutal. The day after Pearl Harbour the Japanese captured Manila. Four months later, the American general Edward King, Jr surrendered at Bataan. The Filipino and American soldiers were divided into smaller groups and forced to march for 65 miles. Disease and mistreatment meant that possibly upwards of 20,000 died en route, with many understandably referring to it as the Bataan Death March. The Japanese were successful in invading various European colonies across East Asia, including Hong Kong, Malaya, Singapore and Burma, all of which were part of the British Empire. India was next on their list.

Between March and July 1944, the battles of Imphal and Kohima in north-east India took place, involving the Fourteenth Army, a mixture of British, Canadian, American and African (Gold Coast) troops, though the majority were Indian. Gian Singh noted the terror he experienced seeing 'our men, who when captured, had been tied to trees by their turbans and used for bayonet practice'. These battles involved fighting in the jungle using hand-to-hand combat, a very different experience to those who had fought in Europe. As with every front, there are a plethora of incredible individual stories. Corporal Musa Banana from the Nigeria regiment was given a Military Medal in 1945. He clearly deserved it, having run through a shower of Japanese grenades to plant his own. He then worked through the night to lead his unit to safety, despite the grenade splinters he was covered in.

The failure of the Japanese to take India was their first major defeat and a huge turning point in the war. But the role of the Fourteenth Army has largely been forgotten. Why? Most news that made it to Britain was from the European fronts, as there was little, if any, media presence in the East. There was, however, some news from the soldiers stationed here in the form of short video messages entitled 'Calling Blighty'. British soldiers fighting in Asia were given around twenty seconds to record a message for their loved ones, part of an attempt to boost the low morale among these troops. They could then choose who would be invited to a cinema screening back home. These reels give such a personal insight into how much these soldiers yearned for home, yet still stayed so positive, with 'cheerio' and 'keep smiling' repeated constantly. The messages are full of reassurances that they were doing well, but also include many of the men pleading for more letters. The messages are slightly awkward but also clearly very sincere, with some cracking jokes about how much they miss fish and chips. Many would not have seen their families for years. Len from the Worcestershire Regiment addressed his children Callum and Wendy by saying, 'I expect you're now tall enough to see me without having to stand on the seat.' While Frank stated, 'Well, son, this is the first time you've ever seen me or heard me talk. Soon I hope to be with you and take you fishing.'

'MODERN' BRITAIN   8

This chapter will focus on a less familiar story, but one much closer to home. The story of the key struggles that marginalised communities in Britain faced in the few decades after the Second World War. As with every chapter, this is by no means a complete or comprehensive history of this period, nor is it claiming to be. What it will give you is an insight into how post-1945 migrants to Britain and the generation that followed fought their very own civil rights movement.

Our shared history: the devastating story of the partition of India

This period saw the disintegration of the British Empire, with the first key loss being the 'jewel in the crown' in 1947. The Indian National Congress had been demanding independence formally since 1928. In the same year, a British-based organisation called the India League followed suit. Fronted by lawyer and activist Krishna Menon, the League held meetings and distributed pamphlets to publicise their arguments. They established local branches across the country and went on a fact-finding mission to India in 1932, resulting in a 534-page report called 'The Condition of India', which was subsequently banned in India for revealing just how repressive measures were within the Raj, including prison conditions and shootings of unarmed demonstrators.

High-profile members of the League included Labour politician Ellen Wilkinson and future Nobel Prize winner Bertrand Russell, and there was an appetite for Indian Independence across the country. To some, however, their arguments fell on deaf ears. Churchill infamously stated in 1942 that he had 'not become the King's First Minister in order to preside over the liquidation of the British Empire', showing how, among so many of the British elite, the demise of the empire was inconceivable. Why then did the British exit India so swiftly five years later, with the rest of the empire following suit thereafter?

The economic impact of the Second World War was hugely significant, with Britain having to take a $3.75 billion loan from America in 1946 in order to keep afloat, which we finally paid back in 2006. The people of Britain made it clear in the 1945 general election that their priorities were domestic and not international, reflected in their decision to vote in Labour's Clement Attlee rather than keep wartime leader Churchill. Labour's manifesto was deeply influenced by the social reforms suggested by the Beveridge Report and included new priorities like a National Health Service.

Politically, India was ready for independence, with the Indian Civil Service now dominated by Indians for the first time since its formation. There was also an intensity of resentment towards the British that had been exacerbated by the war. Nationalists had taken to the streets in 1942, with Aruna Asaf Ali hoisting the Indian flag over the Gowalia Tank Maidan in Mumbai to make their aim clear; they wanted the British to 'Quit India' immediately. The violence was widespread, and the British had to divert 56 battalions to finally supress it. The following year the Bengal famine hit, killing approximately three million people. There's much debate over the causes of the famine, with the impact of crop failures exacerbated by the conditions of the war. The Viceroy at the time described it as 'one of the greatest disasters befallen any people under British rule and damage to our reputation is ... incalculable'.

The empire the British had spent centuries building now felt overextended in the wake of another expensive world war. Attlee's government sent the Cabinet Mission to India in March 1946 with the express intention of helping India to 'attain her freedom as speedily and fully as possible', no doubt influenced by supporters in the India League. And while India did attain her freedom, the promise to 'help to make the transition as smooth and easy as possible' certainly did not.

In 1940 the Muslim League's Lahore Resolution publicly demanded the creation of Pakistan, perhaps more as a bargaining chip rather than believing it could be a reality. By 1946, however, this seemed like a real possibility; the Muslim League withdrew their participation in July, and in August organised a strike known as Direct Action Day. What ensued was violence from both Hindu and Muslim communities, including rioting, lynching and arson, which left 10,000 injured and approximately 4,000 dead in Calcutta. Violence occurred across the country, characterised by abductions, rape and forced conversions, such as in Bihar and Noakhali. Naval uprisings across 1946 exacerbated matters and civil war was feared. Viceroy Wavell's request for troop reinforcements was denied, despite the British government acknowledging (albeit in their own problematic terminology) that an 'animal fury' was ravaging the nation. Plans for the evacuation of British families were drawn up.

The question wasn't whether Britain was leaving; it was a question of when and how. Attlee acted decisively; by March 1947 he had appointed Lord Louis Mountbatten (King Charles' great-uncle) as the new Viceroy with one clear instruction: India was to be independent by June 1948. It was hoped that Mountbatten's appointment would add glamour and gravitas and somewhat distract from the increasingly precarious circumstances in India. By 3 June, Mountbatten had announced that independence would in fact happen at midnight on 14–15 August 1947. The next two months would now be spent rather chaotically deciding how exactly this was going to look, for it would involve partitioning India into East Pakistan, West Pakistan and India, something Mountbatten decided was the only way to resolve the Indian National Congress and Muslim League deadlock at this point. Of all the Indian politicians involved it was perhaps the future prime minister of India, Jawaharlal Nehru, who was the most closely involved politically, and perhaps also personally, as many have since speculated on just how close a relationship he had with Mountbatten's wife, Lady Edwina.

A Partition Council was formed to organise the division of assets between the two new nations, from typewriters to carpets and ceiling fans. Government employees could decide which nation they wanted to work for, with the option to switch over anytime within six months of partition. It was decided that both sides would have access to things that were impossible to divide, like Central Research Institute in Kasauli, where vaccines were manufactured, a reflection of how it was assumed that movement between the two nations would be possible immediately. Some assets were fraught with arguments, however, such as the collection of the Imperial Library.

The geographical boundaries were to be decided exclusively by Britain. Sir Cyril Radcliffe was given the job of deciding where the border lines should go between India and West and East Pakistan. He had never been to India before and made his decisions based on maps and outdated census data, in just five weeks. He also destroyed his notes so his reasoning could not be questioned. Partition split states along religious lines: Punjab in the west and Bengal in the east were split into two according to their Muslim and non-Muslim areas. The announcement of the borders was deliberately left until 17 August, allowing Mountbatten to distance himself and Britain from the fallout, and also so he could attend both independence ceremonies without having to answer questions about borders. Rumours spread and maps were hastily drawn up, often with huge errors.

Partition meant that millions of Muslims found themselves in India, while millions of Sikhs and Hindus were in Pakistan. The new governments were not prepared for such a panicked mass migration as the one that followed – one of the largest in history. Ten million people became refugees as they moved from one country to another. Up to a million were killed in the horrific violence that took place. Some of the worst was in Punjab, where 200,000 people lost their lives. British troops were ordered not to intervene. Entire villages were massacred. Trains would enter their final destination with no living passengers inside. Women were abducted, mutilated, raped and forcibly converted. Tattoos were even used as a method of identification by paranoid families concerned that they would be separated from their loved ones.

Mountbatten was later criticised for rushing the partition process and failing to help stop the violence. No wonder Radcliffe refused to accept any payment for the job. This story, of the birth of these new nations among the mess and chaos of partition, is a shared history of Britain and the Indian subcontinent. Within three months, 8.7 million people had crossed borders. Many migrated to Britain eventually, still feeling both the heavy weight of the trauma they carried, alongside stories of hope and compassion.

One such example is Karam Singh Hamdard, who moved to the UK in 1970. His family home in East Punjab was set on fire by a mob with his mother still inside. She managed to jump out of a window and survive, while his father was shot and killed. One of his sisters survived thanks to the bravery and kindness of a Muslim family, who protected her as well as saving over 30 other women. Karam could never forget the horrors of partition even if he wanted to, with a scar permanently etched on his arm where he was attacked with a poison-soaked spear. The consequences of this shared history are still felt today, with several wars, including the 1971 war which led to the creation of Bangladesh, and the disputed area of Kashmir remains a bone of contention between the two nations. Families are still being reunited over seven decades later.

Operation Legacy was Britain's attempt to save her imperial legacy

In 1945 the Home Office opened a file called 'Compulsory repatriation of undesirable Chinese seamen'. During the Second World War, approximately 20,000 mariners were recruited in Hong Kong, Shanghai and Singapore to help support the British navy to fight against German submarine warfare in particular. Liverpool was a key base for the

Chinese merchant navy. It was here that many sailors met and fell in love with local women. During the war these sailors received less than half the wages of their British shipmates, despite working in the same conditions. They also did not receive the monthly £10 'war risk' bonus. As the Chinese sailors were unionised, they used strike action to pressure for better pay and access to bonuses, which worked. However, after the war these were withdrawn and the Chinese sailors were labelled as 'troublemakers'. The government worked alongside the shipping companies to remove these 'undesirable' men from Liverpool, mostly because they wanted to free up housing. The government relied on the police to round up Chinese seaman and forcibly place them on ships. By March 1946, Home Office files suggest that 2,000 seamen were repatriated in this way. Men with British wives and British-born children were deported, despite legally having the right to stay. Those who were unmarried left behind partners and children. Most ended up in Shanghai or Hong Kong. The British wives of the Chinese seamen who had been repatriated formed a defence association in Liverpool to campaign for the rights of their families, but to little avail. As far as records show, there were no reviews of individual cases, or appeals. In July 2021, the Home Office agreed to look into it.

In the same year that India was partitioned, Attlee's government scoured the rest of the empire looking for somewhere to kickstart a new money-making scheme. They decided Tanganyika (now Tanzania) would be the best option and promptly began clearing millions of hectares of land to grow ... peanuts. Not only would this provide jobs, but it would also help provide oil for an essential British good – margarine. Rationing was still in place in Britain, and would continue until 1954, almost a decade after the end the war, showing just how dire the domestic economic situation was.

Unsurprisingly, the peanut scheme failed from the start for a myriad of reasons, including issues relating to the climate, soil and equipment. Poor planning was key here, coupled with the assumption that the British knew best. Had local people been questioned, they would have quickly realised that the lack of sufficient rain would hamper the scheme irrevocably. In 1951 it had to be abandoned, at the cost of £36 million, equivalent to approximately £1 billion today. British housewives received no increases to their margarine rations.

Just under a decade later, Prime Minister Harold Macmillan made his famous 1960 'wind of change' speech, signalling the Conservative Party's acceptance that, 'Whether we like it or not', the British Empire was changing rapidly as nationalist movements across the remaining colonies demanded independence. This had already happened in the Gold Coast, now Ghana, in 1957, led by nationalist Kwame Nkrumah.

This process of decolonisation involved a highly orchestrated and top-secret administrative undertaking, known as Operation Legacy. In the lead-up to independence days across the empire, files were being categorised. The Colonial Office provided guidance via telegram regarding the 'disposal of classified records and accountable documents' in May 1961. It was made clear that:

> Successor governments should not be given papers which: might embarrass Her Majesty's Government or other governments; might embarrass members of the police, military forces, public servants or others e.g. police informers; might compromise sources of intelligence information; or might be used unethically by Ministers in the successor government.

Documents marked 'Personal' were for UK eyes only. Files marked 'DG' were for the eyes of 'British subjects of European descent', as they may have contained information about political parties, as well as details of 'religious intolerance' and 'racial discrimination'. Anything marked with a red 'W' stamp was a 'Watch' document, meaning it was to be destroyed. In Malaya, lorries were packed and papers taken to a naval base, where they were incinerated. More discreet methods were encouraged, with instructions in Kenya highlighting that 'the waste should be reduced to ash and the ashes broken up', while any that were being dumped at sea must be 'packed in weighted crates and dumped in very deep and current-free water at maximum practicable distance from the coast'. In Belize, the Royal Navy and several gallons of petrol helped one visiting official burn all sensitive files. In British Guiana, it came down to two secretaries using a fire in an oil drum in the grounds of Government House. Eventually the army agreed to lend a hand.

The fact that the name Operation Legacy was first used in 1961 shows that this was the absolute priority: to secure the legacy of empire in the most positive light, apparently via any means necessary. The final decisions on whether files were to be destroyed or not were made on the ground at the time by hundreds, if not thousands of staff who had to ultimately decide whether what they held in their hands was incriminating or not.

Some files were not destroyed, and were instead brought back to Britain. Known as the 'migrated archive', they were moved from Hayes to Hanslope Park in 1995. It wasn't until a legal case was brought against the British government by a small group of elderly Kenyans seeking reparations for their mistreatment in detention camps during the Mau Mau rebellion (1952–60) that their existence was made public. Britain had controlled Kenya since 1895. Increasing African nationalism in the wake of the Second World War led the Mau Mau – the Kenya Land and Freedom Army – to fight violently for their freedom. Atrocities were committed by both sides, with the Mau Mau massacring loyalist troops and their families, for example, while British authorities detained thousands in detention camps. Information in the migrated archive confirmed that suspected insurgents were subjected to brutal treatment in these camps, including rape, torture and lethal beatings by British colonial authorities. In 2013, £19.9 million of compensation was awarded to 5,228 Kenyan claimants. The migrated archive contains information about over 30 other former colonies. Tens of thousands of these documents are still awaiting review before they can be released.

The Windrush generation were invited here

In June 1948, 1,027 passengers disembarked at Tilbury Docks in Essex from the SS *Empire Windrush*. Onboard were 492 passengers from the

Caribbean. The cheapest fare from Jamaica was around £28, approximately £1,000 today. One person who didn't pay out of her own pocket was stowaway Evelyn Wauchope. The 39-year-old dressmaker was no doubt forever grateful that her fellow passengers organised a whip-round, which raised £50, leaving her with enough to cover her fare and have pocket money to spare. These passengers were encouraged to move here with the passing of the 1948 British Nationality Act, which gave anyone from across the British Empire the automatic right to live and work here.

Adverts sprung up all over the Caribbean from organisations that needed workers, including British Rail and the NHS. London Transport (now TfL) even set up a recruitment office in the capital of Barbados, and the Barbadian government would lend recruits the fare to Britain. While the *Windrush* wasn't the first ship to transport immigrants from the Caribbean to the UK, it was the first to dock after the British Nationality Act was passed.

What was it like for the first wave of the Windrush generation? The BBC Caribbean Service broadcast a programme called *Going to Britain?*, which was then made into a pamphlet that provides a unique and fascinating insight into their experience. As you can imagine, the weather features heavily: 'We West Indians believe that we cannot face a cold season without rum. When we get here we find that our belief has no foundation.' Other advice included reminders to shut front doors properly, queuing – 'your place in this Q is Z – that is, at the end of the line' – and keeping your best clothes for your first party in England. Don't overfill the tub, support a football club and embrace the tea-breaks. While the pamphlet did acknowledge that 'your greater problem will be getting on with your white neighbours', the subtitles of this section, 'You are the stranger', 'No offence meant' and 'Politeness the Key', reflect that the advice given to these migrants was essentially to assimilate by any means necessary, even when asked the most offensive of questions, such as if they'd ever worn clothes before coming to England. The pamphlet's 'employment' section alludes to issues newcomers faced with regards to work, advising, 'Take the first job you are offered.'

Due to discriminatory workplace practices, over half of the men who arrived from the Caribbean had to accept jobs with a lower status than they were qualified for. Many had to put up with racist remarks. Sam King recalled that while working for Royal Mail he was greeted with heckles of, 'Send 'em back,' to which he responded with a comeback to make any History teacher proud: 'I'm all in favour of sending them back, as long as you start with the *Mayflower*.' King, who would become the mayor of Southwark, had returned to England via the *Windrush* having already been here as a pilot during the war. He became hugely active in the community, working alongside Claudia Jones to launch the *West Indian Gazette* in March 1958, considered to be Britain's first major Black newspaper.

That summer, the need for community spirit became abundantly clear when rioting broke out in Notting Hill. The 1950s saw the emergence of youth subcultures, including Teddy Boys, known for their signature look of drainpipe trousers, tailored blazers and quiff hairdos. Some held particularly racist views and took offence to immigration and inter-racial relationships, influenced by Oswald Mosley and groups like the White Defence League. At the time, senior officers within the police framed the violence as stemming from 'hooliganism' from both sides. However, confidential files released in 2002 clearly show that the riots stemmed from the actions of hundreds of Teddy Boys and their counterparts, who sought out West Indian residents of Notting Hill, armed with all manner of weapons. Thomas Williams was one example; he was stopped by PC Dennis Feist who found an iron bar down his left trouser leg, a petrol bomb in one pocket and an open razor blade hidden in a comb case in the other.

Miraculously, no one was killed in the violence that ensued. Seymour Manning may well have been, had he not been run into a greengrocer's after being chased by three men, who had already punched and kicked him to the ground. Thankfully the greengrocer's daughter Pat Howcroft bolted the door and faced down what soon became a large crowd demanding that she hand Manning over to them. This was not quite the 'Welcome Home' the *Evening Standard* had promised these 'sons of empire' a decade before. A year later, Antiguan law student Kelso Cochrane was not so lucky. He was stabbed by a gang of white youths in Notting Hill while walking home. No one was ever charged with his murder.

Trinidadian-born Claudia Jones sought to find a way to celebrate the diversity of an area that had been so recently scarred by racially fuelled violence. Jones had grown up in America, but was exiled in 1955 for her communist beliefs. She organised the first London Caribbean festival in 1959, which was televised by the BBC and held in St Pancras Town Hall. This was the forerunner for the Notting Hill Carnival, and it included a performance by the Southlanders, whose singer Harold Wilmot had arrived on the *Windrush* in 1948.

There was a British civil rights movement

1963 was quite the year. JFK made his famous 'Ich Bin ein Berliner' speech in West Berlin, the Beatles went to number one with 'I Want to Hold Your Hand' and the French vetoed the UK's wish to join to European Common Market. It was on 28 August of that year that Martin Luther King Jr delivered his 'I Have a Dream' speech during the march on Washington to a crowd of approximately a quarter of a million. On the same day on the other side of the Atlantic, a group of men of the Windrush generation won their own battle against racial discrimination.

Several years earlier, in January 1955, the Bristol Omnibus Company (BOC), despite facing a shortage of drivers, passed a resolution that 'coloured workers should not be employed as bus crews'. Roy Hackett, Owen Henry, Audley Evans and Prince Brown formed the West Indian Development Council to formalise action against this resolution. Paul Stephenson, Bristol's first Black youth officer, was their talented spokesman, and he decided to test the colour bar outright. He organised for Guy Bailey to be interviewed for a job, which was swiftly rejected when it came to light that Bailey was Jamaican. This was the proof they needed. Stephenson organised a boycott, inspired by the famous Montgomery Bus Boycott, which had been sparked by the arrest of Rosa Parks in 1955. Supporters of the boycott included students and lecturers from the University of Bristol, Labour MP Tony Benn and West Indian cricketer Sir Learie Constantine.

After a four-month boycott, the BOC conceded and ended the colour bar, on the same day that hundreds of thousands were out on the streets of Washington. Just like in America, while this victory by no means ended racist practices in the workplace, it was a step towards the UK's first laws against racial discrimination.

On 17 September, in the same week the Beatles single 'She Loves You' was number one, Raghbir Singh became the first non-white bus conductor in Bristol, passing the company's training school 'with flying colours'. He had moved to Britain from the Punjab in 1959 with his wife and three children. From his first day on the number 8 bus he wore a turban to match his uniform. He was interviewed for the local paper and stated: 'The passengers are so nice, the bus crews are so nice. Everyone is so helpful.' Within the week, two Jamaican and two Pakistani men also became conductors. This would not have been possible without the boycott. Events in the following year provided more connections between the American civil rights movement and its lesser-known British counterpart.

The 1964 general election, won by Harold Wilson's Labour Party, was the backdrop for a particularly controversial constituency battle in Smethwick in the West Midlands. Conservative candidate Peter Griffiths canvassed the local electorate with leaflets emblazoned with: 'If you want a coloured for your neighbour, vote Labour. If you're already burdened with one, vote Tory.' His campaign exploited and exposed the views of many in the community who resented the increasing number of Black and Asian migrants moving to the area, and his views were supported by the colour bar in place in various community establishments like local pubs and labour clubs. He advocated for the repatriation of immigrant residents, and he was also supported by the main local newspaper, the *Smethwick Telephone*, which printed all manner of anti-immigration stories, accusing these new residents of everything from sexual assault to spreading TB and leprosy.

Griffiths won the election, receiving 16,690 votes, and then he and the local council led a campaign to buy up housing on Marshall Street, which had many Sikh residents, although the local paper did not acknowledge this detail, instead running with the headline 'Smethwick will soon be like Mecca'. The plan was to only rent those properties to white tenants. It was also getting increasingly dangerous for immigrant communities in the area, with the launch of a British wing of the Ku Klux Klan in Birmingham and the amount of hate mail residents were receiving from groups like Keep Britain White.

On 12 February 1965, Marshall Street welcomed an unexpected visitor from across the pond: Malcolm X. He had been invited by the local Indian Workers' Association (IWA) to witness first-hand the racism they were experiencing. Originally formed to support the Indian independence movement, in the wake of partition and increasing migration from the Indian subcontinent, local IWAs organised themselves to counter the increasing issues faced by Asian and general immigrant communities. The Southall branch, for example, campaigned for a decade to end the racist education policy of 'bussing' immigrant children to different schools to ensure the number of 'coloured children' in each class was kept below one third. During Malcolm X's short visit he drew parallels between how ethnic minorities were being treated in England and America. Just nine days after his visit to Smethwick, Malcom X was assassinated at a New York ballroom.

The national backlash against Griffiths, coupled with the international exposure of the discrimination in Smethwick thanks to Malcolm X's visit to the area, quite likely contributed to Griffiths losing his seat to Labour in 1966, although he was re-elected several times as he secured his position as the MP for Portsmouth North from 1979 to 1997. There is a blue plaque on Marshall Street which recognises Malcolm X's visit in 1965 to a place that remains today one of the most multicultural areas of Britain.

Life for those who had recently settled in Britain continued to offer challenges, with housing and employment in particular. Frank Crichlow had arrived in Britain in June 1953 on the *SS Colombie*, among the first wave of post-war immigrants from the Caribbean. By

1968 he'd opened the Mangrove restaurant (as well as a coffee bar) in Notting Hill, which attracted a number of celebrities, including Bob Marley, Nina Simone, Diana Ross, Marvin Gaye, Vanessa Redgrave and Jimi Hendrix. It became an important meeting place for Black intellectuals, activists, authors and artists, and also served as the informal head office for the Notting Hill Carnival. In December 1969, Kensington council took away Frank's licence to operate as an all-night cafe – a massive blow, as he did a huge amount of business after midnight. Between January 1969 and July 1970, the Mangrove was raided twelve times by police on 'suspicions' that drugs were being consumed on the premises. Each of the raids resulted in nothing being found.

He wrote to the Race Relations Board, but his complaint was ignored. This is not surprising given that, despite being set up as part of the 1965 Race Relations Act, 734 of its 982 cases were dismissed due to lack of evidence. Frank did not mince his words, writing on the complaint form: 'I know it is because I am a Black citizen that I am discriminated against.'

By the summer of 1970 the community who supported Frank took to the streets, having formed the Action Committee for the Defence of the Mangrove. On 9 August 1970, 150 people marched to the Portnall Road police station, where they were met with violence and arrests. There were 200 policemen ready to challenge the protesters, with another 500 on standby. Darcus Howe, one of the key leaders, said in an interview, 'They [the police] believed, what are these cheeky West Indians doing on the streets challenging our authority with such confidence?'

One of the most iconic images from the protest is of Barbara Beese clutching a pig's head, an anti-police gesture, perhaps more subtle than some of the placards from the protest which said 'Stop Police Brutality or Start Oinking' and 'Calling All Pigs – Freak Out or Get Out'. Nine individuals, including Frank, Darcus and Barbara, were arrested, charged with incitement to riot.

Some of the Mangrove Nine were British Black Panthers, a group inspired by the African American Black Panthers. They were the largest of the British Black Power groups, which included the Black Liberation

Front and the Fasimbas. They served their local communities, providing things like childcare services and Saturday schools, where children were taught Black history. One of their leaflets from 1970 explains why: '[the] British education system purposely distorts our history and never teaches us of the greatness and dignity of our people and their brave struggle against European domination.' Despite this, they were viewed as a threat, illustrated by the existence of the 'Black Power desk', the Scotland Yard unit who kept tabs on them.

Another of the nine was Altheia Jones-Lecointe, who had left Trinidad in 1965 to complete her PhD in biochemistry at UCL. With a strong belief in 'collective leadership', she refused to accept the title of a 'leader' within the British Black Panthers, and under her watchful eye their membership expanded, partly because she worked tirelessly to ensure women were welcomed into the cause.

The Old Bailey was chosen for the trial of the Mangrove Nine, despite usually being reserved for serious crimes like murder and treason. Altheia and Darcus opted to represent themselves, and the Nine collectively cited the 1215 Magna Carta to demand they should be tried by a jury of their peers. Their request eventually led to the dismissal of 63 jurors (and the inclusion of two Black jurors) based on what they understood Black Power to mean.

After a 55-day trial, all nine were acquitted, and the Metropolitan Police failed to have the judicial acknowledgment that there had been 'racial hatred on both sides' removed. This was the first time racism in the police was publicly recognised. But the Mangrove continued to be a target for raids, meaning Frank eventually closed it down. Just like Marshall Street, a blue plaque marks the spot where this hub for the West Indian community once stood.

Women's lib enters the building

Throughout the 1960s and '70s, various pieces of legislation were passed which gave the women of Britain some cause for celebration. For example, from 1967 the contraceptive pill became more widely available to women, irrespective of their marital status. The 1968 Ford machinists strike in Dagenham no doubt paved the way for the 1970 Equal Pay Act, which enshrined the concept of 'equal pay for equal work' into law. Car production at the factory was halted when some female sewing machinists discovered that they were being paid 15 per cent less than the men in the factory who did exactly the same job as them.

Frustration that attitudes towards women weren't changing was made clear in the protests against the 1970 Miss World competition, in the same week 'Bridge Over Troubled Water' hit the charts. Sixty feminists from the women's liberation movement posed as audience members and threw flour bombs and rotten vegetables in unison during the televised contest in London, while shouting, 'We're not ugly! We're not beautiful! We're angry!' This contest was also the first year that a Black woman (Jennifer Hosten) was crowned Miss World.

The issues faced by British women during this period are literally illustrated in an item held by the Black Cultural Archives called Womanopoly. Created by Stella Dadzie and drawn by hand, the spin of the famous board game invites men to play, to help them appreciate what it's like to live 'in a society where the cards are stacked against women'. In the tongue-in-cheek game, women are limited from making progress for reasons that still ring true. Land on 19 as a woman and, despite being up for a promotion, 'Will men work under you? Miss a turn and worry about it.' However, for male players, 'No doubt about you, take an extra turn.' At number 40, men moved forward two spaces for having a 'very high IQ', while the instruction for women states: 'So have you. How embarrassing. Lose a turn for arguing.'

The rise of women's lib in the 1970s saw a huge rise of formalised activism in many forms. Dadzie actually co-founded one such group in 1987, the Organisation of Women of African and Asian Descent (OWAAD), which functioned as an umbrella organisation to directly address the problems faced by Black and Asian women with regards to a variety of issues including health, education and employment. Gail Lewis was a key founder, as was Olive Morris, an activist who was heavily involved in OWAAD, as well as with other groups like the Brixton Black Women's Group.

Born in Jamaica and moving to south London at the age of nine, Olive was propelled into political activism at seventeen, when she intervened to help a Nigerian diplomat who was being accused of stealing a Mercedes when it was, in fact, his own car. She was arrested and subjected to brutal treatment at the hands of the police. She helped set up Sabarr bookshop, the first Black self-help community bookshop in Lambeth, and dedicated the rest of her life to supporting marginalised groups – such as fighting for the rights of squatters, something she herself had experienced. Her grassroots activism meant she worked closely with so many across different communities, making her death at the age of 27 all the more heartbreaking.

The intersectional lens of the OWAAD, reflected in Olive's activism, was addressed from the offset, stating that Black and Asian women had a 'joint historical experience, as victims of Colonialism and our present experience as second-class citizens in a racist society'. Their weekly newsletter 'FOWAAD' reflected their aim to 'show people sisterhood in action', with articles about government immigration proposals, prison welfare, sickle cell anaemia and education cuts. They were involved in direct action too. They joined the campaign to scrap the 'sus' (suspected person) law, the powers that gave the police the right to 'stop and search', which was used disproportionately against young black men.

In 1979, OWAAD, alongside other groups like Southall Black Sisters, organised powerful pickets at Heathrow, protesting the 'virginity tests', which primarily Indian and Pakistani women were subjected to by immigration services on arrival to the UK. Immigration policy at the time stated that anyone moving to Britain with the intention of marrying within three months did not need a visa. Virginity tests were therefore carried out in order to 'prove' these women were unmarried and did not already have children. Male doctors carried out these invasive gynaecological examinations on women as well as teenage girls.

Evidence suggests that at least 80 women were subjected to this in the late 1970s. This became public when an engaged 35-year-old teacher spoke out against such treatment when she arrived in the UK. The issue was written about in the press and was also raised in Parliament in February 1979, which is when the practice was formally banned. Without the mobilisation of immigrant communities, this would not have happened.

Although OWAAD itself disbanded in 1982, many of the women involved were able to continue with their activism via the many organisations they had been associated with. Groups like OWAAD reflect the fact that activists were taking matters into their own hands, rather than waiting for existing women's groups to take on the particular issues these marginalised women faced.

No scabs allowed in 1970s Britain

One such group of women were workers at the Grunwick photo-processing lab in Willesden, London. Many of these women were of South Asian origin and had migrated from East African countries like Uganda and Kenya. Mass migration from Uganda, for example, was triggered in 1972 when leader Idi Amin gave the 80,000 South Asians living in the country (out of population of 10 million) 90 days to leave the country. Indians had first arrived in Uganda as a result of 1890s British colonial policy, which first brought labourers to work on railway projects and eventually led to the creation of a successful professional class. Many of this community were originally from Gujarat, India. Following a policy of 'Africanisation', Amin used a variety of arguments to explain his decision, including that Asians were not integrating within Ugandan society and that many were embroiled in corruption.

One of the key reasons cited was the dominance they had when it came to the economy and business ownership in particular; in the year Ugandan-Asians were expelled, they had contributed 90 per cent of Uganda's tax revenue. They were banned from selling their property and limited to taking what they could fit into a suitcase, alongside just £50 (approximately £700 today). But where could they go? They no longer had any automatic right of entry to the UK due to the 1971 Immigration Act. Edward Heath's government was reluctant to welcome these migrants, instead opting to find a way to settle 'Asians on a suitable island in the dependent territories', and seriously considering the Falkland Islands, Bermuda and the Solomon Islands. When it became clear that none of these were viable options, 28,000 were permitted to move to Britain.

Some areas of Britain protested particularly crudely, with Leicester council issuing an advert in the popular *Uganda Argus* newspaper stating: 'In your own interests and those of your family you should ... not come to Leicester.' The Uganda Resettlement Board countered such attitudes, organising interpreters, social events and language classes to ensure these newcomers to Britain could find housing and employment as soon as possible. They were supported by all manner of organisations, including the Board of Deputies of British Jews, the Catholic Committee for Racial Justice, and the Women's Royal Voluntary Service, who helped source everything from heaters to the specialist utensils needed to cook Indian food.

On 20 August 1976, the week before ABBA's 'Dancing Queen' topped the charts, Jayaben Desai and her son Sunil walked out of the Grunwick factory in protest at the sacking of Devshi Bhudia, who was dismissed for 'working too slowly'. Such arbitrary actions were typical in the factory at the time, where workers had to raise their hands and ask for permission before they could use the toilet. Pregnant women were not given leave for maternity appointments and overtime was compulsory, with no prior notice. Just like the Windrush generation, many of these new migrants found their employment opportunities were limited, despite their qualifications. Workers at the Grunwick factory therefore accepted this low-paid work out of necessity, something the factory owners were fully aware of. This is epitomised by a homemade placard from the strike that followed, emblazoned with the quote 'I can buy a Patel for £15' above images of three bosses, including the factory manager, John Stacey. Underneath the images are three words that ooze defiance: 'NOT ANY MORE'.

The inclusion of Patel is a reference to the fact that many of these women were Gujarati Indians; two Patels working in Grunwick at the time were, in fact, members of my family. The same photo includes Jayaben Desai with a placard stating 'George Amin of Willesden', drawing clear parallels between the managing director of the factory (George Ward) and the Ugandan leader. The protesting workers decided that joining a union would strengthen their case, but the factory refused to recognise their union membership and the 137 workers on strike were sacked.

Unlike previous strikes involving South Asian 'strikers in saris', like the Imperial Typewriters strike in Leicester in 1974, the Grunwick strike had the support of the broader trade union movement. On some days there were 20,000 people out on the streets of Willesden, including big names like National Union of Mineworkers leader Arthur Scargill and Labour minister Shirley Williams. This was partly because a delegation of strikers had toured workplaces all over Britain, drumming up support for their cause and challenging what working-class Britain may have previously assumed about 'little Asian ladies'.

This was the first time the Special Patrol Group (SPG), who were normally used to dealing with public disorder and terrorism, were used in an industrial dispute. Violence did take place, mostly between the SPG and union supporters, with articles from the time alleging that the police set out to deliberately provoke the protestors. The Union of Postal Workers showed true solidarity with the strikers by boycotting postal services to and from the factory. However, momentum began to wane as the Trade Union Congress (TUC), under pressure from the Labour government, essentially withdrew their support for mass picketing. In one last attempt, Jayaben and three other workers staged a hunger strike outside the TUC headquarters, but to no avail. The strike was eventually called off in July 1978.

Despite this, it was the first time that a strike by immigrant workers had received such widespread support, with thousands taking part in marches and shouting slogans like, 'The workers united will never be defeated.' This would not have been possible without the leadership of Jayaben Desai, who later became a teacher. She died in 2010 at the age of 77. It's worth pointing out that Jayaben did all this while standing at the towering height of four-foot-ten, making her an inch shorter than our favourite suffrajitsu instructor Edith Garrud.

'Rather swamped'

The National Front was formed in 1967, and their aims were made abundantly clear from the three groups they originated from: the British National Party, the League of Empire Loyalists, and the Racial Preservation Society. It was in the early 1970s that their membership grew rapidly, in response to growing immigration. Similarly, the 1970s saw the formation of groups like Rock Against Racism and the Anti-Nazi League, who sought to counter those joining far-right organisations.

One of the National Front's key tactics was to organise marches through increasingly multicultural areas, deliberately provoking anti-racist groups to respond. Riot shields were used for the first time in England in August 1977 when the National Front marched through Lewisham, and violence ensued between them, the police and anti-National Front protestors, leaving over a hundred people injured. In 1978, Margaret Thatcher infamously stated during a TV interview that 'people are really rather afraid that this country might be rather swamped by people with a different culture'. She made her views on migrants clear by stating: 'We must hold out the prospect of a clear end to immigration.'

On 23 April 1979, while the National Front held a meeting in Southall, Blair Peach was among approximately 3,000 people who attended an Anti-Nazi League demonstration. Peach, originally from New Zealand, was a 33-year-old primary school teacher with a history of anti-racism activism. As the demonstration turned violent and he attempted to get away from it, Peach was hit on the head by an officer and died from his injuries later that night. His body was embalmed and lay in state in the Dominion Cinema in Southall so that people could pay their respects. It's estimated that over 8,000 people opted to do so, a reflection of what he meant to the local community and beyond. An internal inquiry concluded that one of six officers had killed Peach, but none were prosecuted, confirmed in 2010 when the Metropolitan Police released a report which stated that Peach was likely killed by a member of the Special Patrol Group, who were the riot police present on the day.

In 2021 it came to light that Peach's partner at the time, Celia Stubbs, was under police surveillance for the two decades after his death, with undercover officers of the Special Demonstration Squad monitoring her campaign to seek justice for Peach's death, including demands for a public inquiry. Peach and Stubbs were in fact being monitored prior to his death, due to their affiliation with the Socialist Workers Party. Peach's legacy lives on via the National Education Union's Blair Peach award, which is granted to an NEU member 'who has made an exemplary contribution to their school or union branch's work in any area of equality and diversity', a fitting tribute to this teacher and campaigner.

On 18 January 1981, Yvonne Ruddock and Angela Jackson were celebrating their sixteenth and eighteenth birthdays at a house party in New Cross, south-east London, when a fire broke out. Yvonne and twelve others died in the fire, with another subsequently dying by suicide. There had been arson attacks in the area, as well as witness statements, which led to conclusions being drawn that this was a deliberate racist attack. The subsequent police investigation was marred by controversy, as they tried to focus on how a fight inside the party may have caused the blaze, despite the fact that a fight in fact never occurred. Young victims were being questioned for hours and some were coerced into signing false statements. Some within the police were already disrespecting the tragedy, saying things like, 'New Cross should be renamed Blackfriars.'

The New Cross Massacre Action Committee (NCMAC) was formed to help raise funds for the affected families, as well as to collect their own evidence. There was also increasing frustration at how the case was being handled. Media coverage was sparse and increasingly pointed the finger at the victims, while there were no condolences sent from Prime Minister Thatcher till much later. Grieving families received death threats as well as letters saying their losses were being celebrated, which meant police escorts were needed for the funerals. The NCMAC were granted permission to organise a march, which they planned for a Monday in order to gain as much attention as possible.

The Black People's Day of Action on 2 March was attended by approximately 18,000, and was planned to start at New Cross Road and end in Hyde Park. Echoing similar sentiments from Grunwick, those on the march were chanting, 'Black people united will never be defeated.' Banners were held showing the names and faces of the thirteen young victims along with statements like '13 Dead, Nothing Said', a clear reference to the silence from the establishment. However, when the march reached Blackfriars Bridge, they were met with police in riot gear blocking their way. Scuffles ensued and eventually the protestors made it onto Fleet Street, an important part of the march, as this was the heart of British print media. Protestors found themselves being racially abused by office workers who shouted obscenities at them from their windows.

Despite this, the sheer number of people who attended the march was where the real victory lay, proof that the Black community and their allies would not be silenced. Moreover, the work of the NCMAC may well have prevented innocent victims from being wrongly convicted. To this day, the cause of the fire is still unclear; an inquest in 2004 led to another open verdict. There are numerous memorials, including thirteen trees that were planted in Hackney Downs to remember each of the victims.

Following the New Cross Fire, tensions were running high. This was exacerbated by the launch of Operation Swamp, when hundreds of plain-clothes officers descended on Brixton. The 'sus' law was used disproportionately against young Black men, and within five days almost a thousand people had been stopped and searched, sometimes multiple times a day.

On 10 April, rioting started, sparked by the stabbing of Michael Bailey, who ran into police when he was in need of medical assistance. The police stood accused of hindering rather than helping. Over the next two days the streets of Brixton were a battleground, littered with burned-out cars, buildings and rubble, and almost 300 police officers were injured. Rioting and unrest spread across other major cities, including Leeds, Liverpool and Leicester. In Toxteth, rioting in July lasted for nine days and CS gas grenades were fired by police in order to disperse crowds.

Meanwhile, in June 1981, a month before Charles wed Diana at St Paul's Cathedral, twelve youths of South Asian origin (from Hindu, Muslim and Sikh backgrounds) in Bradford were arrested, accused of plotting to use bombs against the police. A police raid had found these members of the United Black Youth League, a group affiliated with the wider Asian Youth Movement (AYM), were in possession of petrol bombs made from milk bottles. They argued that these were for defence purposes, given rumours of a National Front march in Bradford.

Such groups had been formed in the wake of discrimination and violence. The AYM had been involved in a wide range of activism, including the campaign to grant the children of British-born Anwar Ditta the right to move to Britain from Pakistan. The Home Office did not believe they were her children, and it's thanks to the unity of Black Power groups, trade unions, the Indian Workers' Assocation, the AYM and women's groups that her plight remained in the public eye. In 1981 her children were given the green light after documentary programme *World in Action* took on her case.

There were also regional groups like the Southall Youth Movement (SYM), which was organised as a result of the murder of eighteen-year-old student Gurdip Singh Chaggar in July 1978. He was returning home from school when he was stabbed to death in a racially motivated attack by white youths in front of the Dominion Cinema in Southall, west London. When one passer-by asked a police officer who had been killed, he responded with 'just an Asian'. The former chairman of the National Front, John Kingsley Read, reacted to the murder by stating, 'One down, a million to go.'

There are many parallels between the experience of the Bradford Twelve and other events from this chapter. Like victims of the New

Cross Fire, many of these young men were pressured into signing false statements. The police also queried whether they had any connections with events across the rest of the county, like in Toxteth. The West Yorkshire police may have had another motive for desperately wanting to succeed with this case – their reputation needed a boost, having bungled the Yorkshire Ripper case. They had interviewed the serial killer Peter Sutcliffe a total of nine times, yet still did not catch him, leading to the most expensive manhunt in British history.

Support groups for the Bradford Twelve sprung up across the country, via the AYM, and Anwar Ditta spoke passionately at one of the rallies, saying this was an important case in the fight against state racism. Their trial started in April 1982 and lasted for six weeks. Like the Mangrove Nine, they challenged the composition of the jury, so that it eventually included Black, Asian and white working-class jurors.

Tariq Ali opted to defend himself, which he did passionately and eloquently:

> The whole case against me amounts to nothing but a political prosecution. It is aimed at my political views. It is nothing but to get me off the streets. I fought for my people. I am not a terrorist but a victim of terror.

The Bradford Twelve successfully proved, supported by a huge number of witnesses, that they were living in a climate of fear which led them to seek genuine means of defending themselves. In fact, Tarlochan Gata-Aura stated in court that far from feeling protected by the police, 'the police have always protected the fascists'. He admitted to making 38 petrol bombs but insisted they were 'purely for self-defence', citing recent violence in Southall and the fatal stabbing of Satnam Singh Gill by skinheads in Coventry.

Anwar Ditta took to the stand and explained how she lived in fear of racist attacks due to the number of threats she received; she therefore kept buckets by her front door in case petrol was poured through her letterbox. The fabrication of some of the police statements was confirmed in court, as they were analysed to show that the language and phrasing in them was unlikely to have come from teenagers. Their history of activism was also used to prove they were genuine defenders of the community, not the hooligans the police had made them out to be. The police witnesses' ignorance of national race-related issues, let alone local ones, certainly supported the self-defence argument of the Bradford Twelve.

Across the Atlantic, the Black Women for Wages for Housework organised a picket outside the British Consulate in LA, brandishing placards stating 'Free the Bradford 12' and 'Britain's Bobbies Are No Gentlemen!' The Bradford Twelve's plight had gone global.

They were acquitted on all counts and had been supported by hundreds of organisations, including the Blair Peach Memorial Fund, OWAAD and the Race Today Alliance. The victory was not just for the Bradford Twelve and their families, but for the groups that supported them, from religious groups to bookshops, individual MPs like Tony Benn and trade unions. There was clear solidarity across marginalised communities, shown by the support from groups such as the Gay Liberation Front and the English Collective of Prostitutes. After the trial Tariq Ali said, 'The state made a mountain out of a molehill. In so doing, they made a monument to our beliefs. That is, we will defend ourselves by whatever means necessary.'

Pits and perverts

This coming together of unexpected communities was epitomised in 1984. Thatcher's government announced the closure of 20 pits, which would leave 20,000 people without jobs, and lead to a strike involving over 140,000 miners at its peak. The same year saw the formation of LGSM, Lesbians and Gays Support the Miners, after two gay men, Mark Ashton and Mike Jackson, collected donations for the miners at the 1984 Lesbian and Gay Pride March. The government had frozen funds for the National Union of Mineworkers (NUM), meaning fundraising for mining communities became essential. Mark Ashton said, 'We supported the miners unconditionally because we knew if the trade union rights were taken away or diminished, everyone would suffer. So as an act of solidarity we went to support them.' They held weekly meetings at Gay's the Word bookshop and raised money via bucket collections, jumble sales and sponsored events like 'pedal against pit closures'.

In December 1984, the same month Band Aid went to number one, they held a Pits and Perverts benefit gig in Camden, which raised £5,650, equivalent to £20,000 today. Lesbians Against Pit Closures (LAPC) formed a few months after LGSM as a way to counter the misogyny some women were experiencing in the original group. They fundraised for miners using similar tactics to the LGSM, as well as running soup kitchens and organising food banks.

Funds were given to the mining community of the Dulais Valley in South Wales, who also invited members of LGSM to visit them, forging friendships that lasted far beyond the strike. It wasn't without its mishaps, however, with the 27-strong LGSM contingent arriving at 1am after the three minibuses got lost for several hours. There was apprehension on both sides, but also an amusing collision of cultures, with Christine Powell, the treasurer of the Neath and District Miners Support Group, recalling, 'They told me that they were vegetarian, and I thought, "You might be gay and I can handle that, but what the heck do I do with a vegetarian?"'

At the 1985 Pride march, the same year the first episode of *EastEnders* aired, a huge contingent of men, women and children from the Dulais Valley attended, fronted by a NUM banner. As the largest group present, they were invited to lead the march. Their support for what we would now call LGBT+ rights was proven at the 1985 Labour Party conference, when the NUM block voted in favour of the party promising to protect lesbian and gay rights.

They continued to support the community later on in the 1980s, after the Thatcher government passed the infamous Section 28, which was a piece of legislation that banned the 'promotion of homosexuality' by schools and councils across Britain. This legislation was prompted when a book called *Jenny Lives with Eric and Martin* started being stocked in some school libraries, leading to a tabloid outcry.

Section 28 meant teachers were not allowed to talk about LGBT+ issues and same-sex relationships with their students. Councils were also forbidden from stocking libraries with literature or films that contained gay or lesbian themes. Exactly a year after the legislation was passed, Stonewall was co-founded by actor Ian McKellen, to lobby the government to scrap Section 28. Protests came in all forms, including a group of lesbians who abseiled from the public gallery into the House of Lords using a washing line in February 1988. Section 28 was not repealed until 2003, and was fully turned over with the Equality Act 2010.

CONCLUSION: EVERY DAY IS A SCHOOL DAY

You have now travelled through a historical timeline, encountering a wide range of characters and events – some familiar, others less so. It would be a huge understatement to say a lot has happened between meeting the Ivory Bangle Lady and encountering the British civil rights movement.

From when I first started teaching, one of my favourite topics was the suffragette movement, which was, of course, dominated by window smashing and the Pankhursts. This makes complete sense when we consider that our understanding of the past is shaped by those who have written it. The preservation of some stories over others has inevitably meant that some figures have stayed in the shadows, while others have taken centre stage. My first encounter with Sophia Duleep Singh, a few years into my career, therefore had a profound impact on me. Here was a prominent suffragette who also happened to be an Indian princess, yet her contribution to the cause has been hidden from mainstream view. The presence of a South Asian woman within the unexpected context of classic school history was, for me, where it all started. I hope that while reading this book, you too have experienced that feeling of surprise and have also reflected on why these figures, despite their contributions across these chapters, have not been recognised as much as others.

There is so much evidence about the people featured across this book, from the tournament scroll featuring John Blanke to the documents 'signed' by indentured servants and photographs from the Mangrove protest. Yet these are not well-known stories, despite them all being such a crucial part of Britain's story. Their contributions deserve to be part of our collective understanding of historical contexts like the world wars and suffrage movement. This is our shared history, and widening the lens is crucial. This re-examination of our past can allow us to include all who were there, rather than just some. It is possible to tell a story of Britain which includes the Battle of Hastings, the English Civil War and the Blitz alongside the Slave Compensation Act, the looting of the Benin bronzes and the Grunwick strike.

When people talk to me about which aspects of British history they feel the least confident about, the most frequent knowledge gap they identify is hands down the British Empire. The complex content that comes with that, be it the transatlantic slave trade or the partition of India, hopefully feels less daunting now. This is an incredibly layered part of our nation's history, and yet there are still so many who wish to simplify it into a binary of 'good' or 'bad'. The most challenging chapters to write were therefore the ones that had the empire at the heart of them. Partly because I knew they could be the most unfamiliar to readers, but also because the subject matter evokes such visceral reaction. This is a history that is so ingrained in the fabric of our present, and yet is peculiarly unfamiliar. That unfamiliarity can make people feel many things, from anger to guilt. To those who feel any sense of guilt at not 'knowing' this history, you have to remember that it's not easy to find. I hope this book has been your first step towards bridging that knowledge gap.

This was never going to be a comprehensive history, nor is this a blueprint for the perfect curriculum. What I set out to do was to show you an example of one way that history can be travelled, down a wider and more inclusive path, by providing you with a familiar thread of history as a foundation throughout each chapter, with lesser-known stories and figures then taking up the lion's share of the space.

It's also crucial to acknowledge that for each example chosen within this book, there are many others who could have taken their place. When it came to the empire, for example, my focus was primarily on India and West Africa. In the classroom we have to select case studies through which to teach these historical contexts, and one of the great joys of this writing process has been the opportunity to indulge in research I could immediately share with my students. I recounted the story of Faye Schulman, for example, to my Year 9 class and was delighted that they were just as blown away by the photographs she took as I had been.

Before you leave my classroom, I've got a few final questions.

Which events surprised you the most and are there any that piqued your interest so much that you've gone on to delve deeper into them? I do hope so. Which aspects of the book do you most wish you'd learned about at school, and why? Who are you excited to share your new knowledge with?

Of all the people you've met across these eight chapters, who would you most like to have dinner with? Perhaps it's someone whose story resonated with you, or perhaps it's someone who revealed something unexpected about the past. If you can't pick one, you can pick a few for a History Lessons dinner party. How would the seating plan for a raucous dinner party that went on into the early hours differ to that of a more low-key soirée?

How much do you know about your own, personal history? While I can't technically set you any homework, there is something I'd implore you all to do. We can be the custodians of our own history. With that in mind, if you're able to, start at home. Are there any connections between you and this newly acquired historical understanding? What about your local area – who are your local heroes and are there ways that you can help raise their visibility? You might even find some unexpected connections between your own family history and familiar school history contexts like the First World War. You won't know unless you ask. How else would I have found out that my grandad convinced a fellow passenger to pay for them both to go on a tour of the pyramids during a stopover in Cairo before flying to Britain in 1967 to start a new life?

Now that you've experienced a broader 'school history' experience, where do you go from here? The Confucius quote from 500 BC springs to mind: 'Real knowledge is to know the extent of one's ignorance.' My answer would be to question the lens through which the past has been examined – and going forwards, to interrogate, reflect and reframe. Be open to exploring the assumptions you may hold about the past and embrace the recalibration of your understanding. I hope that reading this book has provided a springboard of sorts, empowering you to continue to pursue new learning. Every day is a school day.

BIBLIOGRAPHY

1. Early History

Arieti, James A., 'Magical Thinking in Medieval Anti-Semitism: Usury and the Blood Libel', *Mediterranean Studies* (2018)

Boynton, T., 'Archaeology: report of the Council of the Yorkshire Philosophical Society, 10 February 1902', *Yorkshire Philosophical Society Annual Reports 1894–1903* Volume 9 (1902)

Brown, Steven T., 'From Woman Warrior to Peripatetic Entertainer: The Multiple Histories of Tomoe', *Harvard Journal of Asiatic Studies* (1998)

Chazan, Robert, *Refugees or Migrants: Pre-Modern Jewish Population Movement* (2018)

Davidson, H. R. Ellis, 'The Legend of Lady Godiva', *Folklore* (1969)

Frankopan, Peter, *The Silk Roads, A New History of the World* (2015)

Goodwin, J., 'The Glory That Was Baghdad,' *The Wilson Quarterly (1976–)* (2003)

Hamdu, S. (ed), *Ibn Battuta in Black Africa* (1975)

Heng, Geraldine, 'England's Dead Boys: Telling Tales of Christian-Jewish Relations Before and After the First European Expulsion of the Jews', *MLN* (2012)

Langer, Lawrence N., 'The Black Death in Russia: Its Effects Upon Urban Labor', *Russian History* (1975)

Lewis, Mary, 'A Lady of York migration, identity, ethnicity in Roman Britain', *Antiquity* (March 2010)

Mackensen, Ruth Stellhorn, 'Four Great Libraries of Medieval Baghdad', *The Library Quarterly: Information, Community* (1932)
Marozzi, J., 'Story of Cities, The Birth of Baghdad was a landmark for civilisation', *Guardian* (6 April 2021)
McCullough, Helen Craig, *The Tale of the Heike* (2013)
Mortimer, Ian, *The Time Traveller's Guide to Medieval England* (2012)
Nehru, Jawaharlal, *Glimpses of World History* (1989)
Ovrut, Barnett D., 'Edward I and the Expulsion of the Jews', *The Jewish Quarterly Review* (1977)
Scales, Len, 'Bread, Cheese and Genocide: Imagining the Destruction of Peoples in Medieval Western Europe', *History* (2007)
Schama, Simon, *The Story of the Jews* (2013)
Spindler, Erik, 'Flemings in the Peasants' Revolt, 1381', *Contact and Exchange in Later Medieval Europe: Essays in Honour of Malcolm Vale* (2012)
Urbanus, Jason, 'The Ongoing Tale of Sutton Hoo', *Archaeology* (2014)
Vericour, De., 'Wat Tyler', *Transactions of the Royal Historical Society* (2021)
Weir, Alison, *Queens of the Conquest* (2017)
Wilkinson, Louise, *Women in Thirteenth-Century Lincolnshire* (2007)

Web Articles

'BBC News – Roman Curse tablets UNESCO' (Accessed 24 October 2022)
https://www.bbc.co.uk/news/uk-england-somerset-28012437
'BBC News – Plague Pit found' (Accessed 13 March 2021)
https://www.bbc.co.uk/news/av/uk-33936629
'BBC World Service: The Fifth Floor – the Manden Charter: Mali's Magna Carta' (Accessed 2021)
https://www.bbc.co.uk/sounds/play/p02tj82x
'Annual Report of the Yorkshire Philosophical Society' (Accessed 2021)
https://www.biodiversitylibrary.org/item/250470#page/112/mode/1up
'British Library – Chronicle of the Black Death' (Accessed 13 March 2021)
https://www.bl.uk/learning/timeline/item103973.html
'British Museum – Sutton Hoo' (Accessed 6 June 2021)
https://www.britishmuseum.org/collection/death-and-memory/anglo-saxon-ship-burial-sutton-hoo

BIBLIOGRAPHY

'Cambridge dictionary – beyond the pale' (Accessed 16 May 2021)
https://dictionary.cambridge.org/dictionary/english/beyond-the-pale
'English Heritage – The Massacre at Clifford's Tower' (Accessed 6 April 2021)
https://www.english-heritage.org.uk/visit/places/cliffords-tower-york/history-and-stories/massacre-of-the-jews/
'English Heritage – Food and Health' (Accessed 7 April 2021)
https://www.english-heritage.org.uk/learn/story-of-england/romans/food-and-health/   'Romans:
'Guardian – Roman York skeleton' (Accessed 10 March 2021)
https://www.theguardian.com/science/2010/feb/26/roman-york-skeleton
'Hadrian's Wall' (Accessed 7 April 2021)
https://hadrianswallcountry.co.uk/hadrians-wall/hadrian's-wall-facts
'History Today – Harrying of the North' (Accessed 7 April 2021)
https://www.historytoday.com/history-matters/harrying-north
'Historic UK – Stone of Destiny' (Accessed 16 May 2021)
https://www.historic-uk.com/HistoryUK/HistoryofScotland/The-Stone-of-Destiny/
'History Extra – Matilda' (Accessed 15 May 2021)
https://www.historyextra.com/period/norman/matilda-william-the-conquerors-queen/
'Historic Royal Palaces – Dataset of Jewish Prisoners' (Accessed June 2021)
https://www.hrp.org.uk/media/3082/dataset-of-jewish-prisoners-refugees-and-staff-at-the-tower.pdf
'Royal Palaces – Jewish Workers and Prisoners' (Accessed June 2021)
https://blog.hrp.org.uk/curators/jewish-workers-and-prisoners-at-the-tower-of-london/ Historic
'History Extra – Peasants Revolt' (Accessed 15 May 2021)
https://www.historyextra.com/period/medieval/your-guide-peasants-revolt-facts-timeline/
'Licoricia of Winchester' (June 2021)
https://jwa.org/encyclopedia/article/licoricia-of-winchester
'Samurai death poems' (Accessed 14 April 2021)
https://katanasforsale.com/samurai-death-poems-that-will-take-your-breath-away/
Licoricia statue (Accessed June 2021)

https://licoricia.org/2022/01/27/statue-of-licoricia-of-winchester-to-be-unveiled-by-hrh-prince-charles-on-10-february/

'Royal Burial Ground at Sutton Hoo, The National Trust' (Accessed 6 April 2021)
https://www.nationaltrust.org.uk/sutton-hoo/features/the-royal-burial-mounds-at-sutton-hoo 'The

'National Archives – Jews in England 1290' (Accessed June 2021)
https://www.nationalarchives.gov.uk/education/resources/jews-in-england-1290/

'National Archives – Statue of Labourers' (Accessed June 2021)
http://www.nationalarchives.gov.uk/pathways/citizenship/citizen_subject/docs/statute_labourers.htm

'OCR, T Green 'African Kingdoms: A Guide to the Kingdoms of Songhay, Kongo, Benin, Oyo and Dahomet c. 1400–c. 1800' (Accessed 2021)
https://www.ocr.org.uk/Images/208299-african-kingdoms-ebook-.pdf, accessed 14/03/21

'Oxford University – Roman Curse tablets' (Accessed 24 October 2022)
https://digital.humanities.ox.ac.uk/project/curse-tablets-roman-britain

'Oxford University - when did cats arrive in Britain?' (Accessed 16 May 2021)
https://www.oxfordsparks.ox.ac.uk/content/when-did-cats-arrive-britain

'Oxford University - Why were Jews expelled from England?' Accessed (June 2021)
https://www.history.ox.ac.uk/::ognode-637356::/files/download-resource-printable-pdf-5

'Reading University – Romans Revealed' (Accessed 10 March 2021)
https://www.reading.ac.uk/web/files/archaeology/Bangle_Lady_script_and_notes_for_teachers.pdf

'Misidentified Roman tablets – Smithsonian magazine' (Accessed March 2021)
https://www.smithsonianmag.com/smart-news/these-misidentified-roman-pendants-were-actually-womens-makeup-tools-180973184/

'Gold – Smithsonian magazine' (Accessed March 2021)
https://www.smithsonianmag.com/smithsonian-institution/why-there-more-gold-meets-eye-180971937/

'Yorkshire Museum Trust – Ivory Bangle Lady' (Accessed 14 March 2021) https://www.yorkshiremuseum.org.uk/collections/collections-highlights/ivory-bangle-lady/

2. The Tudors

Bigelow, William, 'Once Upon a Genocide: Christopher Columbus in Children's Literature', *Language Arts* (1992)

Borman, Tracy, *The Private Lives of the Tudors* (2017)

Brotton, Jerry, *This Orient Isle; Elizabethan England and the Islamic World* (2016)

Cohen, I. Bernard, 'What Columbus "Saw" in 1492', *Scientific American* (1992)

Dasgupta, Biplab, *Bengal in the Middle Ages: As Seen Through Foreign Eyes, European Trade and Colonial Conquest* (2005)

Edwards, John, *Mary I* (2011)

Fryer, Peter, *Staying Power: The History of Black People in Britain* (2010)

Heike, Paul, 'Christopher Columbus and the Myth of 'Discovery', *The Myths That Made America: An Introduction to American Studies,* (2014)

Howey, Catherine L., 'Dressing a Virgin Queen: Court Women, Dress, and Fashioning the Image of England's Queen Elizabeth I', *Early Modern Women* (2009)

Jones, Julie, 'Gold of the Indies', *The Metropolitan Museum of Art Bulletin* (2002)

Kauffman, Miranda, *Black Tudors* (2017)

Keay, John, India (2010)

Kupperman, Karen, 'Elizabethan England Engages the World', *The Jamestown Project (2007)*

Lal, Ruby, *Empress: The Astonishing Reign of Nur Jahan* (2018)

Le Beau, Bryan, 'The Rewriting of America's First Lesson in Heroism: Christopher Columbus on the Eve of the Quincentenary', *American Studies* (1992)

Matusiak, John, *A History of the Tudors in 100 Objects* (2016)

Mortimer, Ian, *The Time Traveller's Guide to Elizabethan England* (2012)

Olairur, Michael, *Britain's Black Past* (2020)

Russell, Phillip, *The Essential History of Mexico: From Pre-Conquest to* Present (2015)

Weir, Alison, *The Six Wives of Henry VIII* (1991)

West, Rebecca, *Survivors in Mexico* (2003)

Web Articles

'BBC – Yasuke the African Samurai' (Accessed 18 April 2021)
https://www.bbc.co.uk/news/world-africa-48542673

'Bed of Roses leaflet' (Accessed 8 April 2021)
http://gio6v3sgme0lorck1bp74b12.wpengine.netdna-cdn.com/wp-content/uploads/2015/03/Bed-of-Roses-leaflet.pdf

'British Library – Book of Martyrs' (Accessed 14 April 2021)
https://www.bl.uk/learning/timeline/item126927.html

'British Library – Portrait of Moorish Ambassador' (Accessed 18 April 2021)
https://www.bl.uk/collection-items/portrait-of-the-moorish-ambassador-to-queen-elizabeth-i

'British Library – Tilbury speech' (Accessed 14 April 2021)
https://www.bl.uk/learning/timeline/item102878.html

'English Heritage – Party like Elizabeth' (Accessed 11 April 2021)
https://blog.english-heritage.org.uk/history-of-fireworks/

'English Heritage – History of Fireworks' (Accessed 11 April 2021)
https://blog.english-heritage.org.uk/party-like-elizabeth/

'Guardian - Christopher Columbus lost documents' (9 April 2021)
https://www.theguardian.com/world/2006/aug/07/books.spain

'Historic Royal Palaces – John Blanke' (Accessed 8 April 2021)
https://www.hrp.org.uk/tower-of-london/history-and-stories/john-blanke/#gs.yb0hbe

'History Extra – Kenilworth Castle' (Accessed 11 April 2021)
https://www.historyextra.com/period/elizabethan/princely-pleasures-at-kenilworth-robert-dudley s-three-week-marriage-proposal-to-elizabeth-i/

'History Extra – Yasuke – first African samurai' (Accessed 18 April 2021)
https://www.historyextra.com/period/tudor/yasuke-who-first-african-samurai-japan/

'Who was La Malinche?' (Accessed 12 April 2021)
https://daily.jstor.org/who-was-la-malinche/
'Mary Rose Recovery' (Accessed 16 April 2021)
https://maryrose.org/blog/historical/museum-blogger/
recovering-the-mary-rose-1545-1552/
'Royal Museums Greenwich – John Hawkins' (Accessed 12 April 2021)
https://www.rmg.co.uk/stories/topics/
john-hawkins-admiral-privateer-slave-trader
'Royal Society – Diversity aboard a Tudor warship: investigating the origins of the Mary Rose crew using multi-isotope analysis' (Accessed 12 April 2021)
https://cdn.roxhillmedia.com/production/
email/attachment/860001_870000/
bf8207e22d2c2ae6c98513643fb118b529f11d8c.pdf
Ruby Lal – Empress Photo gallery (15 April 2021)
https://rubylal.com/empress-photo-gallery/
Smithsonian Magazine – Henry 8ths Marriage Bed (Accessed 8 April 2021)
https://www.smithsonianmag.com/smart-news/
henry-viis-marriage-bed-may-have-spent-15-years-british-hotels
-honeymoon-suite-180971485/
'Yale - Walter Raleigh' (Accessed 15 April 2021)
https://avalon.law.yale.edu/16th_century/raleigh.asp

3. Abolition and the Age of Revolution

Akkerman, Nadine, *Invisible Agents: Women and Espionage in Seventeenth Century Britain* (2018)

Bugg, John, *The Other Interesting Narrative: Olaudah Equiano's Public Book Tour* (2006)

Dadzie, Stella, *A Kick in the Belly* (2020)

Donoghue, John, 'The Curse of Cromwell: Revisiting the Irish Slavery Debate', *History Ireland* (2017)

Fryer, Peter, *Black People in the British Empire* (1988)

Fryer, Peter, *Staying Power: The History of Black People in Britain* (1984)

Goodare, Julian, *The Survey of Scottish Witchcraft* (2003)

Griffin, Emma, *Liberty's Dawn: A People's History of the Industrial Revolution* (2013)

Handler, Jerome S., 'An African-Type Healer/Diviner and His Grave Goods: A Burial from a Plantation Slave Cemetery in Barbados, West Indies', *International Journal of Historical Archaeology*, (1997)

Handler, Jerome S., and Charlotte J. Frisbie. '*Aspects of Slave Life in Barbados: Music and Its Cultural Context*', *Caribbean Studies* (1972)

Heuman, G., Review of *True-Born Maroons*, by K. M. Bilby in *Caribbean Studies* (2008)

Jacobsen, Miriam, *Barbarous Antiquity: Reorienting the Past in the Poetry of Early Modern England* (2014)

Lincoln, Margaret, 'Cromwell: a kill joy regime?', *London and the Seventeenth Century: The Making of the World's Greatest City* (2021)

Mortimer, Ian, *Time Traveller's Guide to Restoration Britain* (2017)

Nevitt, Marcus, *Women and the Pamphlet Culture of Revolutionary England, 1640–1660* (2006)

Olusoga, David, *Black and British: A Forgotten History* (2016)

Prince, Mary, *The History of Mary Prince, a West Indian Slave: Related by Herself* (2017)

Ramdin, Roy, *Reimagining Britain: 500 Years of Black and Asian History* (2000)

Rath, Richard Cullen. 'African Music in Seventeenth-Century Jamaica: Cultural Transit and Transition', *The William and Mary Quarterly* (1993)

Siochrú, Micheál Ó. '"Shipped for the Barbadoes": Cromwell and Irish Migration to the Caribbean', *History Ireland* (2008)

Snyder, Howard A., *Jesus and Pocahontas: Gospel, Mission, and National Myth* (2015)

Tremblay, Gail, 'Reflecting on Pocahontas', *Frontiers: A Journal of Women Studies (2002)*

Thomas, Hugh, *The Slave Trade* (1997)

Tremblay, Gail, 'Reflecting on Pocahontas', *Frontiers: A Journal of Women Studies* (13 June 2021)

Web Articles

'Anti Slavery International – Rebellions' (Accessed July 2021)
https://www.gloucestershire.gov.uk/media/2022/rebellions_1-15906.pdf

BIBLIOGRAPHY

'Bunce Island plaque' (Accessed June 2021)
https://artsandculture.google.com/asset/
plaque-commemorating-the-africans-transported-int
o-slavery-from-bunce-island-bbc/ygGwKYHFyXDZsQ?hl=en
'Ashmolean Museum Oxford – Powhatan Mantle' (Accessed June 2021)
https://www.ashmolean.org/powhatans-mantle#listing_156216_0
'Barbados – Newton Burial ground' (Accessed December 2021)
https://barbados.org/newton-slave-burial-ground.htm#.YPqc2C1Q1QI
'British Library - Brookes Ship' (Accessed June 2021)
https://www.bl.uk/collection-items/diagram-of-the-brookes-slave-ship
'British Library - Charter Trading in Africa' (June 2021)
https://www.bl.uk/collection-items/charter-granted-to-the-company-o
f-royal-adventurers-of-england-relating-to-trade-in-africa-1663
'British Library – Demonology' (Accessed 31 July 2021)
https://www.bl.uk/collection-items/king-james-vi-and-is-demonology-
1597
British Library – Captain Cook – Australian perspective (12 June 2021)
https://www.bl.uk/the-voyages-of-captain-james-cook/articles/
an-indigenous-australian-perspective-on-cooks-arrival
'British Library – Witchcraft pamphlet' (Accessed 12 June 2021)
https://www.bl.uk/collection-items/
witchcraft-pamphlet-news-from-scotland-1591
'BBC Abolition Gallery' (Accessed June 2021)
https://www.bbc.co.uk/liverpool/content/image_galleries/slavery_
liverpool_gallery.shtml?6
'BBC Teach - How did Slave owners shape Britain?' (Accessed
December 2021)
https://www.bbc.co.uk/teach/how-did%20slave-owners-shape-britain/
z67dbdm
'Bunce Island' (Accessed June 2021)
https://www.bunceisland3d.org/visit.html 'Bunce Island 1805'
'British Online Archive – Slave Trade records' (Accessed
12 December 2021)
https://microform.digital/boa/collections/5/
slave-trade-records-from-liverpool-1754-1792/detailed-description
'British Museum – Akan Drum' (Accessed December 2021)

http://teachinghistory100.org/objects/about_the_object/ak
'British Museum – sugar bowl' (Accessed December 2021)
https://www.britishmuseum.org/collection/object/H_2002-0904-1
'Convict Records - Crimes' (Accessed 31 July 2021)
https://convictrecords.com.au/crimes
'Convict Records – John Hughes' (Accessed 31 July 2021)
https://convictrecords.com.au/convicts/hughes/john/72743
'Convict Records – Phillip Cunningham' (Accessed 31 July 2021)
https://convictrecords.com.au/convicts/cunningham/philip/142929
'Edinburgh University – The Survey of Scottish Witchcraft' (June 2021)
http://witches.hca.ed.ac.uk
'Encyclopaedia Virginia – Liverpool and Slavery' (Accessed June 2021)
https://encyclopediavirginia.org/6610hpr-12b8d819d5764e1/
'Future Learn – Slavery in the British Caribbean' (Accessed August 2021)
https://www.futurelearn.com/courses/slavery-in-the-british-caribbean/1/steps/894862
'Glasgow University – Slave Runaways' (Accessed June 2021)
https://www.runaways.gla.ac.uk/database/display/?rid=664
'Guardian – Calls for memorial for executed witches' (Accessed 12 June 2021)
https://www.theguardian.com/uk-news/2019/oct/29/calls-for-memorial-to-scotlands-tortured-and-executed-witches
'Historic England Pocahontas Statue' (Accessed 13 June 2021)
https://historicengland.org.uk/listing/the-list/list-entry/1057700
'Historic England – Liverpool' (Accessed June 2021)
https://historicengland.org.uk/research/inclusive-heritage/the-slave-trade-and-abolition/sites-of-memory/slave-traders-and-plantation-wealth/liverpool-and-the-north-west/
'Historic Royal Palaces – Charles I execution' (Accessed August 2021)
https://www.hrp.org.uk/banqueting-house/history-and-stories/the-execution-of-charles-i/
'History Extra 10 misconceptions about the Civil War' (Accessed June 2021)
https://www.historyextra.com/period/stuart/great-misconceptions-civil-war-oliver-cromwell-charles-i-cavaliers-roundheads-parliament-religion-myths-facts/

'History Extra 10 – Cromwell Hero or Villain?' (Accessed June 2021)
https://www.historyextra.com/period/stuart/oliver-cromwell-hero-or-villain/

'HM Treasury – Slavery Abolition Act 1833' (Accessed July 2021)
https://assets.publishing.service.gov.uk/government/uploads/system/uploads/attachment_data/file/680456/FOI2018-00186_-_Slavery_Abolition_Act_1833_-_pdf_for_disclosure_log__003_.pdf

'Local Roots and Abolition' (Accessed July 2021)
https://lrgr14.wordpress.com/2014/06/27/abney-park-cemetery-and-abolitionists-agency-and-memory-in-the-fight-against-african-enslavement/

'Liverpool Museums – Middle Passage' (Accessed June 2021)
https://www.liverpoolmuseums.org.uk/history-of-slavery/middle-passage#section--log-book-of-the-unity,-176

'National Archives – Olaudah Equiano' (Accessed August 2021)
https://www.nationalarchives.gov.uk/pathways/blackhistory/rights/transcripts/equiano.htm

'National Archives – Rebecca Riots' (Accessed August 2021)
https://www.nationalarchives.gov.uk/education/resources/rebecca-riots/

'National Library of Scotland – Janet Horne' (Accessed July 2021)
https://www.nls.uk/learning-zone/literature-and-language/themes-in-focus/witches/source-6/

'National Museum of Australia – Wedgewood medallion First Fleet' (Accessed 31 July 2021)
https://collectionsearch.nma.gov.au/index.html

National Museum of Australia – Chain gang shackles (Accessed 31 July 2021)
http://collectionsearch.nma.gov.au/object/109322

'National Museum of Royal Navy – African Seaman Royal navy Anti-Slavery campaign' (Accessed 28 July 2021)
https://www.nmrn.org.uk/news-stories

'National Portrait Gallery – Louise de Kroualle' (Accessed December 2021)
https://www.npg.org.uk/collections/search/portrait/mw05102/Louise-de-Kroualle-Duchess-of-Portsmouth-with-an-unknown-female-attendant

'National Trust – Penrhyn Castle' (Accessed 12 December 2021)

https://www.nationaltrust.org.uk/penrhyn-castle/features/penrhyn-castle-and-the-transatlantic-slave-trade
'Old Bailey – Elizabeth Bruce, Elizabeth Anderson' (Accessed 31 July 2021)
https://www.oldbaileyonline.org/browse.jsp?id=t17870110-22-punish122&div=t17870110-22#highlight
'Sam Sharpe Project' (Accessed July 2021)
http://www.samsharpeproject.org/sam-sharpe
'Scone Palace – Dido Belle' (Accessed June 2021)
https://www.scone-palace.co.uk/dido-belle
'Spitalfields Life – Bevis Mark Synagogue' (Accessed August 2021)
https://spitalfieldslife.com/2016/06/15/at-bevis-marks-synagogue/
'UCL – Centre for the Study of the Legacies of British' (Accessed December 2021)
https://www.ucl.ac.uk/lbs/project/details/
'UCL – Centre for the Study of the Legacies of British – Agnes Montgomerie' (Accessed December 2021)
https://www.ucl.ac.uk/lbs/person/view/29898
'UCL – Legacies of British Slavery' (Accessed November 2021)
https://www.ucl.ac.uk/made-at-ucl/stories/legacies-british-slavery
'UCL – Legacies of British Slavery – Richard Watt III' (Accessed November 2021)
https://www.ucl.ac.uk/lbs/person/view/13160
'UCL – Legacies of British Slavery – Vreed-en-hope' (Accessed November 2021)
https://www.ucl.ac.uk/lbs/estate/view/1117
UNESCO (Accessed November 2021)
https://whc.unesco.org/en/tentativelists/5745/

4. Victorians (at Home and Abroad)

Anand, Anita, *Koh-I-Noor* (2017)
Archer, Mildred, *Treasures from India. The Clive Collection at Powis Castle* (1998)
Basu, Shrabani, *Victoria and Abdul* (2010)
Dalrymple, William, *The Anarchy* (2019)
Dalrymple, William, *White Mughals* (2002)

Fryer, Peter, *Black People in the British Empire* (2021)
Goodman, Ruth, *How to Be a Victorian* (2013)
Green, Toby, African Kingdoms (OCR)
Hicks, Dan, *The Brutish Museums* (2020)
Hyam, Ronald, *Britain's Imperial Century, 1815–1914, A Study of Empire and Expansion* (2002)
Jenkins, John Edward, *The coolie: his rights and wrongs* (2010)
Judd, Denis, *The Lion and the Tiger* (2004)
Keay, John, *India* (2010)
Kingscote, Adeline Georgina Isabella, *The English baby in India and how to rear it* (1893)
Manji, Fatima, *Hidden Heritage: Rediscovering Britain's Lost Love of the Orient* (2021)
Mathur, Saloni, *India by Design* (2007)
Olusoga, David, *Black and British: A Forgotten History* (2016)
Patton, Sharon F., 'The Stool and Asante Chieftaincy', *African Arts* (1979)
Sharkey, Heather, 'A Famous Queen Mother from Benin', *Expedition Magazine* 61 (2021)
Shears, Jonathon (ed), *The Great Exhibition, 1851: A Sourcebook* (2017)
Sheridan, R., 'The condition of the slaves on the sugar plantations of Sir John Gladstone in the colony of Demerara, 1812-49', *New West Indian Guide* (2022)
Shubert, Adrian, 'Women Warriors and National Heroes: Agustina De Aragón and Her Indian Sisters', *Journal of World History* (2012)
Taylor, Miles, *Empress: Queen Victoria and India* (2018)

Web Articles

'ABC The British stole the Benin Bronzes' (Accessed November 2021)
https://www.abc.net.au/news/2020-11-30/benin-bronzes-stuff-the-british-stole-museum-history/12837940
'Balmoral Castle' (Accessed August 2021)
https://www.balmoralcastle.com/slideshow-5.htm
'BBC – skull in a pub' (Accessed 12 August 2021)
https://www.bbc.co.uk/news/world-asia-india-43616597
'British Library – the Great Exhibition' (Accessed August 2021)
https://www.bl.uk/victorian-britain/articles/the-great-exhibition

'Brighton Museum' (Accessed August 2021)
https://brightonmuseums.org.uk/hove/exhibitions-displays/jaipur-gate/
'British Library – Indenture to Windrush' (Accessed 13 August 2021)
https://www.bl.uk/windrush/articles/indenture-to-windrush
'British Library – Roshani Begum rebel dancer' (Accessed 4 August 2021)
https://blogs.bl.uk/untoldlives/2021/04/
 roshani-begum-dancer-turned-rebel-from-tipu-sultans-court.html
'British Library Untold Lives – an abandoned Ayah' (Accessed June 2021)
https://blogs.bl.uk/untoldlives/2016/10/an-abandoned-ayah.html
'British Museum - Benin bronzes' (Accessed October 2021)
https://www.britishmuseum.org/about-us/british-museum-story/
 contested-objects-collection/benin-bronzes
'British Museum - Benin plaque' (Accessed October 2021)
https://www.britishmuseum.org/collection/object/E_Af1898-0115-31
'British Museum - Portuguese figure Benin' (Accessed October 2021)
https://www.britishmuseum.org/collection/object/E_Af1928-0112-1
'British Museum Oba Photo' (Accessed October 2021)
https://www.britishmuseum.org/collection/object/EA_Af-A47-70
'Digital Benin – Cargo Collective' (Accessed October 2021)
https://files.cargocollective.com/c696558/Digital_Benin_Press_Kit.pdf
'Choctawnation – Irish Connection' (Accessed 10 July 2022)
https://www.choctawnation.com/about/history/irish-connection/
'Christies Tipu Sultan Jade set pendant' (Accessed 4 August 2021)
https://www.christies.com/lot/lot-6211938
'Christian Missionary Society Archive' (Accessed 25 October 2021)
http://www.ampltd.co.uk/collections_az/cms-4-01/description.aspx
'The Indian Labour Diaspora' (Accessed September 2021)
http://www.coolitude.shca.ed.ac.uk/sites/default/files/
 TheIndianLabourDiaspora-compressed.pdf
Colonial and Indian Exhibition Catalogue 1886 (Accessed 9 August 2021)
https://archive.org/details/cihm_05255/page/n3/mode/1up?view=theater
'English Heritage – Ayahs blue plaque' (Accessed August 2021)
https://www.english-heritage.org.uk/about-us/search-news/
 pr-ayahs-blue-plaque/
'English Heritage – Sarah Forbes Bonetta' (Accessed August 2021)
https://www.english-heritage.org.uk/visit/places/osborne/
 history-and-stories/sarah-forbes-bonetta/

'English Heritage – Queen Victoria diary' (Accessed 29 June 2021)
https://www.english-heritage.org.uk/about-us/search-news/pr-queen-victoria-diary/
'Future Learn – Royal food' (Accessed August 2021)
https://www.futurelearn.com/info/courses/royal-food/0/steps/17095
'Guardian – East India Company – Original Corporate raiders' (Accessed 4 August 2021)
https://www.theguardian.com/world/2015/mar/04/east-india-company-original-corporate-raiders
'Guinness World Record – largest suit of armour made for an animal' (Accessed 4 August 2021)
https://www.guinnessworldrecords.com/world-records/79173-largest-suit-of-armour-made-for-an-animal
'Hansard The Ashanti Expedition' (Accessed October 2021)
https://hansard.parliament.uk/Commons/1901-03-19/debates/19ea3bcc-b7f4-4dab-9afc-0b9abe700ab4/TheAshantiExpedition?highlight=savage
'History Extra – The Great Hunger' Accessed (July 2022)
https://www.historyextra.com/period/victorian/qa-irish-famine-great-hunger-name-usa-ireland-etymology/
'History of Parliament – George Graham' (Accessed 3 August 2021)
http://www.histparl.ac.uk/volume/1754-1790/member/graham-george-1730-1801#footnote1_npwssgo
'Kinross House FAQ' (Accessed 3 August 2021)
https://www.kinrosshouse.com/about/faq
'Manhyia Palace' (Accessed October 2021)
https://manhyiapalace.org
'Met Museum – Queen Mother Pendant Mask' (Accessed October 2021)
https://www.metmuseum.org/art/collection/search/318622
'National Archives – Victorian Britain' (Accessed 9 August 2021)
https://www.nationalarchives.gov.uk/education/victorianbritain/happy/
'National Army Museum – Battle of Plassey' (Accessed 4 August 2021)
https://www.nam.ac.uk/explore/battle-plassey
'National Maritime Museum – How did the EIC change people's lives in Britain?' (Accessed 4 August 2021)
https://www.rmg.co.uk/sites/default/files/KS3-activity3-historical-sources-v3.pdf

'National Trust – Clive Museum at Powis' (Accessed 4 August 2021)
https://www.nationaltrust.org.uk/powis-castle-and-garden/features/the-clive-museum-at-powis
'National Library of Australia – Access by Arrival Date' (Accessed 17 September 2021)
https://www.nla.gov.au/research-guides/indian-emigration-passes-to-fiji-1879-1919/access-by-arrival-date
'Newspaper – Sarah Forbes Bonetta wedding' (Accessed 14 August 2021)
https://www.newspapers.com/article/36616425/wedding-of-sarah-forbes-bonetta/
New York Times – Benin Bronzes (Accessed September 2021)
https://www.nytimes.com/2020/01/23/arts/design/benin-bronze
'Open University – Robert Clive' (Accessed August 2021)
https://www.open.edu/openlearn/history-the-arts/history/hero-and-villain-robert-clive-the-east-india-company
'Open University – Colonial and Indian Exhibition' (Accessed August 2021)
https://www.open.ac.uk/researchprojects/makingbritain/content/colonial-and-indian-exhibition-1886
'Oxford Reference – Tipu Tiger phrase' (Accessed August 2021)
https://www.oxfordreference.com/display/10.1093/acref/9780199539536.001.0001/acref-9780199539536-e-156
'Parliament – The Great Famine' (Accessed July 2022)
https://www.parliament.uk/about/living-heritage/evolutionofparliament/legislativescrutiny/parliamentandireland/overview/the-great-famine/
'Reading University – the Political Economy of Indian Indentured Labour in the 19th Century' (Accessed September 2021)
https://www.reading.ac.uk/web/files/economics/emdp202016.pdf
'Royal Armouries – Stuffed elephant toy' (Accessed 4 August 2021)
https://shop.royalarmouries.org/products/royal-armouries-armoured-elephant-stuffed-toy
Royal Collection Trust – Abdul Karim (Accessed 29 August 2021)
https://www.rct.uk/collection/406915/the-munshi-abdul-karim-1863-1909
'Royal Collection Trust – Bakshiram' (Accessed 9 June 2021)
https://www.rct.uk/collection/403826/bakshiram
'Royal Collection Trust – Carved Leopards' (Accessed October 2021)
https://www.rct.uk/collection/69926/carved-leopards

'Royal Collection Trust – Maharajah Duleep Singh' (Accessed 9 August 2021)
https://www.rct.uk/collection/search#/70/collection/41542/maharaja
'Royal Collection Trust – Queen Victoria journal (Accessed 14 August 2021)
https://www.rct.uk/collection/themes/trails/
  black-and-asian-history-and-victorian-britain/queen-victorias-journal-ra
'Schweppes heritage' (Accessed August 2021)
https://www.schweppesus.com/#our-sparkling-heritage
'Trove – Indian immigration passes 1879-1916' (Accessed September 2021)
https://nla.gov.au/nla.obj-2586944660
'Trove – Indian immigration passes 1879-1916' (Accessed September 2021)
https://nla.gov.au/nla.obj-2750194243/view?partId=nla.
  obj-2750194867#page/n4/mode/1up
'V+A Henry Cole and the Koh-i-Noor' (Accessed August 2021)
https://www.vam.ac.uk/blog/caring-for-our-collections/
  henry-cole-and-the-koh-i-noor-diamond
'V+A Tipu's Tiger' (Accessed August 2021)
https://www.vam.ac.uk/articles/tipus-tiger
Twitter – @singhlions – original letter Duleep Singh to Queen Victoria
https://twitter.com/singhlions/status/889105302762659844?lang=en-GB

5. The Suffragettes

Anand, Anita, *Sophia: Princess, Suffragette, Revolutionary* (2015)
Atkinson, Diane, *Rise Up, Women! The Remarkable Lives of the Suffragettes* (2018)
Lytton, Constance, *Prisons and Prisoners: Some Personal Experience* (1976)
Marlow, Joyce, *Suffragettes, the Fight for Women* (2015)
Purvis, Jane (ed), *Votes for Women* (1999)
Ramdin, Roy, *Reimaging Britain, 500 Years or Black and Asian History* (2000)
Robinson, Jane, *Hearts and Minds: The Untold Story of the Great Pilgrimage and
  How Women Won the Vote* (2018)

Web Articles

'British Library – Cato Street conspiracy' (Accessed 30/12/21)
https://www.bl.uk/collection-items/an-authentic-history-of-the-cat
  o-street-conspiracy

'British Library – Women's suffrage timeline [Accessed 30/12/21]'
https://www.bl.uk/votes-for-women/articles/womens-suffrage-timeline
'Daily Mail historical archive – The Suffragette Athlete' [Accessed 22/01/22]
link.gale.com/apps/doc/EE1866474387/DMHA?u=ucl_ttda&sid=bookmark-DMHA&xid=829391fc
'Fawcett Society, Mary Wollstonecraft' [accessed 30/12/21]
https://www.fawcettsociety.org.uk/blog/celebrate-foremother-feminism-mary-wollstonecraft
'Google Arts and Culture – Emily Davison letter [Accessed 31/12/21]
https://artsandculture.google.com/asset/page-1/qAEKCNy4LfoBnQ?hl=en&childassetid=1wFySksknVnbYw
'Google Arts and Culture – Women's Exhibition refreshments photo' [Accessed 27/12/21]
https://artsandculture.google.com/asset/refreshment-department-at-the-women-s-exhibition-broom-christina/hQG06qlTipbuEQ?hl=en
'Guardian – suffragette trees' [Accessed 02/01/22]
https://www.theguardian.com/environment/2021/oct/08/suffragettes-tree-inspiring-new-generation-aoe
'Historic England – Eagle House' [Accessed 02/01/22]
https://historicengland.org.uk/listing/the-list/list-entry/1115252?section=official-listing
'LSE – Women's Library'
https://lse-atom.arkivum.net/the-womens-library
'LSE Library – Rosa May Billinghurst' [Accessed 02/01/22]
https://www.flickr.com/photos/lselibrary/38666686576/in/album-72157660822880401/
'Manchester Art Gallery – Outrage' [Accessed 22/01/22]
https://manchesterartgallery.org/news/manchester-art-gallery-outrage/
'Museum of London – Bread' [Accessed 27/12/21]
https://collections.museumoflondon.org.uk/online/object/67537.html
'Museum of London – Holloway prison' [Accessed 27/12/21]
https://www.museumoflondon.org.uk/discover/suffragettes-holloway-prison
'National Archives – Black Friday' [Accessed 29/12/21]

https://www.nationalarchives.gov.uk/education/resources/
suffragettes-on-file/black-friday-statement-2/
'National Archives – broken windows' [Accessed 27/12/21]
https://blog.nationalarchives.gov.uk/rather-broken-windows-broken-promises/
'National Archives – postman burnt by accident' [Accessed 27/12/21]
https://www.nationalarchives.gov.uk/education/resources/
suffragettes-on-file/postman-burnt-by-acid/
'National Archives – suffragettes in trousers' [Accessed 27/12/21]
https://www.nationalarchives.gov.uk/education/resources/
suffragettes-in-trousers/source-one-leaflet/
'National Archives – window smashing' [Accessed 27/12/21]
https://www.nationalarchives.gov.uk/education/resources/
suffragettes-on-file/window-smashing-campaign/
'Parliament – Chartist Petitions' [accessed 30/12/21]
https://www.parliament.uk/about/living-heritage/transformingsociety/
electionsvoting/chartists/case-study/the-right-to-vote/
the-chartists-and-birmingham/1842-and-1848-chartist-petitions/
'Parliament – Herbert Asquith speech' [Accessed 02/02/21]
https://www.parliament.uk/contentassets/
e6eada5668704020961caada8e9e8988/filename_sggfpcqzafwffgifrojz.jpg
'Postal Museum – human letters' [Accessed 27/12/21]
https://api.parliament.uk/historic-hansard/commons/1917/mar/28/
mr-speakers-services
'Postal Museum – human letters' [Accessed 27/12/21]
https://www.postalmuseum.org/blog/human-letters/
Suffragette Stories – letter from Mary Blathwayt to Annie Kenney [Accessed 30/12/21]
https://suffragettestories.omeka.net/items/show/39
'Tate - Sylvia Pankhurst' [Accessed 23/01/22]
https://www.tate.org.uk/whats-on/tate-britain/display/
bp-spotlight-sylvia-pankhurst
'William Cuffay' [Accessed 30/12/21]
https://phm.org.uk/blogposts/william-cuffay-black-chartism-and-a-treasured-object/
William Cuffay trial' [Accessed 30/12/21]

https://www.medway.gov.uk/info/200393/cuffay_and_chatham_exhibition/1164/trial_and_aftermath
William Cuffay record [Accessed 30/12/21]
https://convictrecords.com.au/convicts/cuffey/william/40169
'YouTube – Clare Balding – Epsom Derby' [Accessed 25/02/22]
https://www.youtube.com/watch?v=-W_URTWjgR0

6. The Great War and Beyond

Arthur, Max, *Forgotten Voices of the Great War* (2002)
Basu, Shrabani, *For King and Another Country* (2016)
Bourne, Stephen, *Black Poppies* (2014)
Brendon, Piers, *The Rise and Fall of the British Empire* (2007)
Das, Shantanu, *India, Empire and First World War Culture* (2018)
Hanna, Judith Lynne. 'Dance and the 'Women's War', *Dance Research Journal* (1981)
Lawrence, Dorothy, *Sapper Dorothy* (2010)
Newman, Vivien, *We Also Served: The Forgotten Women of the First World* War (2014)
Olusoga, David, *Black and British: A Forgotten History* (2016)
Olusoga, David, *The World's War* (2014)
Sandes, Flora, *An English Woman-Sergeant in the Serbian Army* (1916)
Visram, Rozina, *Asians in Britain* (1997)
Walker, Julian (ed), *Languages and the First World War: Communicating in a Transnational War* (2016)
Wilson, John-Hughes, *A History of the First World War in 100 Objects* (2014)

Web Articles

'Archeologie De La Grande Guerre – Grimsby Chums' [Accessed 12/02/22]
https://archeologie.culture.gouv.fr/archeologie1418/en/grimsby-chums
'BBC – Call to teach 1919 Liverpool Race Riots' [Accessed 17/02/22]
https://www.bbc.com/news/uk-england-merseyside-48527393
'BBC – Munitions Dead remembered' [Accessed 17/02/22]
http://news.bbc.co.uk/1/hi/england/west_yorkshire/4257546.stm

'BBC – Muslim Burial ground' [Accessed 17/02/22]
https://www.bbc.com/news/uk-england-surrey-34792865
'BBC – Teenage soldiers of WW1' [Accessed 12/02/22]
https://www.bbc.com/news/magazine-29934965
'BBC – The Corpse Factory and birth of fake news' [Accessed 12/02/22]
https://www.bbc.com/news/entertainment-arts-38995205
BBC Great War interviews – Shell Shock [Accessed 18/02/22]
https://www.bbc.co.uk/iplayer/episode/p01td29c/the-great-war-interviews-7-mabel-lethbridge
'British Library – Shell Shock [Accessed 18/02/22]
https://www.bl.uk/collection-items/w-h-r-rivers-on-the-treatment-of-shell-shock-from-the-lancet
'First Indian pilot of First World War' [Accessed 18/02/22]
https://www.britishlegion.org.uk
'British Library – British Empire exhibition' [Accessed 18/02/22]
https://www.bl.uk/collection-items/advertisement-for-the-indian-pavilion-and-british-empire-exhibition
'Abe Bevistein' [Accessed 18/02/22]
https://www.britishnewspaperarchive.co.uk
'Commonwealth Graves Commission – Patcham Down' [Accessed 13/02/22]
https://www.cwgc.org/visit-us/find-cemeteries-memorials/cemetery-details/5001087/patcham-down-indian-forces-cremation-memorial/
'Commonwealth Graves Commission – Chinese Cemetery' [accessed 18/02/22]
https://www.cwgc.org/visit-us/find-cemeteries-memorials/cemetery-details/68500/noyelles-sur-mer-chinese-cemetery/
'Commonwealth Graves Commission – Indra Lal Roy' [Accessed 18/02/22]
https://www.cwgc.org/find-records/find-war-dead/casualty-details/325397/indrulal-l-roy/
'Coultard – British Empire exhibition' [Accessed 18/02/22]
https://courtauld.ac.uk/research/research-resources/publications/courtauld-books-online/apocalypse/the-abbey-in-ruins-and-ablaze-staging-disaster-at-the-1924-1925-british-empire-exhibitions/
'English Heritage – Cell block graffiti' [Accessed 13/02/22]

https://www.english-heritage.org.uk/visit/places/richmond-castle/richmond-graffiti/cell-block-graffiti/

'English Heritage – Richmond Sixteen' [Accessed 13/02/22] https://www.english-heritage.org.uk/visit/places/richmond-castle/history-and-stories/richmond-sixteen/

'Government Case Study – Mir Dast' [Accessed 13/02/22] https://www.gov.uk/government/case-studies/ww1-pakistani-vc-recipient-mir-dast

'Guardian – Lusitania' [Accessed 13/02/22] https://www.theguardian.com/world/2015/may/13/anti-german-riots-lusitania-1915-first-world-war

'Historic England – Munitions [Accessed 17/02/22] https://historicengland.org.uk/research/current/discover-and-understand/military/the-first-world-war/first-world-war-home-front/what-we-already-know/land/munitions-factories/

'Historic England – Muslim burial ground' [Accessed 17/02/22] https://historicengland.org.uk/services-skills/education/educational-images/muslim-burial-ground-horsell-common-woking-7986

'Imperial War Museum – Battle of the Somme' [Accessed 13/02/22] https://www.iwm.org.uk/history/what-happened-during-the-battle-of-the-somme

'Imperial War Museum – British Empire troops' [Accessed 13/02/22] https://www.iwm.org.uk/collections/item/object/205078674

'Imperial War Museum – British Empire troops' [Accessed 13/02/22] https://www.iwm.org.uk/collections/item/object/205078675

'Imperial War Museum – Christmas Truce' [Accessed 13/02/22] https://www.iwm.org.uk/history/the-real-story-of-the-christmas-truce

'Imperial War Museum – Lottie Meade' [Accessed 13/02/22] https://www.iwm.org.uk/collections/item/object/205380866

'Imperial War Museum – Munitions Factory' [accessed 13/02/22] https://www.iwm.org.uk/history/9-women-reveal-the-dangers-of-working-in-a-first-world-war-munitions-factory

'Imperial War Museum – Recruitment posters' [accessed 13/02/22] https://www.iwm.org.uk/history/11-amazing-first-world-war-recruitment-posters

'Imperial War Museum – Surprising Laws' [accessed 13/02/22]
https://www.iwm.org.uk/history/10-surprising-laws-passed-during-the-first-world-war

'Imperial War Museum –Health in the trenches' [accessed 13/02/22]
https://www.iwm.org.uk/history/how-to-keep-clean-and-healthy-in-the-trenches

'Imperial War Museum – Young Women of London' [accessed 12/02/22]
https://www.iwm.org.uk/collections/item/object/28305

'Independent - Grimsby Chums article' [accessed 12/02/22]
https://www.independent.co.uk/news/world/europe/farewell-to-the-grimsby-chums-who-died-as-brothers-in-arms-9143224.html

'Library and Archives Canada – George Strangling Wolf' [accessed 13/02/22]
https://www.bac-lac.gc.ca/eng/discover/military-heritage/first-world-war/first-world-war-1914-1918-cef/Pages/item.aspx?IdNumber=255909

'Library of Congress – Bahamas poster' [accessed 12/02/22]
https://www.loc.gov/resource/cph.3g11198/

'Mary Evans – Right to Serve march' [accessed 13/02/22]
https://www.prints-online.com/womens-right-to-serve-march-4385027.html

'National Archives – British Empire exhibition' [accessed 13/02/22]
https://blog.nationalarchives.gov.uk/20speople-a-vast-window-display-the-british-empire-exhibition-of-1924-5/

'National Archives – Walter Tull' [accessed 12/02/22]
https://www.nationalarchives.gov.uk/education/resources/walter-tull/

'National Archives – Great War resource' [accessed 13/02/22]
https://www.nationalarchives.gov.uk/education/resources/great-war-1914-1918/

'National Archives – Indra Lal Roy' [accessed 13/02/22]
https://www.nationalarchives.gov.uk/pathways/firstworldwar/people/lalroy.htm

'National Army Museum - Battle of Loos' [accessed 13/02/22]
https://www.nam.ac.uk/explore/battle-loos

'National Army Museum – Battle of Tsingtao' [accessed 17/02/22]
https://www.nam.ac.uk/explore/siege-tsingtao

'National Army Museum – Gallipoli notes' [accessed 13/02/22]
https://www.nam.ac.uk/sites/default/files/
   learning-resource-files/2018-01/gallipoli-teachers-notes.pdf
'National Army Museum – Western Front notes' [accessed 13/02/22]
https://www.nam.ac.uk/sites/default/files/
   learning-resource-files/2018-01/western-front-teachers-notes.pdf
'National Football Museum – Lily Parr' [accessed 13/02/22]
https://www.nationalfootballmuseum.com/halloffame/lily-parr/
'PM News – Aba Riots' [accessed 27/06/22]
https://pmnewsnigeria.com/2018/03/08/
   iwd-2018-united-nations-recognises-aba-womens-riot/
'RAF 100 – Indra Lal Roy' [accessed 22/02/22]
https://www.raf100schools.org.uk
'RAF Museum – Sargent William Robinson Clarke' [Accessed 12/02/21]
https://www.rafmuseum.org.uk
'Royal Collection Trust – Brighton Pavilion' [accessed 13/02/22]
https://www.rct.uk/collection/themes/trails/
   brighton-pavilion-the-making-of-a-pleasure-palace/pair-of-chandeliers
'Science Museum – British Empire exhibition' [accessed 17/02/22]
https://journal.sciencemuseum.ac.uk/article/experiencing-tropical-africa/#abstract
'Sikh Museum – Kitchener Hospital' [accessed 17/02/22]
https://www.sikhmuseum.com/brighton/doctor/kitchener/morale.html
'Sir John Monash Centre – the origins of Plonk' [accessed 13/02/22]
https://sjmc.gov.au/wine-in-war-the-origins-of-plonk/
'Trove - Wembley Exhibition Strike' [accessed 17/02/22]
https://trove.nla.gov.au/newspaper/article/64202224
'Westminster Abbey – unknown warrior' [accessed 12/02/22]
https://www.westminster-abbey.org/abbey-commemorations/
   commemorations/unknown-warrior
'West Indian Contingent Committee Reports' [accessed 13/02/22]
https://westindiacommittee.org/historyheritageculture/wp-content/
   uploads/2019/06/West-India-Contingent-Committee-Reports-1916-19.
   pdf
'YouTube – The Indian Labour Corps in WW1' [accessed 12/02/22]
https://www.youtube.com/watch?v=O-EqcX8OWrM

7. The Second World War

Basu, Shrabani, *Spy Princess: The Life of Noor Inayat Khan* (2008)
Bourne, Stephen, *The Motherland Calls* (2012)
Bowman, Ghee, *The Indian Contingent, The Forgotten Muslim Soldiers of Dunkirk* (2020)
Khan, Yasmin, *Great Partition, The Making of India and Pakistan* (2007)
Khan, Yasmin, *The Raj at War* (2016)
Mace, Martin, *Unearthing Churchill's Secret Army* (2012)
Millett, Allan Reed, *The Second World War in 100 Objects* (2012)
Panter-Downer, Mollie, *London War Notes* (2015)
Schulman, Faye, *A Partisan's Memoir* (1995)
Smyth, Lyn, *Forgotten Voices of the Holocaust, A New History of in the words of the men and women who survived* (2005)
Trevor-Roper, Hugh, *The Last Days of Hitler* (2013)

Web Articles

'BBC – Art hidden from the Nazis' [Accessed 10/05/22]
https://www.bbc.com/culture/article/20180413-the-art-hidden-from-nazi-bombs
'BBC – Bethnal Green memorial' [Accessed 10/05/22]
https://www.bbc.com/news/av/uk-21646633
'BBC – Chamberlain returns from Munich' [Accessed 10/05/22]
https://www.bbc.com/historyofthebbc/anniversaries/september/chamberlain-returns-from-munich/
'BBC – VE Day broadcasts' [Accessed 10/05/22]
https://www.bbc.com/historyofthebbc/anniversaries/may/ve-day-broadcasts/
'Business Insider – Black WW2 Tank Unit' [Accessed 10/05/22]
https://www.businessinsider.com/story-black-wwii-tank-unit-that-crushed-nazi-forces-2017-4?r=US&IR=T
'Churchill Museum' [Accessed 13/05/22]
https://www.nationalchurchillmuseum.org/disaster-of-the-first-magnitude.html

'Channel 4 – A Cheeky video message from WW2' [Accessed 23/06/22]
https://www.youtube.com/watch?v=0BoI3bnp30I
'German History Museum – Goering' [Accessed 10/05/22]
https://www.dhm.de/datenbank/goering/dhm_goering.php?seite=9
'Google Arts and Culture – Baedecker Raids' [Accessed 10/05/22]
https://artsandculture.google.com/story/baedeker-raids-imperial-war-museums
'Guardian – Auschwitz Liberation' [Accessed 10/05/22]
https://www.theguardian.com/world/2015/jan/27/auschwitz-short-history-liberation-concentration-camp-holocaust
'History Extra – Dunkirk' [Accessed 10/05/22]
https://www.historyextra.com/period/second-world-war/dunkirk-facts-history-east-mole-hitler-halt-order-douglas-jardine/
'Holocaust – Holocaust Memorial Day Trust' [Accessed 10/05/22]
https://www.het.org.uk/hmd-2022-resources
'Holocaust Memorial Day Trust – Auschwitz Birkenau' [Accessed 10/05/22]
https://www.hmd.org.uk/learn-about-the-holocaust-and-genocides/the-holocaust/the-camps/auschwitz-birkenau/
'Holocaust Memorial Day Trust – Babi Yar Massacre' [Accessed 16/06/22]
https://www.hmd.org.uk/resource/the-babi-yar-massacre/
'Holocaust Memorial Day Trust – Death marches and liberation' [Accessed 16/06/22]
https://www.hmd.org.uk/learn-about-the-holocaust-and-genocides/the-holocaust/death-marches-and-liberation/
'Holocaust Memorial Day Trust – Emanuel Ringelbaum' [Accessed 10/05/22]
https://www.hmd.org.uk/resource/emanuel-ringelblum-and-oneg-shabbat-archive/
'Holocaust Memorial Day Trust – Genocide outside the camps' [Accessed 10/05/22]
https://www.hmd.org.uk/learn-about-the-holocaust-and-genocides/the-holocaust/genocide-outside-the-camps/
'Holocaust– Gold Mothers Cross' [Accessed 10/05/22]
https://www.holocaust.org.uk/gold-mothers-cross

'Holocaust Memorial Day Trust– Helene Melanie Lebel' [Accessed 10/05/22]
https://www.hmd.org.uk/resource/helene-melanie-lebel/
'Holocaust Memorial Day Trust – Irena Sendlerowa' [Accessed 16/06/22]
https://www.hmd.org.uk/resource/irena-sendlerowa/
'Holocaust Memorial Day Trust – LGBT History month' [Accessed 16/06/22]
https://www.hmd.org.uk/news/lgbt-history-month-time-remember-nazi-persecution-gay-people/
'Holocaust Memorial Day Trust – Resistance and Rescuers' [Accessed 16/06/22]
https://www.hmd.org.uk/learn-about-the-holocaust-and-genocides/the-holocaust/resistance-rescuers-and-liberation/
'Holocaust Memorial Day Trust – Rudolf Brazda' [Accessed 16/06/22]
https://www.hmd.org.uk/resource/rudolf-brazda/
'Holocaust Memorial Day Trust – 1942 Wannsee Conference' [Accessed 16/06/22]
https://www.hmd.org.uk/resource/20-january-1942-wannsee-conference/
'Imperial War Museum – 6 Stories of the Kinder transport' [Accessed 10/05/22]
https://www.iwm.org.uk/history/6-stories-of-the-kindertransport
'Imperial War Museum – 10 Stories of the Battle of Britain' [Accessed 10/05/22]
https://www.iwm.org.uk/history/10-inspiring-stories-of-bravery-during-the-battle-of-britain
'Imperial War Museum – Calling Blighty from Burma' [Accessed 10/05/22]
https://www.iwm.org.uk/history/calling-blighty-from-burma-in-1945
'Imperial War Museum –D Day' [Accessed 10/05/22]
https://www.iwm.org.uk/history/d-days-parachuting-dummies-and-inflatable-tanks
'Imperial War Museum – Operation Barbarossa' [Accessed 10/05/22]
https://www.iwm.org.uk/history/operation-barbarossa-and-germanys-failure-in-the-soviet-union
'Imperial War Museum – A volunteer from British Guiana' [Accessed 10/05/22]
https://www.iwm.org.uk/collections/item/object/33287

'Imperial War Museum – Indians in Civil Defence' [Accessed 10/05/22]
https://www.iwm.org.uk/collections/item/object/33292
'Imperial War Museum – Indian forces in France' [Accessed 10/05/22]
https://www.iwm.org.uk/collections/item/object/205215002
'Imperial War Museum – Indian WRENS 1945' [Accessed 10/05/22]
https://www.iwm.org.uk/collections/item/object/205187585
'Imperial War Museum – Mahinder Singh Pujji' [Accessed 10/05/22]
https://www.iwm.org.uk/collections/item/object/80026782
'Imperial War Museum – Womens Land Army [Accessed 10/05/22]
https://www.iwm.org.uk/history/what-was-the-womens-land-army
'International Encyclopaedia of World War One' [Accessed 10/05/22]
https://encyclopedia.1914-1918-online.net/article/husen_bayume_mohamed
'Internet Archive Mahinder Singh Pujji' [Accessed 10/05/22]
https://web.archive.org/web/20120801114327/http:/www.bharat-rakshak.com/IAF/History/1940s/Pujji01.html
'LA Times – Leningrad' [Accessed 25/05/22]
https://www.latimes.com/archives/la-xpm-1994-01-27-mn-15973-story.html
'Londonist – London Blitz pies' [Accessed 10/05/22]
https://londonist.com/london/transport/tube-train-pie-refreshment-specials-blitz-london-underground
'MI5 – Agent Garbo' [Accessed 10/05/22]
https://www.mi5.gov.uk/agent-garbo
'National Archives – Forgotten Army in Burma' [Accessed 10/05/22]
https://blog.nationalarchives.gov.uk/the-forgotten-army-west-african-troops-in-burma-1945/
'National Archives – Khan award recommendation' [Accessed 10/05/22]
https://discovery.nationalarchives.gov.uk/details/r/D7357147
'National Archives – Musa Banana' [Accessed 10/05/22]
https://discovery.nationalarchives.gov.uk/details/r/D7366785
'National WW2 Museum – Sophie Scholl' [Accessed 10/05/22]
https://www.nationalww2museum.org/war/articles/sophie-scholl-and-white-rose
'National WW2 Museum – D Day Spies' Accessed 10/05/22]
https://www.nationalww2museum.org/war/articles/d-day-spies

'New Statesman – How WW2 Made Britain Multicultural' [Accessed 10/05/22]
https://www.newstatesman.com/culture/2018/08/how-second-world-war-made-britain-multicultural
'New York Times – Rudolf Brazda' [Accessed 10/05/22]
https://www.nytimes.com/2011/08/06/world/europe/06brazda.html
'Oxford – Mahinder Pujji' [Accessed 10/05/22]
https://www.oxforddnb.com/view/10.1093/ref:odnb/9780198614128.001.0001/odnb-9780198614128-e-103160
'Pattons Panthers' [Accessed 10/05/22]
https://warfarehistorynetwork.com/article/pattons-panthers-the-story-of-the-761st-tank-battalion/
'Riverside Radio – the Blitz in Balham' [Accessed 10/05/22]
https://www.riversideradio.com/news-slides/blitz
'Royal Historical Society – Indian Women's Work in War and Famine'
https://blog.royalhistsoc.org/2021/05/04/the-women-had-saved-the-situation-indian-womens-work-in-war-and-famine/
'The Times – Faye Schulman' [Accessed 10/05/22]
https://www.thetimes.co.uk/article/faye-schulman-obituary-c93csqdlk
'The Times – the girl who fooled the Nazis' [Accessed 10/05/22]
https://www.thetimes.co.uk/article/the-good-time-girl-who-fooled-the-nazis-9mgbknm2wjz
'US Holocaust Memorial Museum – Josef Mengele' [Accessed 13/05/22]
https://encyclopedia.ushmm.org/content/en/article/josef-mengele
'US Holocaust Memorial Museum – Kristallnacht' [Accessed 13/05/22]
https://encyclopedia.ushmm.org/content/en/article/kristallnacht
'US Holocaust Memorial Museum – Molotov Partisan Brigade' [Accessed 13/05/22]
https://collections.ushmm.org/search/catalog/pa1142244
'VADS – A Hindu makes a camera gun' [Accessed 13/05/22]
https://www.vads.ac.uk/digital/collection/IWMPC/id/6630/rec/3
'War and Navy Dept – A Short Guide to Britain' [Accessed 27/05/22]
https://issuu.com/ajarmedia/docs/guide_to_great_britain
'West End at War' [Accessed 13/05/22]
http://westendatwar.org.uk/documents/E._Ita_Ekpenyon_download_version_.pdf

'White Rose 6th leaflet' [Accessed 23/05/22]
https://www.gdw-berlin.de/fileadmin/bilder/publikationen/
  begleitmaterialien/Faksimiles_PDFs_englisch/FS_15.6_ENGL_1.
  Aufl_RZ-web.pdf
'Wilayati Akhbar' [Accessed 20/05/22]
https://ids.si.edu/ids/deliveryService?id=NMAH-AC0433-0005515a
'Women beneath the Surface' [Accessed 13/05/22]
https://www.tandfonline.com/doi/full/10.1080/07292473.2020.1790473
'WW2 SOE Training manual' [Accessed 25/05/22]
https://ironwolf008.files.wordpress.com/2010/07/
  the-wwii-soe-training-manual-rigden.pdf
'Yad Vashem – Ringelblum' [Accessed 20/05/22]
https://www.yadvashem.org/yv/en/exhibitions/ringelblum/index.asp '
'Tape 1 Calling Blighty 2nd & 7th Worchester Rgt 1944' [Accessed
  26/06/22]
https://www.youtube.com/watch?v=Z_oZVc-Kip4

8. 'Modern' Britain

Cobain, Ian, *The History Thieves* (2016)
Grant, Colin, *Homecoming: Voices of the Windrush Generation* (2019)
India League, *Condition of India: Being the Report of the Delegation Sent to India by the India League in 1932* (1933)
Khan, Yasmin, *The Making of India and Pakistan* (2007)
Khan, Yasmin, *The Raj at War* (2015)
Olusoga, David, *Black and British: A Forgotten History* (2016)
Patel, Hasu H., 'General Amin and the Indian Exodus from Uganda', *Issue: A Journal of Opinion* 2, no. 4 (1972)
Puri, Kavita, *Partition Voices* (2019)
Sengupta, Anwesha, 'Of Men and Things: The Administrative Consequences of Partition of British India', *Mahanirban Calcutta Research Group*
Street, Joe, 'Malcolm X, Smethwick, and the Influence of the African American Freedom Struggle on British Race Relations in the 1960s', *Journal of Black Studies* (2008)

Tate, Tim, *Pride: The Inspiring True Story behind the hit film* (2018)

Taylor, Becky, 'Good Citizens? Ugandan Asians, Volunteers and "Race" Relations in 1970s Britain', History Workshop Journal (2018)

Web Articles

'Asians from Uganda – Resettlement document' (Accessed 12/06/22)
http://www.asiansfromuganda.org.uk/images/19.gif

'AQA Mark scheme 2019' (Accessed 12/06/22)
https://filestore.aqa.org.uk/sample-papers-and-mark-schemes/2019/june/AQA-70412S-QP-JUN19.PDF

'BBC – Ugandan Asians advert' (Accessed 12/06/22)
https://www.bbc.com/news/uk-england-leicestershire-19165216

'Black Cultural Archive – Womanopoly' (Accessed 12/05/22)
https://artsandculture.google.com/asset/womanopoly-stella-dadzie/ZwHfTb-kh5Dy4w

'Black Cultural Archive – Black Women's Movement' (Accessed 12/05/22)
https://artsandculture.google.com/story/hAUBVgWeiBZ-Ig

'British Library – How Caribbean migrants rebuilt Britain' (Accessed 05/05/22)
https://www.bl.uk/windrush/articles/how-caribbean-migrants-rebuilt-britain

'BBC – Siblings reunited' (Accessed 05/05/22)
https://www.bbc.com/news/world-asia-india-61548612

'BBC – the pool of blood that changed my life' (Accessed 15/06/22)
https://www.bbc.com/news/magazine-33725217

'British Newspaper Archive – Notting Hill Race Riots 1958' (Accessed 05/05/22)
https://blog.britishnewspaperarchive.co.uk/2022/05/12/exploring-the-notting-hill-race-riots-of-1958/

'British Library – Grunwick dispute' (Accessed 05/05/22)
https://www.bl.uk/collection-items/photographs-from-the-grunwick-dispute

'British Pathe – 70 pickets arrested' (Accessed 05/06/22)
https://www.britishpathe.com/video/VLVA4V3PPO62GWTR3JJFQHR5BETA9-UK-SEVENTY-PICKETS-ARRESTED-AND-30-PEOPLE-INJURED-AS-18000/query/Seventy

'Bristol Museum– Bristol Bus Boycott' (Accessed 05/05/22)
https://www.bristolmuseums.org.uk/stories/bristol-bus-boycott/
'Channel 4 – the day Britain took in 27,000 refugees' (Accessed 05/05/22)
https://www.channel4.com/news/by/jon-snow/blogs/day-britain-27000-refugees
'Channel 4 – Undercover policing' (Accessed 05/05/22)
https://www.channel4.com/news/undercover-policing-blair-peachs-partner-horrified-to-have-been-spied-on
'Creative book – 13 dead, nothing said photos' (Accessed 05/05/22)
https://www.creativeboom.com/news/13-dead-nothing-said-a-south-london-photography-show-marking-black-lives-lost-and-1980s-protest-/
'Fordham Source Book: British Government Statement: Policy in India, 1946' (Accessed 02/05/22)
https://sourcebooks.fordham.edu/mod/1946-india-ukpolicy.asp
'Goldsmiths – Battle of Lewisham' (Accessed 06/05/22)
https://www.gold.ac.uk/history/research/battle-of-lewisham/what-was-the-battle-of-lewisham/
'Guardian – Britain's most racist election' (Accessed 06/05/22)
https://www.theguardian.com/world/2014/oct/15/britains-most-racist-election-smethwick-50-years-on
'Guardian – Ministers hunted for island to house Asians' (Accessed 06/05/22)
https://www.theguardian.com/uk/2003/jan/01/past.politics
'Guardian – Patricia Howcroft obituary' (Accessed 06/05/22)
https://www.theguardian.com/theguardian/2013/dec/13/patricia-howcroft-obituary
'Guardian – Sam King obituary' (Accessed 06/05/22)
https://www.theguardian.com/society/2016/jun/30/sam-king-obituary
'Guardian – Undercover with Paul Lewis and Rob Evans' (Accessed 06/05/22)
https://www.theguardian.com/uk-news/undercover-with-paul-lewis-and-rob-evans/2016/apr/13/covert-police-spied-on-strikers-and-their-supporters-in-iconic-dispute
'Hansard – Forced Repatriation' (Accessed 02/05/22)
https://hansard.parliament.uk/commons/2021-07-21/debates/A72FC416-BDED-4060-9CDF-60061F12B1C6/ForcedRepatriationOfChineseSeamenFromLiverpoolAfterWorldWarTwo

'Hansard – Immigration procedures 1979' (Accessed 02/05/22)
https://hansard.parliament.uk/commons/1979-02-19/
debates/8b08facc-47af-41eb-b071-cce935bbda0b/ImmigrationProcedures
'Hansard – Indian Constitution December 1946' (Accessed 02/05/22)
https://api.parliament.uk/historic-hansard/commons/1946/dec/12/
india-constitution
'Hansard – Ugandan Asians' (Accessed 02/05/22)
https://hansard.parliament.uk/lords/2012-12-06/
debates/12120659000796/UgandanAsians
'History Extra – Idi Amin' (Accessed 02/06/22)
https://www.historyextra.com/period/20th-century/
fleeing-idi-amin-after-uganda-asian-expulsion-arrival-britain/
'Homer Sykes – Blair Peach funeral' (Accessed 02/06/22)
https://homersykes.photoshelter.com/gallery/
BLAIR-PEACH-FUNERAL-SOUTHALL-LONDON-1970S/
G0000nuhgDhSPAig/C0000_5qMC9953Ww
'Indian Workers Association' (Accessed 10/05/22)
https://iwasouthall.org.uk/images/iwa-booklet.pdf
'Institute of Race Relations' (Accessed 05/05/22)
https://irr.org.uk/article/society-in-black-and-white/
'Institute of Race Relations – Virginity Tests' (Accessed 05/06/22)
https://twitter.com/IRR_News/
status/1489539235195625473?s=20&t=MYmiMNqsBCAjYB9cmJvAuA
'Library – Grunwick Strike' (Accessed 05/06/22)
https://libcom.org/article/strikers-saris-grunwick-strike
'New Cross Fire – Hackney' (Accessed 03/07/22)
https://www.londonremembers.com/memorials/new-cross-fire-hackney
'Margaret Thatcher – Granada interview' (Accessed 05/07/22)
https://www.margaretthatcher.org/document/103485
'The campaign to free the Bradford 12' (Accessed 12/07/22)
https://www.marxists.org/history/erol/uk.hightide/b-12-victory-2.pdf
'Metropolitan Police – Investigating the death of Blair Peach' (Accessed 05/07/22)
https://www.met.police.uk/foi-ai/af/accessing-information/met/
investigation-into-the-death-of-blair-peach/
National Archives – Mangrove Nine Protest (Accessed 10/05/22)

https://www.nationalarchives.gov.uk/education/resources/mangrove-nine-protest/source-one/

'National Archives – migrated archives' (Accessed 05/05/22)
https://discovery.nationalarchives.gov.uk/details/r/C12269323

'National Archives – Ugandan Asians 40 years on' (Accessed 05/06/22)
https://www.nationalarchives.gov.uk/education/outreach/projects/ugandan-asians-40-years-on/

'NEU Blair Peach award' (Accessed 05/07/22)
https://neu.org.uk/about/reps/neu-awards

'Stonewall – Our impact' (Accessed 12/07/22)
https://www.stonewall.org.uk/our-impact

'Tandana archive' (Accessed 10/06/22)
http://www.tandana.org/data/Kala%20Tara%20education%20pack.pdf

'TVO – Black Power – A British story of resistance' (Accessed 10/05/22)
https://www.tvo.org/transcript/136021X/black-power-a-british-story-of-resistance

'Pride in London – Mike Jackson from LGSM' (Accessed 10/06/22)
https://www.youtube.com/watch?v=LSuwsuLqIus&t=48s